CW01035103

THE
DEFENDER

THE
DEFENDER

JOSEPH
BELTRAMI

With a foreword by
Sir Nicholas Fairbairn Q C M P
Former Solicitor General for Scotland

M & A THOMSON
1988

The publishers would like to thank the following for kind permission to reproduce copyright photographs:

Ray Beltrami for pages 21, 82 and 270.
Express Newspapers Ltd for page 56 (from the *Scottish Daily Express*).
Glasgow Herald and Evening Times for pages 130 and 233.
The Scotsman Publications Ltd for page 140.
Scottish Daily Record and Sunday Mail Ltd for pages 91 and 196.

© Joseph Beltrami 1980
First published by W & R Chambers Ltd,
Edinburgh, 1980

Revised edition by M & A Thomson, East Kilbride, 1988

Printed in Great Britain by
M & A Thomson Litho Ltd, East Kilbride

ISBN 0 9513963 0 7

Acknowledgements

I would like to express my thanks to the following persons who have assisted me in the course of the preparation of this book:

My wife Delia, the former Solicitor General for Scotland Sir N H Fairbairn Q C M P, the Clerk of Justiciary, and my eldest son Edwin, who is now a barrister in England. I am very grateful for their considerable assistance.

I am especially grateful to William Allsopp for his help with the preparation of the text, and my secretary Miss Angela Reid.

Contents

Sir Nicholas Fairbairn Q C M P

'We are all in his debt'
Foreword
by Sir Nicholas H Fairbairn Q C M P, former Solicitor General for Scotland

The criminal courts have a unique fascination and all that happens in them is a matter of intense public interest, which is heightened if those who practise in the courts have a personality which fascinates the public. It is not easy to define why the criminal courts are so fascinating, but it is probably the gladiatorial nature of the legal process and the doubt as to the outcome which attracts the betting instinct in all of us—and also the wonder as to how Daniel can escape from the lions' den, the sort of James Bond syndrome. And of course the ability of the great pleader to persuade fifteen people that what they know to be black is white. In the words of Pope:

All look on with reverential awe
At crimes which 'scape and triumph over law.

I was called to the Scots Bar in the summer of 1957. In those days there was no criminal Legal Aid in Scotland (although there had been for some years in England) and very few clients could pay. But my heart was set on a criminal practice. I had neither notion nor concept, nor apparently care, that all my efforts had no obvious prospect of reward and possibly no prospect at all. All I wanted was to be a criminal practitioner and to be good at it. In those days, when there was a circuit in prospect in any of the towns in Scotland a library boy would enquire of the very junior members of the bar if they were willing to be put on the list of 'poor counsel' for that circuit. I always volunteered. On such occasions one might have the benefit of being 'instructed' before the circuit began. That is to say, having probably been chosen with a pin from a list of unknowns by a worried solicitor, 'instructions' took the form of a copy of the indictment if you were lucky. Alternatively, you just travelled through to Glasgow and hung about in counsel's room in the hope of being 'instructed' on the spot.

It was on the occasion of my first murder trial in Glasgow in 1958 that I first set eyes on Joseph Beltrami. I remember vividly taking notice of him because he took no notice of me—not yet, as it turned out. He was very young but very brusque, radiating a justified but as yet unproved confidence and an undisguised ambition which merely served to exaggerate my regret that he overlooked me. One day he didn't. I think I was as dismayed to receive his first instructions as I had been upset not to do so before. I knew I must do well or the first case would be the last. Hitherto his regular advocates had been J Irvine Smith and Alistair MacDonald, now Sheriff of the Shetlands, a counsel of immense strength and superiority whose tongue and wit classified all his colleagues with exaggerated accuracy and wicked insight. On his elevation to the shrieval Bench— and on his recommendation—Joseph Beltrami instructed me instead. At that time he had an office in Buchanan Street. It was small, simple, dingy and sparsely furnished. After all, he had so far only one foot on the bottom rung of the ladder. He then had a staff of one, his secretary Therese McBryan, whose huge brown eyes put me at ease in advance of being admitted to the reserved presence.

I was eventually shown in. Joseph Beltrami seemed totally in command of his practice and of himself but, like myself, certainty of the end and uncertainty of the means of achieving that end combined in conflict. There were no pleasantries and certainly no jokes. As the cases in this book show, Joseph Beltrami achieved his monumental success by total dedication to the task in hand. Success has enabled him to release his humour and his many other talents and to allow them to blossom forth, but until success was within his grasp he used *all* his energy only for the case in hand.

2

He spoke with a deep, rasping bark which was about an octave below the voice of anyone else and he repeated most phrases two or three times. He had big, commanding eyes which rolled ceaselessly on his instructed counsel. He smoked often, smiled rarely and had very definite ideas on the course he wished the case to take. His incisive talent was encased in the defensive armour of a distant reserve. His certainty and his uncertainty compelled him to keep people at a distance until he was sure he could meet them on his own terms. He never laughed. Flippancy interfered with his ceaseless concentration. Nonsense scored nil; diversions from the matter in hand even less. Indeed, it was years before I first saw him laugh, though he laughs plenty now. He listened to nothing he did not want to hear and said repeatedly what he wanted to say. The right to deafness was not accorded to his audience. This insistence and concentration was the bedrock of his mastery of the forensic art and the foundation of his legendary constellation of successes. He kept his big, intelligent eyes on the ball of the case in hand, behind which the goal of his ambition was never out of sight. He was about to climb swiftly to the top, to supremacy, never outpacing his rank on the ladder until he could afford to do so. I was about to see why.

We had three clients to see and three cases to discuss. As it happened, we won them all in a row, a hat-trick. It was the beginning of an incomparable partnership and a fulfilling friendship which I have had the privilege of sharing with his delightful family and his many friends. Little did I guess on the occasion of that first awkward and stiff instruction what a remarkable partnership of success and understanding we would have and what a close friendship we would enjoy as the years went on.

Joseph Beltrami first instructed me on a capital murder case in 1961—*Her Majesty's Advocate v Walter Scott Ellis*, the first major case in this book. It was a case which aroused intense interest and righteous indignation, for there appeared to be no motive for the destruction of the life of a good and diligent family man.

We immediately went to the grim fortress of Barlinnie Prison for a consultation. We were shown into the presence of Ellis in the little, bare interview cell in the hospital block—and some presence he had! His face was ashen—as prison faces often are, particularly when in prospect of death. This pallor served to emphasise his sleek black hair, but it was his hard, black, Jesuitical eyes which dominated his expressionless face.

No case ever started with a bleaker prospect. But every case teaches an advocate at least one lesson which the practitioner should never forget. The first rule of the forensic lawyer is that no case is so good that you cannot lose it and no case so bad that you cannot win it. The Ellis case proved the truth of that first rule, for it was difficult to believe it could be won even before the glass evidence appeared on the scene. There then was the lesson: never bow down before what appears to be overwhelming evidence until you have tested its veracity and strength. At Joseph Beltrami's suggestion I did extensive research into the nature and properties of glass. He describes how the research paid off. Ellis was acquitted by a whisker: life continued. There were hysterical scenes outside the court; Ellis was free for a bit and Beltrami was on his way for good.

The lessons that we learned from defending Ellis proved vitally important in the last case of 'gentle' Johnny Ramensky, who had a lifelong compulsion to break into whatever he was outside and out of whatever he was inside, but before I come to it may I recall the irony of the bank-robbery case which is also described in this book? Johnny was a true amateur, almost a caricature, a sort of Laurel-and-Hardy criminal. Not only did he blow an empty safe on that occasion—and use such an excess of TNT that two somnambulant constables strolling half a mile from the bank were knocked on their backs by the explosion—but he overlooked a locked drawer which contained more than £80 000! He just couldn't ever get it right. He was a real Charlie Chaplin character, with the same endearing charm.

4

Unusually for a criminal, he never denied what he had done, only what he hadn't. This made it so easy for those instructed to defend him, and yet so difficult—for, as the last case in which I defended him (for safe-blowing in Lanark) showed, I simply couldn't believe either that he had deceived us or that the abundant evidence provided by the police witnesses could be broken. For a moment I had forgotten the rule that there is no case so bad it cannot be won. As it turned out, the apparently superabundant evidence collapsed under the scrutiny of cross-examination. The Crown wisely drew stumps after the first 'expert' witness rather than put the corroborating 'expert' into the box to confirm dubious testimony and Ramensky was rightly acquitted. He returned to prison, where he died—and where, for most of his life, he had also lived.

If I were to be asked what is the most important element in Joseph Beltrami's success, I would have no hesitation in saying 'thoroughness'. He overlooks nothing, and that is demonstrated by the Leap Year Case. In Scotland there is a rule that a person who is remanded in custody after his committal can only be held for a hundred and ten days thereafter, and by that time his trial must be concluded. As ever, Beltrami had done his arithmetic. And he knew that the hundred-and-ten-day period was up. He had made one mistake the last time this had happened; he had told the client. The client told the turnkey. The turnkey told the court superintendent. He told the police. So the Crown were prepared and we almost lost the case. The second time, Joseph Beltrami made no mistake.

I have often been asked how an advocate can defend a man whom he believes to be guilty. Joseph Beltrami gives you his answer: perhaps I may be permitted to add mine. Firstly may I say that clients do not come and say 'I have just disposed of Granny! Will you get me off?' What they say is 'I didn't dispose of Granny. Please defend me on this false charge!' And it is the duty of the advocate or the lawyer to present his client's case as his client gives it to him—so far as it is consistent with his duty to the court, because a lawyer is first and foremost the servant of justice. Unless the evidence which is in prospect is such as to make the defence frivolous, the instructed lawyer is bound to present his client's position even if it is merely a straight denial of the evidence. Now if a lawyer were to decline a case because he thought his client was guilty, he would become the judge and the jury in the case. And what would be the position of the lawyer if he was equally convinced that a client was innocent and that client was then convicted? He would surely have an equivalent veto on the verdict as he would have on the client's right to a defence.

Our system of law is not perfect. Sometimes the innocent are convicted; sometimes the guilty are acquitted. The latter is the price we pay for minimising the former. But the system depends for its success on the diligence and capability of the solicitors who are instructed for the defence. For it is the knowledge that the most rigorous preparation has been made and that the most probing scrutiny will await the witnesses which stimulates the prosecutor to care and diligence. In applying to himself the principle *nihil nisi optimum* (which happens to be my armorial motto) Joseph Beltrami has made a singular contribution to maintaining the high standards of equity of the criminal law of Scotland. Before I entered Parliament in 1974 we worked in harness for fifteen years. And this book describes some of the exciting episodes on that journey.

Although, inevitably, only a few of his great successes are described in this book, they are sufficient to illustrate the supremacy of the Scottish criminal system whereby the prosecution is laid by an impartial Procurator Fiscal under the instruction of the Lord Advocate. The evidence is tested by the defence and judged by the jury without the distraction of opening speeches, and with closing speeches which are infinitesimally brief compared with the equivalent in England. If the evidence does not satisfy or pass the scrutiny of the defence, then it will fail before a jury. Beltrami is a master at the preparation of that scrutiny.

During the course of a remarkable career in which he has been such a protector and saviour of so many humble people—some more sinning than others, and some more sinned against—Joseph Beltrami has transformed his life as well as theirs. When I first was instructed by him, he lived in a little flat in the Trongate, and stage by stage, he moved to his present delightful mansion in Bothwell. He progressed from a little Renault which he had in 1959 stage by stage to the Mercedes he has now.

Thus he fulfilled the great precept of Adam Smith, that in benefiting himself he benefited many others much more. He has done well not only by himself and his family and clients, he has done well above all by the law of Scotland. For that we are all in his debt.

The Beltrami family

8

'Justice is incomplete without diligent defence'
Introduction
by William Allsopp

When they call the cases at Glasgow Sheriff Court each weekday, and sometimes Saturdays too, Joseph Beltrami, criminal lawyer, is never far away. The odds are that he has a client appearing that morning on some charge, grave or otherwise.

Even during the strike of Scottish courts administration staff early in 1979, when court business came virtually to a standstill, Joe and his clients kept turning up. The courts may have stopped operating fully, but crime hadn't taken a holiday and the constabulary hadn't given up. Sheriffs were still working, processing accused persons—remitting them for further hearings, granting or refusing bail, sometimes effecting summary justice.

On one such morning Joe Beltrami called me over and, between clients, told me he was thinking of writing a book. Perhaps I could help?

To me it was an honour, and to both of us, a challenge. No-one before had written the kind of book that Joe Beltrami had in mind. By the very nature of his clientele, for one thing, few could. It was to be a sound and sober account of a criminal defence solicitor at work—recalling past cases, not necessarily the most sensational but each with a telling, and occasionally unique, legal point to make. It would attempt too, to give the man in the street an insight into real-life courtroom drama.

It would also, I suspected at the time, keep Joe Beltrami from being bored while he waited for the courts to resume normal business in meting out justice to his clients.

This is not a book about Joe Beltrami. But it is very much a book *by* him: these are his cases, his experiences, his own responses to the needs of his clients and the requirements of Scots Law. It is how, as a criminal defence lawyer, Joe Beltrami practises within the purlieus of the law.

As the layman, sandwiched in this book between august legal luminaries, I must insist on my pennyworth . . . so that other laymen will fully appreciate, as I came to appreciate, just how far justice is incomplete without diligent defence. And just how incomplete legal defence is without unabashed respect for the law and its traditions.

Joe Beltrami has upset long-standing law. He has gained two Royal Pardons for clients wrongfully convicted—indeed, wrongfully accused. If the law leaned backward to be fair to an accused, Joe leaned inexorably with it.

In this period of collaboration I learned much about the law, much about a solicitor's approach to client, case and courtroom. I learned a great deal about the astonishing scope and flexibility of Scots Law. And I suppose I was introduced to its imperfections too.

I also learned a little more about Joseph Beltrami.

Although this book is not intended to be biographical or autobiographical, and although Joe Beltrami may need no introduction to the legal profession—or the criminal profession either, for that matter—perhaps the ordinary reader would appreciate a brief pen-portrait. . . .

Almost forty years ago the young Joe Beltrami got on a tramcar in Stockwell Street, Glasgow and rode with it to Gilmorehill, to matriculate as a student at Glasgow University.

When he got on the tram he was going to be a schoolteacher. When he got off he had decided to become a lawyer. His decision to take up the law rather than teaching was made in the space of four tram-stops, between Charing Cross and Gilmorehill.

At Charing Cross a schoolfriend, Kevin Purcell, had boarded the same tram and sat beside him. He told Joe that he was going to matriculate in law—because he had just heard that the Legal Aid (Scotland) Act of 1949 had been passed. And, in his opinion, law was the profession to enter. Joe mulled this over in the course of four tram stages—and matriculated in the Faculty of Law. That was in September 1950.

He had been brought up in Glasgow, living at No 132 Bridgegate, within a stone's throw of Glasgow High Court. The last public hanging, in July 1865, had taken place in Jail Square—a few steps down the Saltmarket from where Joe was to live. His father, of Swiss descent, ran a fish restaurant at Glasgow Cross from the beginning of the war until 1955.

Joe was educated at St Aloysius College, Glasgow, and he graduated Bachelor of Law in June 1953, at the age of twenty-one.

From March 1954 to March 1956 he did his National Service. After basic training he became a Sergeant in the Intelligence Corps, with an immediate posting to Paris as interpreter/translator with the British military delegation to the European Defence Community, based at the British Embassy. Later, he was posted to Taunton in charge of Field Security for the South West District of England.

He started out on his own in November 1958, opening a small office in Buchanan Street, and he still remembers his first client and his first fee. It was for five pounds—all that his client had.

My first acquaintance, as a newspaperman, with Joe Beltrami was during the murder trial of Walter Scott Ellis—described in this book—in which Ellis, who faced the death penalty, was eventually freed on a Not Proven verdict. That case, I now know, sealed Joe's success as a criminal defence lawyer. Since then the 'underworld', a not insubstantial substratum of Glasgow society, has sought Joe's services in time of trouble.

It is said that if there were no bad people there would be no good lawyers. As the leading—and arguably the busiest—criminal lawyer in town, Joe has not his clients to seek. Proving a client's innocence, mitigating an offence or—and he sees this as the most important aspect—testing a prosecution case to the limits is Joe Beltrami's professional *raison d'être.*

Perhaps his endeavours on behalf of Patrick Meehan exemplify a solicitor's concern for his client. In the end he won a Royal Pardon for Meehan, wrongly accused and convicted of murder, who served seven years' imprisonment before being released. That case also revealed the complex nature of the Beltrami criminal practice. Years of day-to-day professional dealings with criminal clients were to culminate in a unique involvement with the 'underworld'. No fewer than six of his regular clients were implicated in one way or another in this sensational murder case. And because of the special code of confidentiality between solicitor and client, Joe was unable to help one client without putting another at risk.

So far as this present book is concerned, may I, as a layman, recommend it to all who are fascinated by crime and courtroom drama, from a safe distance... to all those who, by the grace of God, a little care and lots of luck, have not needed the services of a criminal defence lawyer.

Meehan's case finished successfully in 1984 with an award of £52,000. The book covering the complete saga (1969–84) has been written and will shortly be published.

Beltrami's *Meehan* will make interesting reading and could prove that fact can be stranger, and more interesting, than fiction.

1

'But here, unless I am mistaken, is our client'

Clients and cases come to a criminal lawyer in all kinds of ways. But not all come as direct as the case of Ian Adam. Indeed, you might think my introduction to Ian Adam and a murder case was not unlike the opening scenes of a *Perry Mason* episode.

It was early on a Sunday afternoon when I received a telephone call at my home. I had been relaxing in front of the television set with my family. The caller would not give his name at first, but said that the matter was extremely urgent and that I should see him at once. Because it was Sunday, after all, and not wishing to waste time on something that could possibly wait until office hours, I asked him to give me the gist of it. Cranks do telephone from time to time. . . . He then said that it was about a dead body—which had not, as yet, been discovered by the police.

The caller explained that, when he had got back to his digs that morning after being away for a day and a half he had found the dead body of the man who occupied the flat. He said that the body was badly battered. Knowing that it would soon be discovered, and because he had been living in the same flat with his common-law wife, he had panicked and had put the body in a wardrobe.

I asked him again who and where he was, and he told me that his name was Adam and he was staying in a boarding house in Bath Street, in the centre of Glasgow. I told him to stay where he was and I would come out.

I drove to the boarding house and rang the bell. The landlady opened the door and I told her I wanted to see

Mr Adam. She checked her register and confirmed that she had a Mr Adam. She shouted his name and a tall, dark and extremely well-built man appeared from a downstairs room. He seemed to recognise me and invited me in. I hesitated. The thought occurred to me that this might be some kind of set-up. How easy it would be, I thought, to invent a story to bring me there, get me into a room and then—with the help of some confederate, perhaps—rob me. I looked at Adam's considerable build and decided that he would not even require a confederate....

'No,' I said, 'you can discuss the matter with me at the door here, or we can sit in my car outside.'

Possibly reading my thoughts, he told me that his wife was in the room—but he agreed to get into my car anyway. There he told me that he and his wife had occupied a flat in Alexander Street, Clydebank until the previous day. That morning he had gone back to the flat to pick up some belongings and had seen the occupier, a man called Arthur Friel, lying battered and dead in the living room.

As he had lived in Friel's flat for some seven weeks, he panicked on finding him and had put what he now described as a mutilated and dismembered body into a wardrobe.

He asked me what he should do—then suggested that I drive him to the flat, where I could see for myself the body and the state of the premises. I said it would be a better idea if we went straight to Clydebank police station—and there he could give the police a full statement, in my presence, about his macabre find. He agreed to this, and I drove to Clydebank.

We spoke to the C I D officer in charge, Chief Inspector Gow, whom I knew well. I left Adam in the waiting room and we went into Gow's office. 'Bill,' I said. 'I want to tell you where you can find a mutilated and dismembered body in your area!'

'No, Joe!' he said. 'It's a quiet, sunny Sunday afternoon and most of our staff are off today.' Then he asked 'Are you pulling my leg?'

The thought struck me that I had not actually been to the flat and seen a dead body. It could be a hoax in the very worst taste. However, I reassured myself with the thought that if it were, Adam would surely have told me long before we arrived at the police station.

Gow had a word then with Adam, who repeated his story. Gow said he would go at once to the flat with one of his officers. I told him that I was going back home and he promised to telephone me later regarding developments. I left Adam at the police station.

The police did indeed find a body in the flat, as Adam had described.

As it turned out, Adam eventually admitted killing Friel. He had panicked afterwards and tried to dispose of the body by cutting off the arms and legs and trying to burn parts of the body in the open fireplace. At his trial he pled Guilty to murder and was sentenced to life imprisonment.

Perhaps my oddest introduction to a client, however, was in the early days of my practice, when I still lived in a top-floor flat in a tenement in Glasgow's Trongate.

One morning I opened the door to leave for the nearby Sheriff Court and stumbled over the semi-recumbent body of a man. He had made himself comfortable with his head resting against the wooden wall of the alcove between the inner and outer doors. His bottom was cushioned on my modest doormat. Recovering from my shock, I realised that Victor 'Scarface Jock' Russo urgently required my attention. At least he had had the decency not to interrupt my breakfast—or even, depending how long he had been there, my sleep!

Solicitors are repeatedly phoned at ungodly hours. Sometimes those who have been charged with murder ask the C I D—as is their entitlement—to get in touch with their lawyer. Occasionally too, identification parades have to be held very shortly after arrest, particularly if Service personnel or holidaymakers are to be witnesses, since they may be destined for faraway places the next day.

More often than not, however, it is persons charged with drunk-driving offences in the early morning who ask the police to phone their solicitor. Under the present system of breathalysing, little can be done by solicitors because the eventual outcome depends so much on the blood or urine samples which the police are entitled to demand from the arrested person. At three o'clock in the morning one usually advises the police officer to tell the client to call at the office within, say, seven days. The client is normally released several hours later—in the absence of other non-related offences—and does not make his first court appearance for some weeks. In fairness, the telephoning officer is usually apologetic, explaining that he is duty-bound to accede to the client's request and communicate with his lawyer.

Several years ago I was awakened at 2 a.m. by a police officer phoning to say that a client of mine called McGuinness was being detained on a drunk-driving charge and wanted to see me right away at the station. Rubbing the sleep from my eyes I said, as politely as circumstances permitted, that I saw little point in seeing McGuinness at the station. As an afterthought, I asked where he was being detained. 'Delta Division, London Metropolitan', I was told. Only when I woke up in the morning did I see the funny side!

Many a running battle I've heard over the phone. A wife rings me up and says 'Listen to him—he's trying to kill me!' 'Him', of course, being her husband. Once too, someone phoned me at 4 a.m. to tell me that the police were at his door demanding entry. I could even hear the shouts and thuds at the door. 'What will I do?' he said. Disgruntled, I retorted 'Let them in, of course!'

Some years ago, I recall, Nicholas Fairbairn—then a young advocate—had a hair-raising introduction to a client. He and I had travelled to Barlinnie Prison to have a consultation with a man who was awaiting trial on two unrelated murder charges. The circumstances of the murders were appalling and revealed little motive—and the client was of a somewhat violent and belligerent disposition at the best of times. But he became even more aggressive when he was addresed by his proper surname, Mitchell. Instead, he used an alias—Ramsay—and just before my first-ever meeting with him at the Sheriff Court, the police—to their everlasting credit—pulled me aside and told me that under no circumstances should I call this man Mitchell, but always Ramsay! There was some deep-seated reason for this foible. I gathered that it stemmed from a hatred of his father.

I remember, while driving Fairbairn to the prison, emphasising this fact in no uncertain manner. 'Don't mention the name Mitchell!' I admonished him.

We were ushered into an austere interviewing room in the prison hospital by one of the white-coated attendants, and within seconds our client joined us. Fairbairn, clutching the indictment and other papers (which, of course, referred to the client as 'Mitchell, alias Ramsay') greeted him. 'Good afternoon, Mr Mitchell. I am here to—'

At this juncture Fairbairn was seized by both velvet lapels and most unceremoniously pushed against the stone wall. He was called names that he hasn't heard used even in the House of Commons. He was as pale as a ghost. I shouted out the name 'Ramsay' several times and managed to rescue learned counsel—but the consultation that followed, needless to say, was one of the shortest I have ever attended.

Subsequently, prior to the case being called in the High Court, I advised the Clerk as a matter of urgency that, in calling the case, he should omit all reference to the name Mitchell and merely call my client Ramsay. This was duly done, much to the relief of Mr Fairbairn and—to a lesser extent—myself.

Some clients, of course, come by recommendation from clients I have successfully represented. One of my first excursions into the very different legal and procedural territory of Courts Martial came because a British Army sergeant, stationed in Germany, knew a client of mine,

Arthur Thompson. When Sergeant Karl Dahl, of the Royal Artillery Gunnery Establishment near Celle, faced a charge in 1978 of assaulting a staff sergeant by pointing a loaded Mauser automatic pistol at him and threatening him, he was advised by Thompson to instruct me. It was a successful mission for me, with Dahl being acquitted of the serious charges and retaining his rank and seniority.

Courts Martial were not entirely new to me. I had been instructed in my first General Court Martial—again in Germany—almost twenty years ago. And since the Dahl case I have flown to Dusseldorf to defend at a District Court Martial. Throughout the duration of such proceedings I am vested with the army rank of Major or Colonel— depending on whether the proceedings are District (maximum sentence two years' imprisonment) or General (life)— an aspect of these cases which I must confess I rather enjoy.

I relish also the challenge of the legal procedures, terminology and principles (which are purely English) and the ceremonial and pageantry attached to the affair: swords, full-dress uniform for the military personnel with civilian lawyers in their own compulsory uniform of wide red band around the waist, gown, black jacket, grey silk tie and pin-stripes.

What I did not enjoy during the Dahl case was the ribbing I got in the Officers' Mess! My visit coincided with Scotland's sojourn in Argentina for the World Cup. This event was the main topic of conversation in the Mess and I had to watch our pitiful attempts against Peru and Iran on their TV.

A question that keeps cropping up from laymen is: How can you defend someone when you know he is guilty of the crime charged?

When solicitors see a client for the first time they do not—at least, I do not—ask him whether or not he is guilty of the charge. The matter is put this way: How will you be pleading to the charge—Guilty or Not Guilty? If a client says 'Guilty', then steps are taken to act on this instruction. If he replies 'Not Guilty', then the preparation for the defence begins.

If, in the course of further dealings with the client, he advises me that he *is* guilty of the charge, then I can take one of two courses. I can send him to a solicitor outside my firm, or I can continue to defend him—on the clear understanding that, whereas I can put the Crown to the test with regard to proof beyond reasonable doubt, I cannot lead a substantive defence on his part. This means that I cannot call him as a witness, nor can I call defence witnesses who might try to exculpate him.

The client, of course, may think that his position will be prejudiced in the latter event, in which case he would consult a fresh solicitor about the whole matter.

A solicitor is the agent, or spokesman, for the accused. He is neither judge nor jury. He should be dispassionate and impartial in his approach to a trial, and should not be influenced unduly by his own personal views. An accused person may be a rascal with many previous convictions, but our law states that if he proposes to plead Not Gulity then he will be entitled to a fair trial. This means he is entitled to the application of the law in all its fairness.

A solicitor must try to divorce himself from the enormity of a crime and be clinical in his assessment of the situation. On occasions he may have doubts as to his client's veracity, but he must accept his client's instructions on this matter, provided the client has not confessed to him.

It would be extremely unfair were an accused person in the High Court obliged to represent himself—faced, as he would be, by the Depute, an experienced silk, his assistant, the might of the police force, first choice of doctors, pathologists, psychiatrists—as well as any number of typists available. The situation would be too one-sided. Miscarriages of justice would occur far more often in such circumstances. The power of the Crown and the numerous persons who could be called in to assist on the one hand— with on the other the solicitor and his limited staff—would make it wrong indeed for a certain accused not to be allowed to instruct legal assistance. There would then be a power dictating in advance of the jury.

To sum up the matter: solicitors may, from time to time, defend persons whom they think could be guilty, but nonetheless they will defend them to the best of their ability within the law.

The Glasgow criminal lawyer does come across one type of client who is peculiar to the city. He is the Glasgow 'hard man'. Indeed, a good deal of Glasgow's notoriety as a place of violence probably stems from the existence of this character—aggressive, insensible to the odds against him or to the consequences of his actions. The 'hard man' might well in earlier times have been described as a 'bonny fechter' and admired—always in the van of Scottish soldiery, matching the muskets of the Redcoats with claymores and boulders, seldom countenancing defeat. . . .

Nowadays he is regarded as a hoodlum, with a reputation for explosive reactions. For him the thought is the deed. To think of violence is to carry it out—hang the consequences, the odds, the pain of injury! Indeed, a salient characteristic of the Glasgow 'hardman' seems to be a high pain threshold. And he never appears to know when he is beaten. Along with a phenomenal tolerance for pain usually goes a tolerance too for enormous cargoes of liquor.

The abilities of 'hard men' to involve themselves in reasoned debate are minimal. They are much more inclined to resolve matters by doffing jackets and indulging in a 'square go'.

I have met and represented many 'hard men' and my recollection is that they show little fear of the consequences of their actions and are remarkably calm both on the eve of a trial and at its conclusion. They do not complain much, even following an adverse verdict, but seem to be realistic and philosophical about the outcome.

Some 'hard men' are well-built, while others are remarkably slight—one supposes that the heart, coupled

Colin Beattie

with tradition, is the all-important feature. Their reputation for violence is always at stake.

I do not wish to confuse 'hard men' with Glasgow 'chib men'—those who carry and are prepared to use the 'chib' (knife or razor). Many of the latter are basically cowards, and restrict their activities with weapons to those occasions when their victims are caught unarmed. No-one has any time for 'chib men', but many of us do have a softer spot for the fighting 'hard man'.

He will often be the first to rally to the assistance of someone incapable of looking after himself: 'hard men' do not enjoy liberties being taken with anyone. I have even known situations when they have rallied to the assistance of beleaguered police officers facing insurmountable odds!

'Big Coalie' Beattie from Partick is a 'hard man'. Over the years policemen have expressed the opinion that 'Big Coalie' is one of the hardest and most violent men in Glasgow. Despite this awesome billing, I must admit that he has been one of my favourite long-term clients.

Colin Beattie, to my knowledge, has never been involved in dishonesty or violence with weapons of any type. With his height and build the use of a weapon would hardly be necessary. It would appear, however, that 'Big Coalie' sometimes feels impelled to take the part of the underdog—often a complete stranger to him—and on occasions finishes up by being charged by the police. He just does not like to see one person taking advantage of another person less well-equipped to look after himself. Most of these skirmishes have not been of too serious a nature, although I have been instructed by Beattie at both Sheriff-and-jury and High Court level, with not unfavourable results.

So far as I am concerned, Beattie has always displayed a friendly disposition, never argumentative and particularly easy to deal with as a client. It never ceases to amaze me, too, that despite his many violent 'encounters' his face still bears no visible signs of scarring. He has always accepted my advice about his cases without question, even if this involved pleading Guilty. Mind you, it would be wrong to depict him as some kind of knight in shining armour: even he would be upset if he were so described, and it would be the height of folly to rile him! One cannot condone in any way his resentment towards authority and the forces of law and order. There are clearly two sides to the man, as to most of us. But I believe in taking a person as I find him.

I recall one occasion when 'Big Coalie' even took issue with another client of mine—in the form, luckily, of a mild though telling rebuke—because the other man had addressed me as 'Joe' and not 'Mr Beltrami', as 'Big Coalie' always does!

Over the years he has frequently been charged with police assault in our lower courts. Often these matters resulted from the arrest of someone else—and 'Big Coalie' going to his aid. I have often advised him not to take heed of the plight of others, but to think of his family and himself. No doubt he listens to this advice when I am giving it—but his memory must obviously lapse with time. . . .

More often than not the police, when they go to arrest 'Big Coalie', go in large numbers—I know of occasions when eight officers were detailed to arrest him—and sometimes (and very properly) have used their batons in the course of subduing him. Occasionally the batons have been known to break in the process.

On not a few occasions he has steadfastly refused medical treatment, obviously needed, at hospitals—simply because the arresting officers declined to remove his handcuffs, thus exercising a very wise discretion. However, 'Big Coalie' regarded the matter as one of principle and would rather lose blood unnecessarily than conform. On one such occasion, nearly twenty years ago, he required to be taken—albeit reluctantly—from the prison hospital block to the Royal Infirmary, where he was detained for three weeks suffering from serious head injuries following violent resistance to arrest. I remember visiting him there, in the casualty ward, and what a sorry sight he was! He had numerous lacerations to his head, and his nose had been fractured. He duly appeared in court at a later stage— his recovery powers must be remarkable—when he was very properly sentenced to a prison term on charges of assaulting six police officers. The medical evidence I adduced on his behalf probably helped in mitigating the sentence to one of nine months' imprisonment!

And finally, perhaps the oddest interaction between solicitor and client I remember was the case of Richard Forde, who pled Guilty to a charge of stealing three blazers and three clothes hangers from an Argyle Street store. Forde was due for trial on an entirely different matter the following week and, speaking in mitigation of the theft charge, I was obliged to admit to the Sheriff that I was partly responsible for my client's present predicament. He had, in fact, stolen the blazers in order to raise the money for my fee so that I would be properly instructed to defend him at his forthcoming trial. . . .

2
The Trial of Walter Scott Ellis

In 1961 there were some five or six experienced criminal lawyers of proven stature in Scotland. Alas, I was not one of them, although my name had been heard of in comparatively minor skirmishes in court for about five years. I had been successful in five capital murder cases over the years preceding 1961, but in all honesty there had been nothing special about them. Any number of young lawyers, with suitable counsel, would have achieved similar results. There are some cases which, failing serious blunders, cannot be lost. I had come, however, to enjoy the exciting cut-and-thrust involved in these knife-edge capital charges, when conviction meant the unmentionable—the death sentence. I have been instructed in several hundred non-capital murder cases and the feeling, I must say, is not quite the same. There was much more strain for lawyer and counsel involved in cases of a capital murder—not to mention the accused.

In 1957 the Homicide Act categorised murder in such a way that the death penalty could apply in certain circumstances. Under Section 5 of the Act it was a capital offence to commit murder in the furtherance of theft; to commit murder by shooting or by using explosives; to murder a policeman in the execution of his duty; and to murder in the course of resisting arrest. Under Section 6 it was also a capital offence to commit more than one murder.

I disagreed with the Homicide Act. I recall a case in 1962 when two clients were charged with kicking a tramp to death in Glasgow. They were also charged, jointly, with stealing the sum of ten shillings from him. During the pre-trial preparations, which lasted three months, both clients were more concerned about being acquitted on the trifling charge of the theft of ten shillings than they seemed to be about the extremely grave charge of kicking a person to death—because the theft of ten shillings made the matter a capital offence. Matters were thus put badly out of focus by this ridiculous categorisation.

So far as the section dealing with murder by shooting or using explosives is concerned, it is my experience that most murders are caused by stabbing—using knives, bayonets and the like—and not by the use of guns or explosives. Why distinguish between murder by shooting and murder by stabbing someone through the heart? I saw no logical reason for this distinction. The powers that be have said that the root cause of violence in our country is the possession of weapons, such as knives— yet the Homicide Act did not encompass the use of knives, except in the furtherance of theft or in cases of more than one murder.

In 1965 the Homicide Act was repealed by the Murder (Abolition of the Death Penalty) Act 1965. It had had a trial run of eight years.

I have often felt that the possession of offensive weapons should be treated much more seriously by the courts; at the moment a person charged with this offence is almost invariably fined in our summary courts. To stamp out violence we must get to the root—and that is possession of offensive weapons. After all, if a person has a reasonable excuse for having a weapon, he will be acquitted—but potential murderers seldom have a reasonable excuse. The number of people charged with 'carrying an offensive weapon' has been a scourge in this country for the past thirty years.

But back to 1961, when murder was capital in certain circumstances, such as the use of a firearm. . . .

Walter Ellis senior, father of a man called Walter Scott Ellis who had been arrested and charged with capital murder for allegedly shooting a Glasgow taxi driver in Castlemilk, was looking for a lawyer to represent his son.

In those days there was no Legal Aid and lawyers and counsel were not paid by the State for the work done by them. The accused had to pay for legal services, although in fairness to our profession, many lawyers and counsel were prepared to do these cases for the challenge and for little else in the way of remuneration. There was in existence at the time a Central Legal Aid Fund, out of which counsel— and occasionally a solicitor—could apply for a hardship payment (generally in the region of twenty pounds) provided the facts justified it. The whole situation is entirely different now.

There would be no problem, of course, if the accused or his relations were in possession of substantial funds, but this was seldom the case—and Walter Scott Ellis did not fall into that category.

His father—now dead—told me, when he first consulted me on behalf of his son, that he had already been to two well-known criminal lawyers before coming to me. For various reasons, these lawyers had declined to take the case. I admired him for telling me this. He went on to say that he could only afford a very modest fee. The sum he offered—one hundred pounds—could not possibly have covered even my own time, far less that of senior and junior counsel too, who would have to be instructed in such a case. A solicitor had to arrange acceptable fees for both counsel and this, on occasions, meant deducting a portion of his own personal remuneration.

Despite the lack of monetary incentive, I rose to the challenge. I already knew from reading the Press that this was to be a very big case indeed, and honestly felt proud at being asked to handle Mr Ellis's son's future. I knew also that the Crown would have a reasonable case against him, but decided to take the brief, third choice or not. From that day on until the conclusion of the trial, Mr Ellis senior conferred with me on numerous occasions. He was most attentive to his son's interests.

On the following day I interviewed Walter Scott Ellis for the first time—in Barlinnie Prison. I had never dealt with him in the past, although I had heard of him.

He was then nearly thirty years old, slightly built, of average height and quite good-looking. He had jet black hair with a side parting and was always clean and smartly turned out. He struck me as quiet and soft-spoken. His manners were good, and I experienced no difficulties in all my dealings with him. He was not argumentative—as many accused are—and allowed his advisers to make the decisions, knowing that they acted in his best interests.

Ellis showed me his copy of the charges against him—capital murder and the possession of a number of live bullets at his home in Rockcliffe Street, Bridgeton. He was frank in telling me that he would have little answer to the second and much more trivial charge, but so far as the main matter was concerned, he strongly denied—and continued to do so—having been involved in the shooting.

I told him of his father's visit to my office and of his instructions to me, but pointed out that it was not his father who had been charged. Did he, Walter Scott Ellis, wish me to represent him at his trial?

He must have been told by his father of his difficulty in obtaining a lawyer, and possibly thought that he had little alternative but to brief a willing and eager me. It was, I suppose, a case of Hobson's choice—I was literally his sole lifeline. He said that he did indeed wish me to represent him, and so began a three-month period of extensive preparation—and worry.

I took a detailed statement from Ellis as to his movements on the night of the murder and obtained names and addresses of witnesses who could, according to my client, vouch for these movements. I saw him regularly during the period before the trial. He was demanding—but who could blame him, in view of the awesome penalty he faced? He intended to plead alibi in respect of the serious charge, and dutifully I prepared this and interviewed the witnesses he proposed to call in support of it. He maintained that on the night of the murder he had been attending a party at the home of a man called Brady in Mill Street, Bridgeton. Afterwards he had gone by taxi to his home in Rockliffe Street, also in Bridgeton, where he had spent the night.

By this time I had already started up a professional relationship with Nicholas Fairbairn, then a young advocate of only some two years' standing. Together we had had a run of marked success during his short spell at the Bar, and I briefed him to take this serious capital case.

Although Fairbairn had accepted the brief, I was informed by the Dean of the Faculty of Advocates only three weeks before the trial that I must also instruct a senior counsel. I explained that my client, Fairbairn and myself were pleased with the existing arrangement—but there was to be no exception to this rule of the Bar. I was given a list of three Q Cs who would be available, and I went through to Edinburgh and instructed Ronnie A Bennett Q C to lead the defence.

Meanwhile, Fairbairn and I had had many meetings about the case, particularly on the forensic and technical side. There was to be vital and crucial evidence concerning glass and ballistics. We also studied the post mortem report. Since we were already advanced in our preparation on those aspects, I decided to take a most unusual course of action. I would split the defence, so that Fairbairn could concentrate on the extensive technical aspects of the evidence while Bennett would cover all the straightforward factual questions. Prior to the trial, Lord Patrick approved our unique motion to do this, as a result of which, each counsel was to cross-examine in the sphere allotted to him. Perhaps the motion was superfluous, in that, where there are two counsel, junior counsel does on occasion deal with formal, noncontentious evidence in order to gain experience. In this particular case, however, most of the evidence was extremely important, and the trial judge was advised in advance as a matter of courtesy.

The final jury summing-up was, as was usual, to be done by Bennett—after due consultation with both Fairbairn and myself.

This is the only occasion when I have insisted on such a line as instructing solicitor. Teamwork at this trial had to be of the best—and it proved to be just that.

Three weeks before the start of the trial, scheduled for 30 October 1961, I received the indictment.

The final charges agaist Ellis were 'That [my client] did....on 23 July 1961, in Tormusk Road, Glasgow, near No 11 thereof, assault John M Walkinshaw, 6 Horndean Crescent, Glasgow, the driver of a motor taxi-cab, and did discharge at him a loaded firearm and shoot him in the shoulder and head, and that [he] did murder him, and such is Capital Murder within the meaning of the Homicide Act 1957, Section 5', and 'On 27 July 1961, in the house occupied by [him] at 31 Rockcliffe Street, Glasgow, [he] did have in [his] possession ammunition for a firearm, namely eight .22 cartridges and three .32 cartridges, without holding a Firearm Certificate, contrary to the Firearms Act 1937, Section 1.'

There were one hundred and twenty-five witnesses on the prosecution list—I remember this because I interviewed most of them at least twice—and there were some seventy-three productions. But no gun was produced, as it had never been found.

The rest of the *dramatis personae* at the trial were to be:

—the late Lord Patrick, the judge, then seventy-two years old and a lawyer of the highest calibre. He was an extremely fair judge, well-known for his total impartiality and 'straight-down-the-middle' jury charges.

—Norman R Wylie, Advocate Depute, heading the prosecution. He later became a Tory MP and Lord Advocate, and is now Lord Wylie, Senator of the College of Justice.

The wood—known as Glen Wood—which separates Tormusk Road from Ardencraig Road was of absolutely vital importance in this case. And it often pays to visit the scene of the crime. Fairbairn and I must have been through that wood on at least six different occasions, and very often returned home up to our ankles in mud. The significance of the wood will be made clear later on, in the course of the evidence. We had also visited Pilkington's, the English glass experts, and the Scottish Central Glassworks of Alloa.

The police had done a number of trial runs by car from and to various points between Bridgeton—where, undoubtedly, Ellis had been that night—and Castlemilk. The timing of these runs was to be of importance—indeed, it turned out to be crucial—so I engaged the services of a Glasgow taxi-driving client, Wolf Stringer, who did the same (and additional) runs for me. Wolf was later to be called as a defence witness.

At the Pleading Diet on 20 October I duly appeared and tendered pleas of Not Guilty to both charges. I also lodged a Special Defence of Alibi, in which it was claimed that my client had been not at Tormusk Road but at Rockcliffe Street at the time of the capital crime. The strain of preparation was certainly taking its toll and I remember eventually having a nightmare about six days before the start of the trial—waking up about three o'clock in the morning, in a cold sweat, just as a faceless man was being executed on a mental interpretation of the gallows. I say, 'mental interpretation' because I have never seen the gallows, nor do I ever wish to do so.

Two days before the start of this memorable trial, Bennett, Fairbairn and I had our final consultation with Ellis at Barlinnie. The lengthy, rigorous preparation was now complete.

The Crown case on the main charge was a classic circumstantial one. There were no eye-witnesses to identify Ellis at Tormusk road, but there was a succession of small adminicles, or pieces of evidence; not one of them cast-iron in itself, but each forming a tiny link in a rather weighty chain of evidence. As the chain was formed link by link, so—the Crown hoped—inferences would be drawn until finally the accused would be so enmeshed and fettered in it that his guilt would be plain.

Very often, it is said, the picture painted by circumstantial evidence can be even more certain and conclusive than that of eye witnesses who can, after all, be cross-examined closely—but how can one cross-examine, for example, a piece of glass or a fingerprint? In this case, the defence intention was to render the ultimate inference impotent by neutralising as many of the links as possible. In short we were aiming to persuade the jury to draw inferences which excluded the accused—indeed, exculpated him—from the various diffused pieces of evidence. It was also intended to highlight the omissions in the Crown case—such as the non-appearance of the accused's fingerprints among the many found in the taxi. And the fact that the only two possible eye-witnesses had identified someone else at the identification parade, a person who was to be on our defence list of witnesses because he bore so little resemblance to Ellis.

There were many other sound defence points, which will be dealt with at a later stage. . . .Nevertheless, the Crown case required to be treated with the utmost respect.

The trial opened rather dramatically. For good reason—we had even then decided that, all things being equal, Ellis should not be called as a witness in his own defence—the Special Defence of Alibi was withdrawn. We knew, from the lengthy statement that we had taken from Ellis, that if called he might dispute comparitively minor points of the Crown evidence and so put his own credibility in the melting pot. The points with which he might join issue were not all material to the outcome of the trial. We felt generally that we could now break the Crown chain at more than one point without requiring the benefit of our client's testimony and it would have been tactically wrong to proceed with an alibi defence without calling the accused in support of it.

You can imagine the difficulties involved in arriving at this decision—to begin a capital murder trial having already decided that the accused would not be called! The reasons had been fully explained to Ellis, a man of considerable intelligence, and we took him along with us on this difficult and onerous decision. In the event, we were amply justified.

I felt almost relieved when battle was joined. The three of us could not have done more for the accused. We were now on the home straight. In about three days' time we would know if our tactics and planning had borne fruit. Having said that, we fully appreciated that numerous meetings lay in front of us. Other spontaneous decisions would have to be made in the course of the trial and I prayed that we would not be found wanting in any of them.

The Advocate Depute, Mr Norman Wylie, opened his case by calling the dead man's widow, Mrs Helen Walkinshaw. She was quite composed when giving her evidence, but was dressed in black.

She told the court that her late husband had been the owner of five radio-taxis. He had left home by about 10 p.m. to drive one of his cabs. She had expected him home about 1 a.m., and sat up waiting for him. At three o'clock she had been called to the Victoria Infirmary, but learned when she arrived that her husband had been transferred to Killearn Hospital. She saw him there. He was unconscious, and died later in the morning.

Everyone in the courtroom was extremely sympathetic, and somewhat moved by her evidence, so tragic was the case. Clearly, John Walkinshaw had been an excellent husband and father. He had obviously worked hard to build up his taxi fleet.

The next witness was an official from the City Architect's Department who produced a large-scale map of the Castlemilk area. Mr Bennett, for the defence, asked him about the distance by road over two separate routes from Mill Street, Bridgeton to Tormusk Road. The witness replied that by one route it was a little over three miles and by the other, four and a half miles.

After him came Mrs Jean Finlayson, of 9 Tormusk Road, who told the court that there had been a small party at her home that evening. At about 1.30 a.m. the party began to break up and her husband Ronald telephoned for a taxi for his guests at about 1.40. He was told that a cab would arrive in about ten minutes.

Minutes later Mrs Finlayson had gone out on to her verandah to see if the taxi had drawn up, but it had not. She left the verandah and about a minute afterwards returned to it as she could hear the sound of a vehicle's engine. She saw a taxi draw up nearby, on her side of the road. She told her husband, who went downstairs to engage it. Seconds later he ran back to the house, saying that there was something wrong with the cab driver. He asked her to dial 999 for the police.

When he approached the taxi-cab, which was parked outside No 11, Ronald Finlayson said the driver was slumped over the wheel, with his face covered in blood. The engine was still running and the radio was operating. There was a crackling from it, and he could hear voices. No-one was in the cab. The taxi was pulled into the kerb at a slight angle. Questioned by the Crown, Finlayson said that about ten minutes after telephoning for a taxi, and before he had left the house, he had heard two shots. He looked out of his living room window, which was one storey up, and saw a man running across the grass verge in front of his house and making for the Glen Wood, which was on the opposite side of the road. At the other end of this wood was Ardencraig Road. 'The man was carrying something white in his right hand,' he told the court. 'I did not know what it was, but, from the distance, it looked like a handkerchief.'

Finlayson went on to say that the man was running very fast and must have known where he was going because there was a small burn at that part of the wood, and not many knew that there was also a small stone bridge over it close to that point.

Asked about a description of the running man, he said that he was of medium height and size. He had lost sight of the man after he had entered the wood—'because it was very dark there'. Minutes after seeing all this, he had gone outside to look for the taxi.

Mr Wylie was about to sit down, having exhausted his examination of the witness, when the Procurator

Fiscal, who was assisting him, appeared to suggest that he put one final question to the witness. As a general rule, such questions should not be asked unless the questioner has a fair idea of the answer he will receive. How many times has a final question proved to be disastrous?

From later evidence it was to be conceded—and amply proved—that Ellis had been wearing a very dark suit that evening. Witnesses at the party he had attended earlier that night described his clothing. The Crown knew about this— and with the best will in the world all that the Fiscal was seeking to do was to establish that the running man had been wearing a dark suit.

And so the Advocate Depute asked 'Finally, what was the colour of the suit worn by the running man?'

'He was wearing a very light-coloured suit,' replied Finlayson.

Had the Crown visited the locus of the crime at night they would have realised that the street lighting was of the orange sodium type, under which colour and shades are distorted and there can be little accuracy as to whether things are light or dark. As it was, the first telling point had come at the expense of the Crown.

In cross-examination, Mr Bennett asked Finlayson if he had attended an identification parade at Southern Police Headquarters about a week after the incident. He said he had, and had picked out a man who looked like the running man.

He went on to say that the man he had identified had given the name 'Hart'.

Did you say that there was no other man on the parade who was like the man seen by you?'

'Yes,' said Finlayson. And it was common knowledge that Ellis had been on that parade, along with five other people including Hart.

Further questioned about the object he had seen in the running man's hand, Finlayson said that it *could* have been a gun but he was inclined to the view that it had been of a cloth fabric rather than metal.

Another witness, William Allison, who had been at Finlayson's party, said that he had gone to the window along with Ronald Finlayson and had seen a man running across the road towards the wood. He said that the man was carrying something which glittered. I noticed that, on this occasion, the Crown did not ask Allison as to the colour of the suit worn by the running man. Nor did the defence!

It emerged that Allison, too, had identified a man called Hart at the parade as being like the man he had seen running into the wood. (There must have been a stage at that parade when Hart began to have doubts about the wisdom of volunteering himself as a stand-in!)

Other people living in the immediate vicinity were called—some of whom had heard the sound of two shots. They estimated the time at about 1.45 a.m. Another resident said that she had been awakened by a taxi outside her window. She was sure it was a taxi, because she heard a radio. She went on to say that she also heard two male voices. 'It was like someone speaking and someone answering,' she said. Then she had heard a bang, like glass breaking, after which she had dozed off. She was awakened by another bang. 'I thought it was a taxi door being slammed.'

Under cross-examination, she said she had heard footsteps before the second bang, as if someone had approached the taxi and was going into it. She heard the footsteps after a crash of glass and assumed that the taxi would be leaving with a passenger. The engine had been running all the time.

Another taxi driver, John Devine, of 15 Tormusk Road, had parked his own taxi for the night outside his close (the common passage to his house) at about 1.30 a.m. He went into his house and began to read a newspaper. Fifteen minutes later he heard another taxi draw up nearby. It stopped with the engine running, and this was followed by 'two definite bangs'. He looked out of his window and to the right, where he saw a taxi. All seemed to be well, so he went back to reading his newspaper. He then heard a message being relayed through

Key to Map

➤ position and direction of Walkinshaw's taxi when last contacted
1 where Ellis and Brady hired a taxi
2 Ellis's flat in Rockcliffe Street
3 scene of the murder
4 where 'Ellis' was picked up by McLeod
5 where McLeod set 'Ellis' down
6 Ellis's parents' house
■■ shortest route from Mill Street to Stravannan Road
－－ route alleged to have been followed by Ellis through Glen Wood

BRIDGETON

River Clyde

RUTHERGLEN

KING'S PARK

Croftfoot Roundabout

CASTLEMILK

Glen Wood

the taxi's radio system, and minutes later a number of other cabs arrived outside. He went out and discovered that one of his colleagues was in trouble. Mr Devine said that he noticed the figures 10/4*d* showing on the meter, although he could not remember whether or not it had been in the 'stop' position.

By this point in the trial, the general concensus of evidence had established that the murder had occurred about 1.45 a.m., that two shots had been fired and that the probable assailant had run frantically into Glen Wood carrying something in his right hand.

Donald Crerar, the taxi radio controller who had given Walkinshaw his last instructions over the air, said he got a call for a taxi for a person called Baillie at No 9 Tormusk Road. ('Baillie' was the name on the Finlaysons' door.) He said the call came at a peak period on a Sunday morning for taxi traffic, and he had begun by putting over a radio call for any driver in the Castlemilk area. There was no reply, so he put out another call, for any driver proceeding to, or dropping in, that area. This call had been answered by Walkinshaw, who came on the air and said he was in Myrtle Park and heading towards Aitkenhead Road. The time was about 2 a.m.

Crerar said that he recognised Walkinshaw's voice plainly and passed on to him the instruction to go to No 9 Tormusk Road after dropping his fare. Walkinshaw had replied 'Roger'. A few minutes later, Crerar said, he was relieved for a tea-break but had remained in the control room and could hear the radio traffic. He had been present in the room when an emergency call came over the air and a strange voice asked for an ambulance and said that a taxi driver was 'in a bad way'. The controller then put out a general alarm call for all other cabs in the area to proceed to the spot in Tormusk Road.

Mrs Mary Buchan, of 30 Tormusk Road, said she looked out of the window of her house and saw a taxi standing outside. It was about 1.45 a.m. Asked how she knew the time, she said that she was up late with the baby, which had just fallen asleep. She had looked at her watch, which she had checked with the wireless on the previous evening.

There was a dramatic moment early in the evidence of the next witness, a taxi driver called John McLeod. He pointed to Ellis in the dock and said that he had picked him up in his taxi in the early morning of that same Sunday. McLeod said he had dropped a fare in Ardencraig Street, Castlemilk shortly after 2 a.m. He made a U-turn to go back to the city. By this time it must have been 2.05. He had been flagged down by Ellis, McLeod said, in Ardencraig Road, near Glen Wood. When he picked him up, Ellis had been wearing no coat and no hat. 'I got the impression that he was carrying a handkerchief when he boarded the taxi, but it was only an impression I gained from the fact that when he paid the fare Ellis changed a handkerchief from one hand to the other.' On being asked where he wished to be taken, Ellis had said 'Up the Drive'. McLeod understood that to mean that Ellis wanted to go up Castlemilk Drive. They had had some conversation. Ellis has asked him if he did not like short hires. McLeod had said that one hire was no different from another— 'We are out to make money.' He had proceeded along Ardencraig Road, turned into Castlemilk Drive and then turned right into Ardmeleish Road. There he was directed to a T-junction at Stravannan Road, where Ellis paid him off. He had been given rather a large tip for such a particularly short journey and had then proceeded to the Croftfoot Roundabout, where he arrived at 2.15 a.m.

McLeod was asked by the Advocate Depute if he had noticed where Ellis had gone on leaving the taxi at Stravannan Road. McLeod said that he had not been really interested and did not know. At no time did Ellis mention the name 'Stravannan Road'—which was where his parents lived.

Mr Wylie then asked McLeod if he could identify Mill Street, Bridgeton from a map which had been handed to him. When he said he could, he was asked to indicate the route which would normally be taken by a taxi driver going from Mill Street to Stravannan Road. McLeod said that there were two routes he, as a taxi driver, would be likely to use, and demonstrated these on the map. One of them would be by Shawfield Drive, Polmadie Road, Aitkenhead Road and Carmunnock Road to the Croftfoot Roundabout, and then into Dougrie Road.

Shortly after Ellis had been arrested McLeod had picked him out firmly at an identification parade as being the fare he had taken up in Ardencraig Road. He was absolutely certain as to his identity. He was asked if he could remember anything about the clothing worn by Ellis, and he said that Ellis had been wearing a dark suit.

Incidentally, at all our consulations with Ellis he had always denied hailing a taxi-cab in Ardencraig Road that morning. And in cross-examination Mr Bennett suggested to McLeod that he was mistaken in identifying Ellis. But McLeod would make no concession on this point.

He was asked how he came to pick up Ellis. McLeod said that he saw a man walking along Ardencraig Road in the same direction as he was travelling. The man waved to him to stop. The distance McLeod took him was about three quarters of a mile. The hire was only two shillings, but he had been handed five. 'I told him he was off his head, giving me five shillings for a two-shilling hire and I gave him back some change, which left me with three-and-six.'

McLeod confirmed for Bennett that the man, whoever he was, had been in a quiet and pleasant mood. On being asked if there had been anything odd about the passenger, McLeod said 'No.' Asked if the man had been out of breath, as if he had been running earlier, McLeod again said no. Had he noticed any sign of vegetation about his clothing or shoes? No, he hadn't. Had there been excess mud on his shoes? No.

McLeod went on to say that he had reported the fact of his Ardencraig Road hire to the Police that same morning—as soon as he heard about the shooting of his colleague. He had given a description of the man he had picked up, and the description had fitted the accused. He had not been shown a photograph of Ellis before the identification parade.

Another witness said she had been the fare taken to her home by McLeod and that she had arrived at her house at about 2 a.m.

Fingerprint experts were called by the prosecution and stated that they had carefully examined Walkinshaw's taxi for impressions. They had found none 'of any value.' In cross-examination by Mr Bennett, the experts said that they had found seven impressions in all but that two were later eliminated as having been made by Walkinshaw's drivers.

A police officer in charge of the case was then called—Chief Inspector Thomas Joyce, who revealed that he was called to the scene of the crime early that Sunday morning and had initiated enquiries. Police had formed the view that the killer might be a local person, and so 1430 houses in the area were visited by a team of officers. These visits took place within two days of the crime and questionnaires were completed by the occupants, in which they were asked to account for their movements from 9 p.m. on the Saturday until 3 a.m. on the Sunday. One of the thousands of persons questioned had been Walter Scott Ellis. In his form he had stated that he was at his parents' home in Stravannan Road, Castlemilk from 11 p.m. on the Saturday until Sunday midday. He had been there along with his parents, with whom he often stayed although he had a flat in Bridgeton.

Chief Inspector Joyce also said that he examined the area in Tormusk Road where the taxi had been found. He had found many small pieces of glass close to the offside front wheel of the taxi. The windscreen had shattered after being struck by a bullet, and the pieces of glass consisted of clear glass and green glass. A broken Younger's of Alloa beer bottle had been seen at the kerb.

Within hours of starting enquiries Joyce had learned from witnesses that Ellis had been at a house in Mill Street Bridgeton, on the Saturday night and had left by taxi. Joyce had advertised in the national Press for the driver who had picked up a fare in Mill Street at around midnight on Saturday to come forward and assist the police. No-one had done so.

Joyce told the court of the way in which he had arrested Ellis on 27 July on a capital murder charge. He had called at a house in Rockcliffe Street, but there was no-one there. He managed to gain entry, but the house did not appear to have been inhabited because, for one thing, there were no beds. Indeed, the only furniture was two chairs. Later that day he called at Stravannan Road, Castlemilk, the home of Ellis's parents. He saw the accused there—at this point he identified Ellis in the dock. He charged him, but Ellis made no reply. As Ellis was being driven to the Southern Police Station—and while he was under caution—he said, according to Mr Joyce, 'I was never in a taxi at the weekend. I was in the house at the weekend and my family will prove it.'

In cross-examination, Joyce admitted that there had been a great deal of publicity in the newspapers about the crime, and that the fact that it was a taxi driver who had been shot had been extremely prominent. This publicity had taken place over a period of three days before Ellis's arrest.

Joyce was followed by Detective Inspector Raeside of the Southern Division, who told the court about a visit he had made to Ellis's house in Rockcliffe Street on 27 July. There he had found a matchbox containing eleven live cartridges. It had been on an easy chair in the kitchen and had been hidden by clothing.

Inspector Raeside and some colleagues had carried out a test in order to estimate the time it would take to trot from Tormusk Road to Ardencraig Road through Glen Wood. He said that, all watches being properly synchronised, it took them exactly six and a half minutes.

The inspector had also made a test run in a taxi from Mill Street to Tormusk Road, stopping at No 11. In this time the meter—which had been tested and proved to be accurate—changed to 8/ – when the taxi stopped there. The run had taken exactly ten minutes.

He had waited in the taxi until the meter registered 10/4*d*, the figure quoted that night of the shooting. 'This represented seven periods of three minutes' waiting time. From the tests, I concluded that the taxi was actually standing in Tormusk Road not less than twenty-one minutes and not more than twenty-four minutes before the amount on the meter was noted at the time of the shooting.'

Raeside stated that when Ellis was charged under the Firearms Act with possession of bullets in Rockcliffe Street he had replied 'Nothing to say.'

Another witness said that he had been at a party in Mill Street, Bridgeton where he saw Ellis and a man called John Brady. 'I saw Brady getting out of a taxi—and Ellis was still in it. The time must have been around 1.30 a.m.' he said.

John Brady told the court that he and Ellis had walked to the top of Mill Street at Main Street, where he, Brady, hired a taxi. It took them to another address in Mill Street, where Brady got out. Ellis must have stayed in the taxi, Brady said. He added that Ellis had told him next day that he had jumped out of the taxi in Bridgeton because he didn't have enough money to pay for the fare to Castlemilk. Questioned by Mr Bennett for the defence, Brady admitted that he had been very drunk that evening.

A number of witnesses were called who had attended the party in Mill Street. They said that Brady and Ellis had left at about 1.15 a.m. and that Brady had been seen stopping a taxi nearby. Both Ellis and Brady had driven off in the taxi along Mill Street. In cross-examination, these witnesses said that they knew that Ellis had recently acquired a flat in Rockcliffe Street and that he could have been going home to there. They also said that very often he lived with his parents in Castlemilk.

Evidence, by this time, had shown that the police had advertised for the driver who picked up Brady and Ellis—but had received no replies. The Crown inference was that, by a process of elimination, the driver must have been Walkinshaw—who was of course, unable to get in touch with them. The police said that 1220 registered taxi drivers had been interviewed and that not one of them had said he had picked up a fare in Mill Street. These taxi drivers were not cited as witnesses, and by the time of the trial about fifty of them had left the country for one reason or another.

Other witnesses from the party told the court that when Ellis left the house he was carrying a small brown parcel and that he had seemed concerned about it. They were of the opinion that the parcel contained a half-bottle of wine.

Several neighbours were called who lived in Stravannan Road and who said that they had heard someone enter the close-mouth of No 48 (where the Ellises lived) at about 2 a.m. on the night in question. But they had not seen who it was.

One of the key Crown witnesses was Detective Superintendent James K McLellan B Sc, who at that time had completed twenty-five years' police service attached to the Identification Bureau. He had several forensic qualifications and was an acknowledged police expert in this field. He told the court he had examined a pair of shoes taken from Ellis and that embedded in the left heel and welt he had found tiny fragments of glass. Some of the fragments were coloured green and others were clear. He compared these fragments with other pieces of glass taken from the scene of the crime. He said that it was his opinion that the pieces found embedded in the heel and welt of Ellis's left shoe could have been from the same source as those found at the kerbside in Tormusk Road. The samples were identical in colour and type of glass.

He was also shown one of the bullets from the matchbox found in the flat at Rockcliffe Street, and compared these with the fragments taken from the taxi driver's head. He said that these were not the same and that the bullets in the matchbox did not come from the same batch of lead as those found to have caused Walkinshaw's death. All the bullets found in the matchbox, he said, were of a solid-nosed type whereas the two bullets fired by the assailant were hollow-nosed. The lead, tin and copper content of the respective samples was different.

On being questioned by Fairbairn for the defence, Mr McLellan agreed that no adverse conclusion could be drawn from the alleged possession by Ellis of the bullets contained in the matchbox. The killer bullets were entirely different in age and content from those found in Ellis's house.

Fairbairn then went on to cross-examine this expert witness in a highly knowledgeable way about the density and refractive index of glass. There were many puzzled faces among the jury of eleven men and four women as questions and answers flashed back and forth.

McLellan said that nearly all plain glass in this country was manufactured by one firm—Pilkington's. Although windscreen glass is of a reinforced type, there is no way of differentiating, when it is shattered, between glass that is reinforced and glass that is not. The shattering of the glass destroys the evidence of reinforcement and, accordingly, all that could be said of the clear glass found at the kerbside was that it was of a very common type, mainly supplied by one firm. He agreed with Mr Fairbairn that two fragments of green glass—which, he said, had come from Ellis's left heel— had at one time formed part of a beer bottle. There were initials on the glass which might mean that these were manufactured by the Scottish Central Glassworks of Alloa.

'Do you know that that firm supplies bottles to three of the largest breweries in Scotland?'

'Yes.'

'Would you then agree that there are possibly thousands, if not millions, of such bottles?'

'Yes.'

'Would you say that there are inevitably, in the roads and streets of towns and cities, hundreds of fragments of similar glass?'

'Yes.'

It should be pointed out at this stage that the Crown carefully examined plain and green glass by spectrometer and worked out the refractive index down to four decimal figures. To this level there was no variation whatsoever in density. But beer-bottle glass made by the Scottish Central Glassworks was supplied to Tennant's, Younger's and McLaughlin's breweries—who turned out at that time more than seven thousand gross weekly between them. It was clear that the fact that the respective samples of clear and green glass had similar density was of little value and was exactly what was to be expected.

McLellan also agreed with Fairbairn that McLeod's taxi had not been tested for fingerprints as one would have expected under the circumstances. Had these tests been carried out on the taxi-cab, and had no prints been found traceable to Ellis, this would most certainly have strengthened the cross-examination of McLeod on the point of his identificaton of the accused.

Inspector George Cook followed McLellan into the witness box and he too had formidable forensic qualifications. He said that the clear-glass particles found in the left heel and welt of Ellis's shoe had similar density and refractive index to the particles found at the kerbside. He also said that, so far as the green bottle-glass was concerned, he would expect most of the bottles made by the Scottish Central Glassworks of Alloa to show similar density, because of their bulk manufacture. Fairbairn questioned Inspector Cook on this point—and the witness said that the police did not always take percentage accuracy into account when conducting their experiments. When Fairbairn asked if it was not the case that no experiment could be valid unless the percentage accuracy had been calculated, the Inspector hesitated for a moment, then replied that he did not agree that this was necessarily so.

There then followed a most technical line of questioning, with phrases like 'the Becke-line', 'spectrometer' and 'dissertations on the degree of error in experiments taken to the fourth decimal place'.

Inspector Cook finally agreed that there would be many millions of sheets of glass supplied by Pilkington's all within the same fractional refractive index. The same could be said of properties in the green bottle-glass manufactured at Alloa. As Inspector Cook left the witness box, it was obvious that much of the sting had been taken out of the 'glass evidence'. There was, however, still the combination of the two distinctly different types of glass to be considered. This was, to say the least, extremely coincidental.

Detective Inspector Sowter, a police firearms expert, gave evidence next. The court was hushed as a sliver of bone taken from the dead man's brain tissue was handed up to him in the witness box. Sowter said that this piece of bone had been 'punched' inwards. This sort of injury could only come from an open-ended bullet—or a hollow-nosed bullet that had been cut down. He went on to say that the bullets found in the matchbox in Rockcliffe Street were entirely different from those used in the crime. The Rockcliffe bullets had all been solid-nosed. He was satisfied, he said in conclusion, that the type of weapon used in the crime was a little pocket revolver.

Detective Chief Superintendent Tom Goodall, Head of Glasgow C I D, followed Sowter into the box. In his evidence, he said 'I had certain information published in Glasgow newspapers, to the effect that we wanted to interview any taxi driver who had lifted a fare in Mill Street, Bridgeton, near Main Street, early on the morning of July 23rd.' He was handed a copy of the *Scottish Daily Express,* dated Saturday 16 August. After reading from the newspaper, he told the court there had been no response to his appeal. 'Thereafter, I subsequently published in all Glasgow Sunday newspapers and the evening and daily newspapers. There was still no response. After this, I made a note of all registered Glasgow taxi drivers and sent each of them a circular letter, giving details of the appeal. Again, the results were negative.'

Mr Goodall said that he had been present when several officers had jogged through Glen Wood from Tormusk Road to its exit at Ardencraig Road. The time

47

taken had been exactly six and a half minutes. He then described how the whole area of the wood had been searched for a weapon, using mine-detectors. The search had met with no success. Later the water was drained from a nearby reservoir—without finding the gun.

In cross-examination Bennett asked him how many registered taxi drivers there were in the Glasgow area at that time. Goodall replied that there were 1279, and two in Rutherglen. He said he had sent circular letters to all of those. He was asked if fifty circulars had been returned marked 'Gone away'. Yes, Goodall said. Some drivers had gone to Canada and others to Australia and America by the time the trial started.

Bennett also asked if plaster casts had been taken of footprints in the mud of Glen Wood. Goodall said that this had not been done. 'Had this been done' remarked Mr Bennett 'you might have been in a position to eliminate Ellis from your enquiries.'

Police Constable Henry Golightly said that he worked in the Firearms Department of Police Headquarters. He was handed a heavily-bound volume and asked to identify it. He said that it was the Firearms Register, and that he had checked through it to find if a Walter Scott Ellis had been issued with a Firearms Certificate. There was no trace of any such certificate having been issued to Ellis.

The Advocate Depute, Mr Norman Wylie, then closed the case for the prosecution. It was the third day of the trial.

Mr Bennett opened the case for the defence by calling Maurice Hart, who had been asked to attend an identification parade in the Southern Police Office late in July. Two witnesses had picked him out at this parade. He agreed that Walter Ellis had been part of the line-up, although he did not know him.

In cross-examination, the Advocate Depute asked, 'Did the first man say you were of the same build as the man he was trying to identify?' Hart answered 'Yes.'

'And did the second man say you were of his general appearance?' 'Yes.'

The next defence witness was a taxi driver, Thomas Docherty, who said that he was the first person on the scene after the shooting of Walkinshaw. This man had been on the prosecution list of witnesses, but had not been called by the Crown. Docherty said that Walkinshaw was lying with his head on the runners of the window, face down in broken glass. Blood was dripping from his head into the cab. He had moved Walkinshaw to a position where he was leaning against the steering wheel. He then picked up the microphone in the cab, which was hanging loose, and notified base that 'this appears to be a serious assault and that the police and ambulance should be advised at once'. He also asked that other cab drivers in the area should be told of what he had found.

Docherty said that he had been on the scene three or four minutes before anyone else arrived. Asked if he had moved Walkinshaw again, after the arrival of some of his colleagues, Docherty said that several other taxi drivers thought he should be moved into a more comfortable position. In the end, Walkinshaw was taken from the cab and laid on the pavement.

He said that both offside doors of the cab had been lying open when he arrived. When he eventually noticed the meter in the cab, he saw that it was in the 'stop' position and that the fare had been registered as 10/4d.

The defence had called Docherty because the fragments of clear glass found near the kerbside at the time of the murder could have been dislodged some time after the crime—and at a time when the assailant had disappeared. If there had been no particles of clear glass at the kerbside at the time of the murder, then the forensic evidence with regard to the glass in the heel of Ellis's shoe would have lost all significance.

Another taxi driver, Wolf Stringer, spoke of the experiments he had carried out for us, and of the times taken between Mill Street and Tormusk Road by the two known routes. After the direct trip between these two points, the meter had shown a fare of only 6/–.

Another witness, John Craig, said that not long before the arrest of Ellis he had been drinking with him in a public house. Craig said that two men had accidentally knocked a pint of beer off the bar. The glass was smashed and fell close to Ellis's feet.

Ellis himself, as had been decided, was not called by the defence, which then closed its case.

The Advocate Depute addressed the jury on behalf of the prosecution. He opened the Crown summing-up on a somewhat sensational note-by dropping the lesser charge of possessing live bullets without having the necessary Firearms Certificate.

He pointed out to the jury that this was a trivial charge compared with the first one and that it was a statutory offence. He wished the jury to focus all their attention on the major capital charge and so magnanimously abandoned the second matter—to which there had been little defence offered. I considered this move to be a good prosecution tactic, showing that the Crown was not interested in trivialities.

After this, however, Mr Wylie began summing up his case on the main charge very strongly indeed. He omitted few telling points. He pointed out early in his address that the evidence as to the exact time of the shooting was conflicting—but, he said, few of the witnesses had occasion to register the time. There was one witness who was very definite about the time of the shooting—and that was Mrs Mary Buchan, who had said she had been looking out of her window at 1.45 a.m. and saw the taxi sitting in the street. She was the only witness who had actually pinpointed the time by registering it with her watch.

Mr Wylie went on to explain to the jury that they should approach the case in two phases.

One allegation was that a murder had been committed in Tormusk Road, and the second was that it had been committed by the man in the dock. 'The Crown case is that Ellis boarded Walkinshaw's taxi in Main Street, near Mill Street, Bridgeton, and took it to Tormusk Road, and he was the person who shot Walkinshaw. My case consists of circumstantial evidence, but such evidence is a perfectly valid way of establishing a criminal offence.'

Mr Wylie said that the witness Brady and Ellis boarded a taxi, that the taxi went to 74 Mill Street—where Brady got out—and that the taxi did a U-turn and went back to Main Street. 'There is evidence that I urge you to accept which establishes that that taxi was destined to go to Castlemilk, to the home of Ellis's parents at 48 Stravannan Road.'

The next concrete evidence, he said, was that about half an hour late Ellis was picked up by the witness McLeod in Ardencraig Road, between Tormusk Road and Ellis's home in Stravannan Road. He reminded the jury that McLeod was not to be shaken in his identification of Ellis.

'Is it not strange that Ellis should have required two taxis to take him home? My submission is that the reason he changed taxis is perfectly obvious—because he shot the driver who took him in the first place to Tormusk Road.'

Mr Wylie also reminded the jury that several witnesses had seen a man running into Glen Wood, 'about a thousand yards away from where Ellis was picked up by McLeod, the other taxi driver.'

The Advocate Depute followed this up by summarising. 'We have a murderer running into a wood—and a quarter of an hour later you find the accused, Ellis, standing at the opposite end of the wood looking for a taxi.'

Turning to the forensic evidence, and referring to the ballistics aspect of it, Mr Wylie said 'It is the duty of the Crown to give any relevant evidence, whether it directly supports the Crown case or not. You have heard the evidence of the police experts, that the bullet which killed Walkinshaw was a hollow-nosed bullet while the bullets found in the accused's flat in Rockcliffe Street were of the solid-nosed type. The defence is perfectly entitled to make a point of that—but, of course, bullets were found in the accused's possession, and you may well ask what he was doing with them in the first place.

'It is yet another strand of the circumstantial chain. Is it all coincidence, that Ellis was at Mill Street at 1.30 a.m. and in another taxi at Ardencraig Road at two o'clock? Is it coincidence that a man with no hat and no coat was seen running into one end of Glen Wood? Is it coincidence that he happened to have bullets in his possession at Rockcliffe Street, Bridgeton?'

Mr Wylie also made much reference to the two types of glass found embedded in the left heel and welt of Ellis's shoe following his arrest. Did that evidence not place Ellis beside Walkinshaw's taxi-cab?

The Advocate Depute addressed the jury for an hour, and was followed by Mr Bennett, who made a motion to the trial judge before beginning his jury speech. The jury were asked to retire. Mr Bennett proceeded to ask his Lordship to direct the jury that the evidence led by the Crown was insufficient in law to convict the accused of the crime. 'In my view, there is insufficient evidence established by the Crown on six points. These points are motive, evidence of guilty intention, evidence of preparation for the crime, evidence of opportunity and ability to carry out the crime, evidence of identification, and evidence of the conduct of the accused after the crime.'

Lord Patrick responded with one brief sentence. 'I cannot give that direction.' And so the jury were returned to the courtroom and the case continued.

Bennett, Fairbairn and I had spent hours together collecting all the relevant information gleaned from the numerous witnesses called in the case. The 'prototype' and nucleus of the defence speech to the jury had been carefully worked out, each of us contributing to it. Eventually, all the relevant points were tabulated in a particular order, which enabled the speech to flow in a natural course.

Mr Bennett began by reminding the jury that this was a charge of capital murder and that the penalty was death by hanging. He said that he did not need to remind the jury of the terrible consequences which would follow a decision against the accused. He also reminded them that the onus of proof was on the Crown, and that the standard was 'proof beyond reasonable doubt'.

However, there was no question in the first instance that it had been proved beyond reasonable doubt that the unfortunate John Walkinshaw had been murdered that early morning. 'But are you satisfied that it has been proved to the required standard that he was murdered by Walter Scott Ellis, and, what is more, are you satisfied beyond reasonable doubt on that fact?'

Mr Bennett then submitted to the jury that it was some other man who must have committed the crime. Referring to a map of Glasgow, he pointed out that at one stage in the early morning Walkinshaw had reported to his controller that he was at Myrtle Park, on Aikenhead Road. At that stage he had said that he was dropping a fare at Tormusk Road. Using the map, Bennett pointed out that it was unlikely that the man in the taxi could have been picked up in Main Street, Bridgeton, as Myrtle Park was not on a direct route from there to Castlemilk. He submitted that the murderer must have come from the other direction, somewhere in the Paisley Road area—in any case, on the south side of the river.

Bennett emphasised that no fingerprints or palm prints had been found in either Walkinshaw's taxi-cab or McLeod's. 'And it is extraordinary, in a shooting, that no weapon has been found despite the most meticulous search. It has not been shown either, that Ellis had a gun that evening—or at any other time. The fact that no gun was ever found tends to show that the accused was not the assailant.

'The bullets which killed Walkinshaw did not come from the batch of eleven found at Rockcliffe Street. No marks of burnt powder, such as would have been found if he had discharged a firearm, were found on Ellis's clothing.

'The murderer was seen running away from the scene of the shooting, and the evidence was that he ran very fast. Ellis, that night, according to a number of witnesses at the party in Mill Street, had taken quite a lot of drink. You must consider whether or not a man who had drunk so much could run like a scared rabbit.

'The two witnesses who saw the assailant running into Glen Wood identified someone else at the parade—someone who bore no resemblance to Ellis.

'Much has been said by the police of the considerable number of taxi drivers circulated by them, but they have not been called in evidence to say whether or not any one of them had picked up a fare at Main Street near Mill Street that morning. In any event, quite a number of drivers had already left the country for one reason or another.

'The eye-witnesss Finlayson told you that the running man had a light-coloured suit. McLeod said that Ellis was wearing a dark suit. McLeod told you that Ellis looked normal, not out of breath, not having any signs of vegetation or dirt on his clothing or shoes.'

At this point Bennett posed another question for the jury.

'Would a killer attract attention to himself by hailing another taxi for a distance of only a few hundred yards and in the near vicinity of his crime?'

Bennett said that, had Ellis been in Walkinshaw's taxi-cab at the time when the windscreen was smashed, one would expect to find on his nose or face evidence of slight cuts, following upon his being peppered with tiny glass particles. There was no trace of glass injuries on him, nor was there any trace of glass on his suit.

Mr Bennett then turned to the forensic evidence, especially with regard to the tiny particles of glass found in Ellis's shoe-heel.

'There has been evidence, which is not in dispute, that most clear glass is made by one firm—Pilkington's. That being so, little can be drawn from the fact that the clear glass found in the heel was of similar density to the same type of glass found at the scene of the crime. Equally, the green beer-bottle glass was manufactured by the Scottish Central Glassworks of Alloa, who are the main suppliers to a number of breweries. These beer bottles are very common indeed, and the density of them cannot really vary to any marked extent.'

Bennett then quoted a piece of evidence led by the defence in the person of Wolf Stringer. 'This witness did test runs with the defence from Mill Street, Bridgeton to Tormusk Road, and these runs showed 6/– on the meter. Nothing like the 10/4*d* shown on Walkinshaw's meter.'

Then the court listened even more intently as Mr Bennett made references to the case of Peter Manuel, whose trial for murder had taken place three years earlier.

'It is true that Ellis seems to have told the police a lie when he said that he was not out that weekend. There are many reasons why men do not tell the truth—not wanting their wives to know where they have been, for example, or covering up for petty crimes. A lot of people in Glasgow have not forgotten that Mr William Watt was arrested and confined to Barlinnie Prison for sixty-one days, having been charged with several murders which were later found and proved to have been committed by Peter Manuel. It was only when Manuel was later convicted that William Watt was properly cleared. People are not so naïve as to suppose that the police are infallible.

'It is not sufficient for you to say that he might have done it. Before convicting, you would require to be satisfied beyond reasonable doubt that he had done it.'

Having ended on this telling point, Mr Bennettt thanked the jury for their attention and concluded an excellent address.

Following Mr Bennett, Lord Patrick charged the jury. 'The proof in the case, if there was proof, would depend, wholly on circumstantial evidence. People sneer at that,' he said. 'But these are uninformed people who do not understand that it is every bit as reliable as other evidence. Very often there are no eye-witnesses to a crime, and everything depends on circumstantial evidence.'

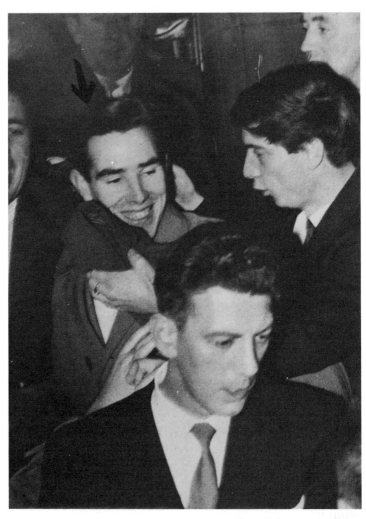

A press photographer catches the mood of elation as Ellis (arrowed), William Allsopp and Joseph Beltrami (foreground) leave the court

Lord Patrick reminded the jury that the only remaining charge they had to consider was a very grave one indeed. It was a charge of murder, and a very intricate one at that. There was only one penalty for such a crime under the Homicide Act, and that was death by hanging. 'If the accused is found guilty he will be hanged by the neck. But that is not a concern of yours or mine. You are here to hear the evidence and make up your minds on that.'

Leaning on one elbow, Lord Patrick spoke slowly to the jury—and I noticed that Ellis was listening attentively with his hands clasped.

'It is important that you, the jury, should pay attention to the question of the burden of proof. You must be satisfied beyond reasonable doubt of the accused's guilt before you would be justified in bringing in a Guilty verdict. It is not necessary to prove motivation. It is quite true, as both Crown and defence have indicated, that the time factor is important. The theory of the Crown is that Ellis got in Walkinshaw's taxi in Main Street, Bridgeton and travelled to the scene of the crime, where he shot Walkinshaw—and then, in another street, nearby, hired another taxi.

'Mrs Buchan has given you a very fair approximation of the time when Walkinshaw was shot. That would be about 1.45 a.m., when she looked out of the window and saw the taxi with the door open. Other timings in this case are merely approximations and might well be out by five or ten minutes either way.'

The judge proceeded to sum up all the evidence in his usual impeccably fair manner.

Dealing with the fact that Ellis told lies to the police— if the police were to be believed in connection with the statement allegedly made about his being with his parents—Lord Patrick said 'Even if you hold that Ellis told lies to the police, that does not prove that he was there at the scene of the crime and committed it. There could be a number of reasons for Ellis's lying to the police unconnected with involvement in this crime.

'In this country suspicion will not do, proof on a balance of probabilities will not do—the Crown must prove matters beyond all reasonable doubt.'

Lord Patrick referred to the fact that the type of glass found in the heel and welt of Ellis's shoe was of a very common origin.

'The Crown ask you to place emphasis not so much on the common type and similar densities, but on the combination and finding of both types of glass, both clear and green.'

The judge finished his summing up and the jury retired to their own room in order to deliberate upon their verdict.

During the half hour of their retirement, I, unaccompanied by counsel, spoke to my client in the police cells below the High Court building. Everyone participating in this trial had, by this time, shown a measure of strain—and the accused was, naturally, no exception. He was almost as pale as I was. He asked me, as I have been asked by hundreds of clients in similar circumstances, what I thought the jury's verdict would be. I told him that I was confident, and this seemed to alleviate the strain from which he was obviously suffering.

The jury bell duly rang and we all assembled in court for the last time. The court had been packed throughout the four days of the trial, but when the tall, bespectacled foreman of the jury was asked to deliver his verdict, not a sound was to be heard. One can readily imagine the relief experienced by the defence when, in a loud voice, he announced 'Not proven—unanimously.'

Within a minute Ellis had been discharged from the dock and was allowed to walk free from the court building. The time was 4.31 p.m. When I accompanied him outside into Clyde Street I saw that more than three hundred people had lined the street, such was the interest in the case.

On the following day there were various newspaper articles ascribed to Ellis. One of his comments was 'I think John Walkinshaw was shot by a roving madman lurking in the Castlemilk woods—by a man who may strike again. I had nothing at all to do with this ghastly, pointless murder.'

3
A Gangplank Too Far

John Thomas Murphy was looking forward to his winter world cruise on the luxury liner *Canberra*.

His ticket—which had cost him over eleven hundred pounds—was in his pocket and his well-equipped cabin awaited him on the P & O cruise ship as she lay alongside the quay in Southampton Docks. Life looked rosy indeed for Murphy.

But his dream trip was never to take place. His life-long ambition to sail in luxury to sunny climes and faraway places was shattered in the passenger access at Berth 106 of Southampton Docks. There, with one foot already on the gangway, Murphy was stopped by two police officers. They said they had a warrant for his arrest and they took Murphy from the docks to the Civic Centre police station in Southampton. The *Canberra* sailed on the next tide—while Murphy sat in a police station, listening to policemen charging him with an offence he had never heard of before! Indeed, few people were aware of the existence of the charge which the hapless Murphy found himself facing that day. . . .

Murphy's troubles began three months earlier. On 16 October 1974 he walked into the premises of Thomas Cook & Sons, travel agents, at 15 Gordon Street, Glasgow and booked a berth on a winter cruise ship due to leave Southampton on 8 January. He handed over £200 in banknotes by way of a deposit.

On 18 November Murphy was back again—handing over £910 in banknotes to pay off the balance of the cost of the cruise.

On each of these occasions Murphy fell foul, had he but known it, of Glasgow Corporation Consolidation (General Powers) Order Confirmation Act 1960, Section 155–(1) iii. . . .

Under Section 155 of this order, any person who has been convicted of robbery, theft, reset, theft by housebreaking, attempted theft by housebreaking, or fraud, is categorised as a 'known thief'. And under sub-Section (1) iii of this Order such a person, who has in his possession any money or article, without being able to give a satisfactory account of his possession, shall be guilty of an offence, which will involve a penalty, in addition to forfeiture or confiscation of the money or article in his possession.

As can be seen, a known thief is in a somewhat invidious position under Scots Law! Technically, if he is found in possession of even a modest sum of money— say, £5—he will be required to give a satisfactory account of this possession at a trial. If he fails to do so, he is liable to be sentenced to sixty days' imprisonment, and to have his money confiscated.

Normally, all such cases have been taken in the old Police Court—now the District Court. But for the first time in my experience the case of John Thomas Murphy—my client by then—was prosecuted in Glasgow Sheriff Court.

The case had such far-reaching importance, in fact, that an eventual appeal against conviction was reported in our *Scots Law Times* of July 1975.

Now it would appear to be oppressive were a 'known thief' asked to account for possession of as little as £5. The fact that he had at least one previous conviction for dishonesty would clearly militate against him when he gave evidence—especially as he would be described on the charge, damningly, as a known thief! And, in this peculiar type of charge, the onus rests with the accused.

In Scotland, the onus of proof in a criminal matter normally rests with the prosecution. Accordingly, the prosecution cannot succeed unless the charge against the accused is proved 'beyond reasonable doubt'. By this is meant that the evidence adduced by the prosecution must bear the characteristics of greatest weight, un-challengeable sufficiency and most cogent effect—as the law likes to put it!

The reason for such a high standard of proof being required is that in our law, unlike that of France, Russia and other European countries, there is a presumption of innocence so far as the accused is concerned—but not if you are a known thief!

Transactions under the known-thief regulations form an exception to the general rule, and in those cases it is for the accused to establish his innocence by proving that the sum of money found in his possession was legitimately obtained.

My own feeling is that, in the interests of fairness and common-sense, guide-lines should be laid down. Under the Order referred to there is no financial limit in respect of such charges. Taking the matter to a totally illogical conclusion, a known thief could be charged with being in possession of a pound note, locked up and brought to trial on this nugatory matter. One might see the pos-sibility of oppression rearing its head in such situations. Police officers could pursue relentlessly persons with a conviction for dishonesty, persistently searching them and charging them with being in possession of trifling sums of money. In normal circumstances, however, a police officer would not consider reporting known thieves found in possession of insignificant sums—but it is unfortunate that the Order does not incorporate a financial limit.

So much for the background to this unusual type of prosecution . . . but how fared John Thomas Murphy, whose fabulous ship sailed without him?

Murphy's two trips to Cook's travel office had come to the notice of the Glasgow police—and they obtained a warrant for his arrest on Christmas Eve 1974. This they despatched to the Hampshire Police, who executed it just as Murphy was about to go up the gangway.

In the police station, a Hampshire detective told Murphy 'For your information, this is the position. The police at Glasgow allege that you have declared to the National Insurance authority that you cannot pay your stamps, but you have paid out eleven hundred pounds for this cruise you were about to go on.'

Murphy: 'I see what it is all about now.'

Detective: 'Do you wish to account for possession of the money which you paid for the cruise?'

Murphy: 'I belong to the Casino in Glasgow. If you look in my belongings you will see there is a membership card there.'

Detective: 'Is that where the money came from?'

Murphy: 'Sometimes a guy can have a lucky streak, that's all.'

Despite this explanation, Murphy was brought back to Glasgow. The charge against him was that 'Having been convicted of theft and fraud, and a known thief, [he was] in the premises of Thomas Cook & Sons on October 16, 1974, in possession of banknotes to the value of £200, and on November 18, 1974, banknotes to the value of £910; without being able to give a satisfactory account of [his] possession thereof; contrary to the Glasgow Consolidation (General Powers) Order Confirmation Act 1960, Section 155.'

We defended Murphy at his trial before Sheriff C H Johnston Q C in Glasgow.

That our client had a number of convictions for dishonesty, and was a known thief within the meaning of the order, was not disputed by us. Nor did we lead evidence on his behalf. Following upon the prosecution's evidence, however, I made submissions to the trial judge.

I said that my client was not obliged, on 8 January or at the trial, to give an account of his possession of the sums of money mentioned in the charge on the dates on which they were in his possession. And I added that my client, if he *were* obliged to give an account, had given it in the course of his conversation with the detective in Southampton police station.

I went on to argue—unsuccessfully, as it turned out—that Murphy had at no time been found in possession of a sum of money. The question of possession, I explained, arose merely by inference—in that Murphy had obviously paid, in two instalments, the sum of £1110 to Cook's—but that he had not been questioned by the police at the time when he made those payments and that his possession was of a retrospective nature. Therefore, I said, he did not require to explain it.

I argued that, under the Order, the law stated that he required to satisfy the court concerning his possession 'if he has'—not 'had'—on his person any money without being able to give a satisfactory account of such possession. I pointed out that, by a similar analogy, the prosecution could learn that a known thief had paid £10 as a deposit for a washing machine twelve months earlier, could check on this and charge such a man with possession of this sum of money—thereby putting the onus on him to establish that his possession was legitimate.

This, I said, could obviously cause oppression if the Crown contention were correct.

The spirit of the Act clearly indicated that 'possession of money' should mean an *inordinate* sum of money (although this was not defined in the Act) and that the person charged should require to be found in possession by the police and was obliged only at that stage to account for it. In this case, I said, my client had not been found in possession of the money and was asked months later to account for his earlier possession. I considered that this was an entirely different state of affairs which was not covered by the Corporation Consolidation Order.

The Sheriff, however, did not agree with me, and my client was convicted and sentenced to forty days' imprisonment. It was further ordered that the money in question would be confiscated. After a conviction on a charge such as that against Murphy, there can be little argument with the Sheriff if he exercises his discretion to confiscate.

After a few words with Murphy, I marked an appeal that same day—and Sheriff Johnston agreed to interim liberation of my client pending his appeal before three judges in Edinburgh. This was heard later that year before Lords Cameron, Johnston and Avonside. Lord Cameron was in the chair. In view of the legal importance of the case and its possible far-reaching consequences, I had instructed two advocates to prepare our arguments. At the appeal it was pointed out that the facts of the case were not really in dispute. Reference was then made to the term 'has' in Section 155 (1) iii, as opposed to 'had'—the present, as against the past, tense. This was the point I had argued before the Sheriff.

It was further stated by the appeal judges that the statute was a penal statute, and should therefore be subject to a strict interpretation—and when there was doubt as to the extent of its application it should always be constituted so as to produce an interpretation in favour of the liberty of the subject.

The judges went on to say that what the statute clearly intended was that there should be instant explanations sought and given. In these circumstances, the appeal judges ruled, the evidence upon which the Sherriff proceeded to convict fell far short of what was necessary to comply with the requirements of the statute. It was, therefore, insufficient to support conviction and so the conviction imposed must, of necessity, be quashed. In view of the fact that my client was not 'found' in possession at Cook's premises, he was held to be under no obligation to give an explanation at a later stage—and, accordingly, the appeal was successful. The appeal judges also stated that it was impossible to forfeit money which had already been paid away to third parties. Murphy's conviction was quashed and the order for confiscation of the sum of money was recalled. In addition, expenses were awarded against the Crown.

But we weren't finished yet. . . . Hadn't Murphy paid over £1110 for a luxury cruise on a ship that went off without him?

I applied to Cook's for payment of the sum of £1110.

However, in this field there were civil difficulties. It was pointed out that Murphy could only be reimbursed were his calling-off due to health reasons—not because he had been, albeit wrongfully, arrested by policemen!

I then learned that Murphy had taken out an insurance policy with a reputable company, and I got in touch with them, explaining the full circumstances. The policy was sent to us and, as very often happens, when we checked the small print on the policy we discovered that it also did not include such a contingency as being arrested at the foot of the gangway. The insurance company would not be held responsible for the actions of the police, nor of the travel agents—nor, indeed, of P & O themselves.

So at the end of the day, although Murphy's conviction was overturned in the Court of Criminal Appeal in this leading case under the known-thief regulations, he had lost out on his cruise and his money was not refunded.

Mind you, we did consider a possible action against the police for arresting Murphy without a *prima facie* case in law against him. But I decided not to pursue this because, after all, a Sheriff had granted a warrant for his arrest and the police had simply seen fit to execute this warrant just prior to his cruise.

I must confess that I could not see why the warrant could not have been executed after the *Canberra*—and Murphy—had arrived back at Southampton! I still can't.

But it is not all high drama, pain and distress in the courtroom. Human foibles and frailties are often exposed there, as raw life and character pass through daily. Humour is there, and drollery and obtuseness and misunderstanding—and often, too, the exhilarating flash of Glasgow wit. . . .

An old lag was destined to appear regularly in Hamilton Sheriff Court on repeated charges of breach of the peace and wife assault. Naturally, he was well-known to the presiding Sheriff.

One morning he appeared before the Sheriff yet again, charged with the same offences and pleading Guilty. By this time, of course, he had an extensive record—although the charges were never very grave. He had also run out of lawyers to defend him and represented himself.

This morning, after the fiscal's narration of the facts of the case, he was asked by the Sheriff if he had anything to say.

'Yes, I know what my trouble is. It is drink. When I commit these offences I am always drunk. Drink makes me a different personality. Yes, that's it—a dual personality! It is like Dr Jekyll and Mr Hyde, and I feel that I am entitled to a final last chance from you.'

'So far as Dr Jekyll is concerned,' pronounced the Sheriff, 'I am prepared to admonish you on these charges. . . . In respect of you, Hyde, I sentence you to six months' imprisonment.'

4
Prerogative Royal

The man wearing sunglasses entered the St George's Cross branch of the Bank of Scotland in Maryhill Road, Glasgow, shortly after it opened for the day, and walked up to a teller's counter.

He handed a piece of paper to the teller. It was a printed note, and it read 'I want money. Look at what I am carrying in the waistband of my trousers.' When the teller looked up he saw that the man had opened his jacket and the butt of an automatic pistol was visible.

The man then handed over a briefcase and the teller filled it with banknotes—£2700 worth, as it turned out—and handed it back. The bank robber took the briefcase, pushed through the swing doors of the bank and walked away. It was just after 9.45 a.m. on Friday 26 April 1974.

When the police arrived they took statements from the teller and his assistant, who had also seen the bank robber—significantly, as it later transpired. Police scientific branch officers came and took some two hundred finger and palm prints from various parts of the bank premises.

Later, the tellers were shown a series of photographs from the Criminal Records Office. They picked out one picture as being like the bank robber. The files identified the photograph as being that of Maurice Swanson.

Early next morning Swanson was arrested at his home in Raeberry Street, Maryhill, not all that far from the bank that had been robbed. When charged with the robbery he replied 'I had nothing to do with this crime.'

Swanson, who was then in his mid-forties, had been born in Latvia and settled in this country after the war. He was a handsome, well-built man, six feet tall, with blond, curly hair. On the day he was arrested, two of his Polish friends—one of them a client of mine—came to me and asked me to represent him. That same day I appeared for Swanson when he was brought before Glasgow Sheriff Court, charged with the bank robbery. Swanson was detained in Barlinnie Prison for seven days before I was successful in obtaining bail and then he was released, pending trial.

In the meantime I had attended an identification parade at Maryhill police station, where Swanson was most positively identified by the two tellers from the bank, as well as by a woman who had been standing at a bus queue fifty yards from the bank and had had a rear view of the robber leaving it. With two such positive identifications and a rear view sighting, the case against Swanson looked very strong. But from my first meeting with Swanson he firmly denied the charge and protested his innocence in the matter. Knowing Swanson as I did, I was impressed by his denials of the crime. In earlier cases where he had been charged with offences he had not been nearly so vehement.

He was quick to tell me that at the time of the robbery he had been at Glasgow Corporation Works premises in Brand Street, in the presence of three of his Polish friends. His Rover car had also been parked at these premises. I sent our office manager, Michael McDonald, to the Corporation Works exactly one week after the robbery and at about 9.30 in the morning—knowing that the procedure would be the same as the previous week and that the various workers would be presenting themselves for their weekly wages as they would have done on the morning of the robbery.

Mr McDonald interviewed five witnesses, three of whom were Poles. Although they had been living in this country for years they spoke limited English. All five remembered the previous Friday and the fact that Swanson had been there before 9.30 a.m., and had driven off after 10 a.m. in his Rover car—giving one of the witnesses, Josef Katarba, a lift home. This was an undoubted alibi: the robbery, as we knew from the police, had taken place at 9.45 a.m. some two to three miles away.

Full statements were taken by Mr McDonald, who was very experienced in this, having taken thousands in his day.

The reason that I had insisted that these witnesses be sought out and questioned at the scene of the alibi exactly one week later was obvious—it made it ever so much easier for them to cast their minds back over a short period of time with that degree of reliability expected in a court of law. To delay the operation and have them interviewed months after the incident causes obvious difficulties. The first question an experienced prosecutor would ask them at the trial would be 'How can you cast your mind back three months or so and state with any degree of certainty that you are recalling Friday the twenty-sixth of April, as opposed to Friday the twelfth, the nineteenth or, indeed, Friday the third of May?' He would follow this up by asking 'How can you pinpoint this particular Friday, the twenty-sixth? Couldn't Swanson have been there and have been seen by you on a previous or subsequent week?'

I have heard this line taken very often in the past—so often, in fact, that I seldom lodge a Special Defence of Alibi unless it is really good and cogent. If not, it can backfire in an embarrassing way.

At this time, I also took a detailed statement from Swanson—without reference to the others—as to his movements on the morning of Friday 26th. After the defence statements had been typed I checked them all personally and then they were put into Swanson's file and we awaited the indictment.

The indictment was served three months later. It is only on receipt of this document, giving the names and addresses of crown witnesses, that the defence can proceed to have them interviewed and precognosced to find out what their evidence is likely to be in Court. The final terms of the charge are also contained in the indictment, along with a list of Crown productions, if any.

I had a fair idea of what the evidence of the prosecution witnesses would be—the issue, as was clear from the identification parade, centred on Swanson being picked out. There was nothing else.

In the meantime Swanson had called frequently at my office and almost overwhelmed me with protestations of complete innocence. 'I swear to it', he would say, with monotonous regularity. He had never been quite like this before—so concerned and anxious.

Two weeks before the trial he called to see me once more. He had been making his own enquiries, he said, as to who had actually robbed the bank. It was, indeed, something one would expect an innocent person to do.

Swanson had many underworld contacts—not having been entirely the clean potato himself. He was able to tell me that whoever the bank robber was, he had no criminal record and so the police would not have him on file—there would be no fingerprints or photographs. He did not know the man, he said, but had gleaned information to the effect that he was considerably younger than himself and had committed one bank robbery since the one at St George's Cross.

Swanson thought that after each robbery the man went completely to ground—and made tracks for somewhere in Spain until the heat was off. He was also able to tell me something which was already fairly obvious to me—the robber was a cool customer who planned his robberies with precision and no small measure of acumen.

This was all very well—and although Swanson, from his demeanour and piteous desperation, had convinced me that this was a case of mistaken identity, I would not be on the jury. Such information as he gave me about the mysterious and successful Mr X was of a purely hearsay nature and of no value in court. We had still to face two and a half positive identifications at his trial. So much must hinge on his own evidence and that of the supporting alibi witnesses. Could these alibi witnesses be broken in the course of cross-examination by the Crown? Could the two bank tellers be broken in the course of ours? Those answers would not be known until the time of the trial.

The case was an extremely anxious one for me, and when I formally gave the Crown the five names and addresses of my alibi witnesses I added another name— that of my office manager, Michael McDonald. It was to be one of the very few occasions that a member of my staff was called for the defence.

I had thought carefully before deciding that his evidence could do nothing but assist Swanson. Had we left him out, I reasoned, the Court or Crown might well ask why the five alibi witnesses had been precognosced so early in the case. They would possibly wish to know who had arranged this, and McDonald could answer that. With the benefit of hindsight, and the knowledge of McDonald's lack of experience in the witness box, I would today, in a similar situation, instruct someone more removed from the case (such as a private investigator) to obtain the necessary information. . . .

We instructed Bert Kerrigan, Advocate, as counsel for the defence—and he too was impressed by Swanson when he met him at the pre-trial consultation. Kerrigan has been instructed in many of my High Court cases, including a number of murder trials. He was formerly Lecturer in Criminal Law at the University of Edinburgh and presently, as well as practising in Scotland, is Visiting Professor at the University of Southern California. He appeared as one of the defence counsel in the well-known mercenaries trial in Angola several years back.

The trial opened on 27 August before Lord Stott, a former Lord Advocate and a sharp and intelligent judge.

Both bank tellers gave their evidence in a most positive manner, and their respective identifications of Swanson could not have been more certain. They were cross-examined with skill by Mr Kerrigan, but with little success in disturbing their identification. Their minds, it was clear, were made up. The woman at the bus-stop was also good for the prosecution, in identifying the rear view of the robber as being 'very like Swanson'.

Police witnesses who were called told of Swanson's unqualified denial of the charge. A pair of sunglasses—and sunglasses had seemed to be the bank robber's only disguise—had been found in Swanson's house. These sunglasses were of an ordinary and very common type, and even the tellers were unable to say if the sunglasses were the same as those worn by the robber. I imagine that sunglasses would be found in most homes, in any event.

The police had done trial runs from Brand Street, where the Corporation Works premises were, to St George's Cross, using the Clydeside Expressway. They said that this trip could be done in a matter of minutes. The Crown's line was thus clear—even if Swanson had been at Brand Street after 9 a.m., he could still have robbed the bank forty-five minutes later. The Crown would want to know later, from the alibi evidence, if Swanson could have left the Works premises at, say, 9.30 a.m. In their statements the witnesses were certain that he did not leave until after ten o'clock.

The Crown, I thought, might argue that Swanson had gone to Brand Street in order to set up an alibi in advance. I had had this happen in a case before.

We called Swanson as first witness for the defence. He was quite certain as to his movements on the morning of the robbery, he said. He knew nothing about the robbery.

The Polish alibi witnesses were then called, beginning with Josef Katarba. He was a shifty-looking customer, to put it mildly, a man of most unprepossessing appearance who found great difficulty in looking anyone in the eye. (Several years later Katarba was found stabbed to death in his flat. I represented the woman charged with his murder and she was acquitted on the grounds of self-defence.)

Katarba's broken English did not help matters, but he stuck to his guns and ended by saying that Swanson had driven him home from the Works premises (where he had been a nightshift worker) shortly after 10 a.m. on the 26th. Asked if he could be mistaken, Katarba said no—all the witnesses had been at the Works office for their pay, although Swanson was only there as a friend and was not employed by the Corporation.

The next witness—another Pole, Victor Griss—was to cause a little stir in court during his testimony. He gave evidence along the same lines as Katarba, but added—apparently—'I know Maurice was at the pay office in Brand Street that morning because I saw him outside at ten o'clock with the robber.'

Even the judge nearly dropped his pen at this. 'With whom?' Lord Stott asked.

'The robber,' repeated Griss.

He was being examined at this time by Mr Kerrigan who, after a hurried conversation with me, eventually gleaned from the witness that what he was trying to say was 'the Rover'. With his limited grasp of English— Katarba, Swanson and he always conversed in Polish— Griss found the letter 'v' unpronounceable, and substituted a 'b'. He also pronounced 'o' soft—so that the name of the car came out as 'robber'!

The matter was soon clarified. And the defence breathed a sigh of relief.

The other alibi witnesses followed—both appalling witnesses, although, with hindsight, truthful—and then Michael McDonald went into the witness box. He had a most uncomfortable time there. The Crown wanted to know why he had gone to Brand Street to see the witnesses so soon after the robbery. The fact that I had instructed him to go there did not seem to satisfy the Crown.

'Why weren't these important witnesses seen in your office? What, if anything, was so different in this case? Why the urgency?' Michael did his best to explain.

The one inference that could be drawn from the Crown's line of questioning was that McDonald had helped to concoct an alibi by seeing witnesses at the place where the alibi was to be set. It was a most unfair inference to suggest. As he left the box I realised that my tactics in putting Mr McDonald's name forward on the defence list of witnesses had been wrong. His evidence had not assisted my client's case at all—on the contrary, it had probably harmed it.

In due course the jury returned a verdict of guilty— by a majority. My heart sank. Swanson was sentenced to five years' imprisonment.

To say that Swanson was distressed at the verdict and sentence would be an understatement. The news from us that there could be no appeal brought tears to his eyes, but the issue had been very much one for the jury— identification relates to matters of fact. The judge's charge to the jury had been unimpeachable. There were no grounds for appeal against conviction, and it would have been the height of folly to appeal against a sentence which had been far from excessive. I would have expected a sentence of seven years. Bank robberies had been extremely prevalent in the Glasgow area at this time, and one would expect condign sentences to follow. Swanson took my advice, negative though it was, and no appeal was marked. It is to be remembered that when one appeals against conviction only—particularly with solid reasons for so doing—an Appeal Court, in rejecting the appeal, can then proceed to review the sentence. In Swanson's case, I felt that an abortive appeal might bring about an increase in sentence. That would have been the very end! This anomaly has been since altered by Parliament.

Both Kerrigan and I were disturbed at the outcome. We felt that an innocent man might have been convicted—although neither of us could be sure. We consoled ourselves by saying that if the tellers had been correct in their identification, then the conviction was a good one. Swanson's file was stored away.

And then occurred one of those extraordinary twists of fate. . . .

Eight months after Swanson had been found guilty and sent to prison, a man we'll call 'McGregor' appeared before Edinburgh Sheriff Court. He had been arrested after an abortive bank robbery there and had been charged with that and four other bank robberies. These four had taken place in both Glasgow and Edinburgh, and the police had a strong case against him on all five counts. He had been caught red-handed in the attempted bank robbery and had been successfully identified—at two parades—for the four other robberies. Furthermore he had given a self-incriminating statement to the police, embracing all the charges against him. McGregor had never appeared in court before his Edinburgh arrest—after which the police had duly taken his finger and palm prints and photographed him for their records.

When he came before the court in Edinburgh for the first time, on Petition—his first judicial examination—McGregor applied successfully for Legal Aid and nominated me as his solicitor. He also intimated, through the duty lawyer, that he intended to plead Guilty to all charges. The relevant documents were sent to me and I duly instructed an assistant, Jim Penman, to see McGregor in Saughton Prison, Edinburgh. McGregor there signed the necessary papers, indicating a Guilty plea, which meant that the case would be dealt with quickly.

Jim Penman took a full statement from him to be used in mitigation of his offence and within seven days an indictment was served on McGregor by the Edinburgh Fiscal, Edwin G Smith. This indictment indicated an early date for disposal of the case.

The disposal date fell on a Monday, at Edinburgh Sheriff Court, from where McGregor would, no doubt, be remitted to the High Court for sentence. Although he had no previous convictions, the charges were extremely grave—and in view of this I decided to see McGregor on the Saturday afternoon before the hearing. I made arrangements to travel to Edinburgh and interview him myself for the first time.

Before leaving my office on Saturday morning I studied McGregor's file. In particular, I studied the full hand-written notes taken by Jim Penman a week earlier. Towards the end of the second page of notes I noticed a rough sketch of Maryhill Road, Glasgow, at St George's Cross. There was an X marking the location of the Bank of Scotland there. I glanced at the charges against him and saw that there was none relating to this bank.

Reading on, after the sketch there was the following in Penman's handwriting: 'My first-ever bank robbery took place at the Bank of Scotland, St George's Cross, Glasgow. Like the other ones, I passed a note and was handed about £2500. This was about nine months ago.'

I sent for Penman, a former police sergeant with many years service, and asked him to explain these entries, as well as the sketch.

He told me that after obtaining background information from McGregor, and his agreement to plead Guilty to the five bank charges, he had asked McGregor if these charges 'cleared the slate' against him. 'Is there anything else that you've been responsible for? It would be in your best interests to tell me, so that everything can be disposed of at once,' Penman had said.

McGregor had then said that there had been one other robbery, involving a bank at St George's Cross, about nine months earlier. Penman had taken a note of this. McGregor had told Penman that this had been his first excursion into bank robbery and he had not been charged with it. He now wished that that robbery should be taken into account with the other five.

Possibly because I had been busy in court, or out of town, Penman had not brought this information to my notice earlier. He had not been with me at the time of the Swanson case and knew nothing about the circumstances of it.

After hearing what Penman had to say, I hurried to my strong room and looked out Swanson's file, which was now gathering dust. I checked the date, locus, the amount of money stolen. I remembered the evidence taken at the trial of the note that was handed to the bank teller. I also remembered Swanson's consistent pleas of innocence.

I was excited, realising that these developments were dramatic to say the least. I was to see McGregor that same afternoon and I would take both files with me to the prison.

Before leaving the office I dictated a letter to Swanson, who was in Peterhead Prison, stating that I did not wish to build up his hopes—I emphasised this—but that there had been a startling new development, which I was pursuing on his behalf. I told him nothing else at that time.

I could not make Saughton Prison fast enough. I had time, however, for a quick snack at home—and could not stop myself from telling my wife Delia, of the morning's exciting discovery. At 3.30 p.m. I was in Saughton Prison, interviewing McGregor.

I well remember that first meeting.

I noticed that, although much younger and a little smaller, McGregor was not unlike Swanson in appearance. Their facial expressions were very similar, their hair-styles identical. My mind's eyes conjured up a picture of McGregor wearing sunglasses. Yes, the likeness was there—despite considerable difference in years.

I was still excited—but the first point I raised with him was a prosaic one. 'Do you know a Maurice Swanson?' He replied 'No.' I asked him if he knew a Maurice Borkowski. (Swanson had changed his name a number of years earlier.) He said he had never heard of such a person.

What I had to guard against was this: from time to time it is possible for two prisoners, even lodged in different prisons, to put their heads together in an endeavour to assist one or the other. From the way in which the somewhat bewildered McGregor answered my questions, however, I felt that this man had no knowledge of the existence of my other client.

I then went over Penman's statement with him and confirmed the various mitigating factors. Having done this, I questioned him about the sketch and the information relating to the bank at St George's Cross. McGregor confirmed the information he had given to Penman. And he said that he wanted this robbery included in the indictment, so that all his depredations would be disposed of at the same time. He would then, he said, be clear to resume a normal life when he finished his prison sentence.

It was then I told him that a client of mine, Swanson, had been convicted of this particular crime the previous August and sentenced to five years' imprisonment. I told him that Swanson had persistently claimed his innocence—and it would appear from what he had said that it was he, McGregor, who had committed the crime. I advised him that he did not require to insist on pleading Guilty to the St George's Cross robbery, because he had not been charged with it. But if he did, then he might well assist a person whom I considered to be innocent and wrongly convicted.

McGregor was quiet for a moment, and then said he understood the situation and was anxious to offer a Guilty plea to Swanson's charge, irrespective of the possible consequences, and to make all necessary disclosures to the authorities.

I realised at that stage, of course, that I was now very much involved in the interests of two clients at once. In order to be scrupulously fair to McGregor I told him I would return to see him the following day, Sunday, and bring with me the counsel who had represented Swanson at his trial. I thought this would be a suitable safeguard, as I did not want to be accused of overemphasising the situation that Swanson found himself in to the detriment of McGregor. On leaving the prison I telephoned Bert Kerrigan and briefly explained the novel circumstances to him. I arranged to meet him outside Saughton Prison on the Sunday afternoon.

When we met I showed him McGregor's file and drew his attention to the statement Penman had taken, as well as my own notes. I also gave him Swanson's file. Within half an hour Kerrigan had assimilated all the facts, and we entered the prison to interview McGregor. Kerrigan took full notes of this interview and was at pains to explain McGregor's rights to him—and in particular his right to different representation if he desired it.

Neither of us was in a position to advise McGregor as to what might happen after we told the Fiscal of his intention to plead to an additional matter with which he had not been charged. But we arranged to confer with him again prior to the Monday hearing in Edinburgh Sheriff Court.

Next morning Mr Kerrigan and I discussed the matter at some length with a senior Fiscal, Mr Taylor Wilson, as Edwin Smith was not available. We put him fully in the picture about the recent developments, and it was decided that it would not be proper to proceed at such short notice with our plea of Guilty on McGregor's behalf in respect of the five charges on the indictment. Accordingly, when the case was called that morning, the indictment was deserted in the meantime by the Crown.

After this Mr Kerrigan and I prepared a fifteen-page dossier, including the handwritten notes by Mr Penman. This document we presented to the Solicitor General for Scotland, Lord McCluskey. It was, of course, given Lord McCluskey's undivided attention, and some time later I was advised by the Procurator Fiscal of Glasgow, Mr Henry Herron, that the Crown had decided to hold an identification parade in Saughton prison, where the two bank tellers who had given evidence against Swanson would be asked to view a parade which included McGregor. This parade was not to include Swanson.

When I learned this I got in touch with another Glasgow solicitor, Paul Burns, who was not connected with my firm, and asked him to accompany me to the parade and look after, in particular, the interests of McGregor. I felt that by this time it was only proper for an independent solicitor to handle McGregor's case.

We travelled through to Edinburgh together, and at the prison we met Henry Herron, Detective Inspector Sinclair Paterson and other officers involved in the Swanson case. We were shown into a church within the prison, where the parade was to take place. McGregor himself had assisted by choosing five other people of similar height and build to his own. Sunglasses were worn by all persons standing on the parade.

Before the start of the parade I conferred with Mr Herron, as a result of which both of us, along with a senior police officer, entered a small room where the two bank tellers were waiting. I told them what the parade was about and advised them that this was another parade in connection with the robbery at their bank nine months previously, and that there was a possibility that an innocent man had been convicted of the robbery because of the evidence given by them at his trial. I pointed out that we were all human and capable of making mistakes but that in the circumstances, and in the interests of justice, if mistakes on identification had been made by them there would be no recriminations. They would not be blamed in any way for having wrongly identified an innocent person.

As soon as I had finished one of the tellers said 'If we don't pick out anyone at this parade, will anything happen?'

I did not answer this, but I realised immediately that it was possible that the witnesses had no intention at that stage of altering their evidence. It is sometimes very difficult for people to admit an error—particularly if the error involved the wrongful imprisonment of a fellow human being.

The second teller was called into the improvised parade room first and, it seemed to me, viewed the line-up somewhat briefly. He turned to the officer in charge of the parade and said 'He's not there.'

The teller from whom the money had been taken then entered the room and looked at the parade.

I was watching him very carefully and, as he looked at the various members of the parade, he paused momentarily at No 5, who happened to be McGregor. Their eyes met. Then he went on to glance at No 6, and told the officer in charge, 'The man is not there.'

As he was leaving the room, McGregor moved forward from his No 5 position and said to me, pointing to the teller, 'He is the man who handed me over the money.' The officers made a note of this remark.

Maurice Swanson with his framed Royal Pardon

This was an identification parade in reverse. We had the unusual situation of the suspect identifying one of the witnesses! But, all the same, things looked bleak. I remember meeting Detective Inspector Paterson at the prison exit. I was despondent, and thought that the release of Swanson was now a forlorn hope. Mr Paterson seemed to share my view.

On the drive back to Glasgow with my legal colleague, hardly a word was spoken. I felt shattered. My hopes had been built up. I was grateful to the prosecution for having arranged the parade—yet it had all been to no avail. We were back to square one.

For the next few weeks nothing happened, apart from the fact that McGregor pled Guilty to the first five charges and was sentenced to nine years' imprisonment. I noted that the St George's Cross charge had not been included on his indictment.

What I did not know was that Detective Inspector Paterson was very concerned about the whole situation and had been giving it a good deal of thought. Then one night a few weeks after the parade, he suddenly woke up at two o'clock in the morning, asking himself 'What have I not done that I ought to have done?' He told me later that he sat and thought and thought until, after about an hour, an answer flashed through his mind. He remembered that numerous photographs and finger and palm prints had been taken at the bank after the robbery.

First thing the next morning he telephoned a Detective Sergeant John Robertson of the Glasgow Police fingerprint department. Paterson asked if there was a chance that prints taken from the bank ten months earlier might still be in existence. Or had these been destroyed? After all, the case was officially over and had been for some time. Later that day Detective Inspector Paterson was told that all the prints had been recovered and were available. He immediately handed over McGregor's finger and palm prints for comparison.

There were some two hundred prints—and, Sergeant Robertson was to tell me afterwards, one of the last to be compared was a palm print taken from the finger-plate on the inside of the bank's swing door. It was McGregor's. No two palm prints have the necessary sixteen points of identical comparison unless made by the same person. Clearly, and beyond peradventure McGregor had been at the bank.

Detective Inspector Paterson had checked at the time of the robbery that the bank cleaners had polished the door finger-plates each evening. McGregor's prints could only have been left there on 26 April . . . and the bank had been open to the public only fifteen minutes before the robbery.

I knew nothing of this at the time, but I learned that Inspector Paterson—armed with the evidence—went through to Edinburgh the following day to see the Solicitor General. He had with him a precognition from the fingerprint expert to the effect that the palm print found on the bank's door was McGregor's. Within days, thanks to the expeditious way in which the matter was handled by Lord McCluskey, decisions were taken at the highest level. These meetings and decisions culminated in the pardon of Swanson on 23 July 1975.

The first I knew of this development was on 23 July when I received a phone call from George Saunders, a senior Court reporter on *The Scotsman*. He was able to tell me that Swanson was to be pardoned two days later. He also told me that the Pardon itself was on the Queen's desk at Buckingham Palace for signature that same day, 23 July, but that she was at Badminton Horse Trials and was therefore unable to do the necessary deed. It is interesting to note, in support of this information, that when I received the official certified copy of the Pardon it was dated the 23rd, although it was not released for two more days. I suppose that two days did not amount to much for Swanson when put against five years in prison.

In the early afternoon of 25 July a member of the Secretary of State for Scotland's office telephoned me from Westminster and told me the terms of a statement which would be made at 4 p.m. that same day by the Scottish Secretary. I knew then that my client's release was more than just imminent. I was delighted.

Maurice Swanson became the first person in Scotland this century to be pardoned by a monarch on a matter of substantive crime. Later, on 19 May 1976, the second such pardon was granted by the Queen to Patrick C Meehan. But that's another story....

It is worth pointing out here an error that has been perpetuated in many newpapers: the celebrated case of Oscar Slater, released from Peterhead Prison in 1927 after nineteen years in prison, did not end with a Royal Pardon. Slater, who was convicted in 1909 of the murder of eighty-three-year-old Miss Marion Gilchrist at her home in Glasgow, had his conviction quashed by the Court of Criminal Appeal. The court had just been formed at the time when it heard additional evidence that had come to light about Oscar Slater's case and the existence of certain errors which had prejudiced his position at his trial. Indeed, the draftsmen of the Criminal Appeal (Scotland) Act of 1926, which set up the modern Appeal Court, had the Slater travesty very much in mind when finalising that forum.

Like Swanson, Slater was also compensated for his nineteen years' wrongful detention in custody, with the then considerable sum of £6000.

Swanson's Pardon was couched in the following terms:

ELIZABETH THE SECOND, by the Grace of God of the United Kingdom of Great Britain and Northern Ireland, and of Our other Realms and Territories, QUEEN Head of the Commonwealth, Defender of the Faith, to all to whom these Presents shall come,
GREETING:

WHEREAS Maurice Swanson or Borkowski was at the High Court holden at Glasgow on the twenty eighth day of August 1974 convicted of robbery and sentenced to five years imprisonment;
NOW KNOW YE that We in consideration of some circumstances humbly represented unto Us and to Our Pre-

rogative Royal, Proper Motion, and Royal Clemency, are graciously pleased to extend Our Grace and Mercy to the said Maurice Swanson or Borkowski and to grant him Our Free Pardon in respect of the said conviction thereby pardoning, remitting and releasing unto him all pains, penalties and punishments whatsoever that from the said conviction may come.

Given at Our Court at St James the 23rd day of July 1975 in the Twenty-fourth year of Our Reign

This document was superscribed by the Queen, *Elizabeth R*, and subscribed by the then Secretary of State for Scotland, Willie Ross.

Although I did not agree with the terminology and would have preferred it made clear that the conviction had been wrongous and was being expunged, nonetheless there was no doubt in the minds of the authorities as to the merit and tenor of the document. I accepted, as did my client, the spirit of the Pardon. This was an occasion when the law was not afraid to admit to error and opened the doors of Peterhead Prison to allow Swanson to walk out a free man.

The reasonable figure of £5000 was awarded in compensation by the Assessor appointed by the Scottish Secretary, Mr James Law QC, after evidence as to Swanson's loss, deterioration in health and the fact that his hair had turned completely white over the eleven-month period of his imprisonment was laid before him by me some weeks later.

Swanson was duly released at 4 p.m. on the day of the pardon, and came to see me the next day. I had not seen him since his conviction and I must confess I barely recognised him. He had lost a lot of weight and, as mentioned above, his hair had turned white. I have seldom seen such a change in a person over such a short period, illness excepted.

Although Swanson was my client at the time of his arrest, trial and pardon (and had been on previous occasions, although he had never been accused of acts of violence), and I triggered off the action which led to his freedom, there must be no doubt who was most responsible for this historic legal success. It was, of course, manifestly attributable to Glasgow Police—and, in particular, to the officer in charge of the case, Detective Inspector Sinclair Paterson. He is now retired from the force which he graced so well for so many years. I have known him since his very early days as a detective constable, and still see him, from time to time, in his present capacity as security officer for British Transport Hotels. He was one of the fairest, yet most dedicated, police officers I ever knew.

As a matter of interest, there was a difference of almost twenty years between Swanson and McGregor. Swanson was some four inches taller, but in 1974 his hair and hairstyle were similar to McGregor's. There was certainly a facial resemblance between the two of them, despite the disparity in ages, especially in the bone structure. Their slightly prominent cheek bones were alike, as was the shape of the forehead. The colour of the eyes was the same. Looking at them standing together, they could easily be distinguished, but it would have been more difficult when they were apart.

We eventually gleaned from McGregor that after some of the robberies—and, in particular, the St George's Cross robbery—he had indeed travelled to Spain and taken up part-time employment as a barman. Swanson's informants had been correct. It is worth noting that Swanson has never been before the courts since his release—and one hopes that he never again will be.

5
Believing Your Eyes

Twenty-one people passed slowly down the line of men at an identification parade at Glasgow's Southern Police Station and pointed to No 4—'That's the man.'

No 4 had been arrested by the police and accused of passing dud cheques in shops on the city's South Side— and No 4 was my client, Derek Bingham. . . .

Bingham had denied the charges but had agreed to take part in an identification parade at which shop assistants, about thirty of them, were asked to pick out the man who paid with worthless cheques. I had been phoned by the police, who said that Bingham wanted me to come and represent him at the parade.

Imagine my dismay as, one after the other, the shop assistants gave the six look-alike men in the line-up a casual glance and then promptly identified my client twenty-one times!

Halfway through the parade I felt like calling it off, to avoid further embarrassment. I could see a number of police officers looking in my direction, no doubt watching my reaction as the nails were most assuredly hammered into Bingham's coffin, so to speak. At the end of the parade the officer in charge approached me and asked formally if I was satisfied with the conduct and composition of the parade. Trying not to betray any of the defeatism I felt, I barked 'Most certainly' and 'Thank you'.

Bingham and I hastily retreated to the interview room, where I said something about the situation 'not looking good'. Bingham just laughed. I stared at him— he was bouncy with confidence. 'These charges will never prove,' he said.

I asked him to let me into the secret.

'Check up with the Governor of Walton Jail in Liverpool,' he told me. 'You'll find out that I was sentenced to six months at the end of February this year for driving a car while disqualified and uninsured. I was only released at the end of June!'

If this were so, I thought, then we had a truly remarkable situation. The charges against Bingham related to offences which had occurred over a period of two and a half months—and Bingham, according to his account, had only been at liberty for a fortnight. And the handwriting on all the cheques had been the same!

When the complaints had begun coming into the police from about twenty shops, all within a radius of three miles, a pattern was detected. Police officers know the *modus operandi* of most criminals, and offences fall into distinct categories. In this case they would have turned at once to their file on 'con men'.

The shop assistants had said that the man passing the dud cheques had an English accent. This could have cut down the number of suspects. They described him as a slim, balding man aged about thirty—and this would have further reduced the number of possibles.

When I met Bingham just before the parade I saw a man of about average height, well dressed, slim and prematurely bald, with a modicum of brown hair on each side of his head. He was thirty-two years old and spoke with a North-of-England accent you might hear any day on the Promenade at Blackpool. And no doubt, prior to my client's arrest, his photograph—from the Criminal Records Office—would have been shown to at least one of the eye-witnesses.

When they eventually arrested Bingham, the police must have been pretty confident—so confident, in fact, that they had not even taken a sample of his handwriting.

That same afternoon I telephoned the Governor at Walton Jail and he confirmed verbally what Bingham had claimed. I asked him if he would send me an official letter to that effect, telling him why I required it. He said he would.

The next day I duly appeared in court to represent Bingham. He was charged on Petition with offences of a fraudulent nature, had bail refused and was remanded to Barlinnie Prison.

On the following day, I received the official communication from Walton's Governor, who had also added the name of the court at which Bingham had been sentenced. This was all I needed. I immediately forwarded this information, duly certified by the Governor himself, to the Lord Advocate in Edinburgh with a copy of the charges (giving the dates) and a covering letter setting out the unusual circumstances.

I also invited the Lord Advocate to have a sample of Bingham's handwriting taken, so that this could be compared with the signatures on the various cheques. I pointed out that Bingham would be pleased to write the signature 'J Cowan' which had appeared on all the cheques. Only three had been passed since Bingham came out of prison.

Two days later Bingham was released from Barlinnie and told that the matter was at an end.

My confidence in eye-witness testimony has never been quite the same since that episode— which is hardly surprising. The case of Derek Bingham exposes a myth—that the identification of a number of eye-witnesses cannot be wrong. The principle of 'the more there are, the better for the Crown' is acceptable up to a point, but I am never truly happy about such a situation unless there is other evidence supporting the identification. This could take the form of:

Statements to the police

Possession of something traceable to the theft or robbery, if this is the charge

Possession of clothing accurately described by eye-witnesses

Flight

Bloodstaining on clothes of suspect, if the charge is one of violence

The interior of Block C, Barlinnie Prison, where untried prisoners are held

Evidence from near confederates of planning the crime

Evidence of handwriting or fingerprints, if available

Incriminating circumstances of the arrest, etc.

Many celebrated authorities in England and Scotland have criticised cases based purely on identification, and the view has often been expressed that where identification evidence is concerned juries must be extremely careful. The reasons for this are obvious—many people can look alike, particularly if they are not seen together and if the period of identification covers less than a minute, as is often the case.

Eye-witnesses are human, and even with the best will in the world are capable of making mistakes. Having committed themselves at an identification parade they are loth to recant at the subsequent trial. No-one wishes to appear fickle or uncertain.

At many parades I have seen an eye-witness, try as she or he might, prove totally unable to identify anyone on the parade—and then turn to the officer in charge and apologise profusely for, as it were, letting him down! I have seen others patently making a guess at a number, rather than appear to disappoint the police. With any luck, those guesses may not incriminate the suspect, although he stands with only another four or five persons—one could calculate the odds. Frequently, too, at a parade a witness may say 'I think Number Three'— but more often than not, at the trial the word 'think' disappears from that witness's vocabulary. There is much more certainty because, by that time, someone has been duly brought to trial.

It is even worse when there has not been an identity parade and an eye-witness is asked to look around the court from the witness box, to see if he can identify the person he is speaking about. As soon as he looks in the general direction of the public and Press benches he cannot fail to spot, like a beacon shining in the dark, a grim-faced, pale and anxious accused sitting in the dock between two smartly-dressed police constables wearing spotless white gloves, batons drawn!

There is one major difference, on the subject of identification, between Scotland and England. In England they do not allow dock identification—unless the witness purporting to identify has already done so at an earlier and properly constituted parade. In Scotland, despite the absence of a parade beforehand, a witness can still be asked to point out the accused in court from the witness box. The English rule about identification in court was brought into being as a result of a Working Group chaired by Lord Devlin in 1974—a Working Group similar to one set up by the Scottish Secretary about twelve years ago, presided over by Sheriff Principal W J Bryden Q C (now Sir William Bryden) to look into and report on identification procedure. The more comprehensive Thomson Report was issued some time later.

The English report was published in 1976 and recommended, along with other things, that only in exceptional circumstances should a person be convicted on the basis of identification evidence unsupported by other substantial evidence. It added that an identification parade should normally be held in preference to other methods of identification.

Having instructed in trials both north and south of the Border, I appreciate the benefit of the English system of fairness on this latter point. This, I may say, is no mean concession from a Scottish criminal lawyer who, by and large, much prefers our system of criminal law, with its considerable safeguards against possible miscarriages of justice.

The Scottish Working Committee, in its report, continued to allow dock identifications, even in the absence of a properly constituted and earlier identification parade—pointing out in the process that, unlike England, we in Scotland have a second acquittal verdict, that of Not Proven. It was satisfied that this additional acquittal verdict counterbalanced matters.

Nicholas Church was seventeen years old and innocent. Yet he was arrested, charged along with three men he had never seen before, tried, found guilty and convicted.

How did that happen? Because, yet again, evidence of identification by eye-witnesses, unsupported by any other evidence, was upheld—and his own plea and evidence of innocence rejected.

The law and Nicholas Church caused so much controversy that two responsible Procurators Fiscal were to make totally conflicting statements on the merits of the lad's 'conviction'.

Nicky Church was a boy who had never been in court before. He held a responsible job. He lived at that time in Glasgow's High Street.

Hours before Nicky Church was arrested three uniformed police officers had seen two persons climbing out of a window of the Nag's Head public house in London Road, Glasgow. They were carrying spirits and cigarettes. Realising that they were housebreakers, the policemen gave chase, but both culprits made good their escape. The thieves had had a start of more than a hundred yards over the constables and disappeared into the night, complete with booty. All three officers, however, had recognised one of them at once as being a particular thorn in their flesh, a man called Crummer who had previous convictions for dishonesty. The other man they did not recognise at all. A search was begun immediately for Crummer and his associate.

Just over two and a half hours later the police received information that Crummer was in a house in nearby Charlotte Street, with the proceeds of the crime. They hurried there in a patrol van—and arrived at the close-mouth just in time to see Nicholas Church walking in. Church was immediately arrested and then taken to the house where the police expected Crummer to be.

Although the close-mouth gave access to a number of tenement houses, the officers thought, no doubt, that Church was going to the house about which they had had information. No doubt too the associate of Crummer, seen fleeing from the pub, had looked like Church from a distance.

The police were not disappointed. With Church in their custody, they entered the house and arrested

Crummer, along with two other men, and also took possession of a quantity of stolen alcohol and cigarettes. Church, meanwhile, was protesting his innocence—but to no avail. He told the police that he had witnesses further up Charlotte Street, whom he had just left, and that he had not been going to this particular house in the first place.

Even the three men in the house, including Crummer, told the police that they did not know Church. All four, however, were taken to the van outside and driven to the Central Police Headquarters. There they were charged with breaking into the Nag's Head on the previous evening, and stealing alcohol and cigarettes to the value of £560.

By now it was well after midnight. Church's father was notified of his son's arrest and arrived at the police headquarters at 2.30 a.m. He was puzzled when told by the officer at the bar counter of the details of the charge against his son. He knew that Nicky had gone to a dance on the previous evening—and he did not know the three others charged along with his son. From the information given to him, he understood that they were grown men, years older than his boy.

The father said that there must have been a mistake made somewhere along the line. He asked if Nicky could get bail. This request was refused, and neither was he allowed to see or speak to his son. He was told that Nicholas would appear at the Sheriff Court later that morning. At the court all four were remanded on petition, and in custody, to Barlinnie Prison. On the same afternoon I was consulted by the distraught father, who was bewildered by what was happening.

Following instructions, I visited the prison and interviewed the boy. He appeared to know nothing at all about the break-in, and told me his movements on the previous night—about the dance, his two male friends, his girlfriend and her mother....He gave me their names and addresses and said that they would support his alibi. He stressed that he did not even know his three co-accused.

The whole matter seemed strange to me—but even more peculiar events were to follow.

Seven days later, two of the original four were released, without comment, and only Crummer and Church appeared again on the original charge. The case had now been reduced to summary procedure—that is, a less serious offence that would be heard without a jury—and both tendered pleas of Not Guilty to the charge. Bail was granted to Church in the sum of £5, but Crummer's bail was set at a much higher figure. This being so, Crummer promptly changed his plea to Guilty—and was summarily sentenced to three months' imprisonment.

Trial was fixed for Church—now alone on the charge—for early December 1961.

I proceeded to prepare his case. He was interviewed at my office on a number of occasions, along with his four alibi witnesses. They were all quite clear as to Church's movements on that May evening, and certain of his non-involvement in the charge preferred against him.

Eventually the trial date arrived, and the case against Nicholas Church was called. The presiding Sheriff was Ronald King-Murray (now Lord Murray, Senator of the College of Justice, a former Lord Advocate and Labour MP for Leith). He was a man of great legal distinction. The Procurator Fiscal was Mr John Grimes, a man of considerable experience in that service and some thirty years my senior.

At the outset, I intimated a Special Defence of Alibi and named three witnesses, over and above the accused, in support of it.

The three police officers gave evidence.

Two of them said that they recognised Church as being one of the two 'men' they had seen climbing out of the side window of the pub, carrying stolen material. In cross-examination they conceded that the circumstances of their observations were not of the very best. It had been dark, in an ill-lit area, and they had only caught 'a fleeting glimpse of both men'. Both 'men' had made good their escape— but they knew and recognised Crummer, and immediately began their search for him. They said that they had been more than a hundred yards away from the window when they saw the two persons leave—and that was why they had avoided capture at the time.

I suggested to them that this whole matter was a case of mistaken identity, but they would have none of that. Indeed, they were adamant. 'We were right about Crummer, and we are also correct about identification of Church.'

I pointed out to them that they knew Crummer well, but they did not even know Church at all at the time. 'Can you exclude the possiblity of error in your identification of Church?' I asked them. 'Yes,' each replied resolutely. They said that they had been of the view that Church had entered the close-mouth to join up with his criminal associates—who were already in the house to which they took him.

I cannot help thinking now how revealing it would have been had the police allowed Church to reach his destination instead of intercepting him before he did so. . . .

The third police witness merely said that Church was 'like the other man', but he could not be certain. The fact that the police were discriminating in this way did not, I felt, help matters. The uncertainty of the third bolstered, if anything, the positive identification of the other two.

Friscal Grimes then closed his case—and I opened the defence by calling Nicholas Church.

He said that he had not been in any way involved, and did not know Crummer—or the other two, for that matter. He had gone to a dance on the evening of 5 May along with two pals. He had met a girlfriend, Agnes McAnena, there. Afterwards, along with his two friends, he had walked with Agnes to the fish restaurant where her mother worked, and they chatted. From there—and this was well after the crime had been committed—they had walked to the corner of Charlotte

Street and London Road. Miss McAnena lived further down Charlotte Street, but they had waited at the corner of the street, as arranged, for the girl's mother to join them.

While the four of them were standing at the corner, watching for Mrs McAnena, Church had left them to go to Agnes's house to use the toilet. He had walked the necessary twenty yards and entered her close, where a number of families lived. He had been followed into the close by three policemen, who had jumped out of a police vehicle. And he had been arrested.

He was then taken to another house in the same tenement, where he saw three strange men drinking from bottles of spirits. All four were taken out to the police vehicle and driven to police headquarters—despite Church's protests and requests that they should confer with the two lads and the girl McAnena, who were still standing at the corner of the street.

Church gave his evidence clearly and was unshakeable in cross-examination, despite the experience and perspicacity of Fiscal Grimes. Church impressed me with his evidence and how he gave it.

He was followed by Agnes McAnena, who supported his evidence in every detail. She too seemed extremely credible in her demeanour.

By now I was more than confident and, on Miss McAnena leaving the witness box, I made the following statement to the Bench: 'I have his two male friends and Mrs McAnena waiting outside in the witness room. They are all of unimpeachable character. They will give precisely the same version and in the same unflinching manner. However, I do not think that it will be necessary to take up more of the Court's time, so I close the case for the defence at this stage.'

My reasoning was that if the Sheriff believed Church and McAnena—and I thought he would—then the other three witnesses were quite unnecessary. If he had not accepted them, the others were pointless in any event. However, when the Sheriff gave his verdict, I felt like kicking myself. I had been far too over-confident....

98

Meanwhile, Grimes and I summed up our respective cases.

Grimes seemed unduly mild in his approach, and really left the matter of decision entirely up to the Sheriff.

I emphasised the possibility of error on the part of the two identifying constables and pressed the demeanour and certitude of the two defence witnesses.

'You cannot decide this issue by counting heads—have the Crown discharged the onus of proof? The defence requires to prove nothing—both sets of witnesses were good and unshakeable, so the verdict must either be Not Guilty or Not Proven,' I said.

The Sheriff retired for about twenty minutes. When he returned he stated 'This is an exceptionally difficult case to decide but, in the end, I have come to the conclusion that the police evidence is accurate.' He found Nicholas Church Guilty, and continued the case for three weeks, in order to obtain a probation report. Church, however, was not detained.

As soon as the Sheriff left the bench, I discussed the case with John Grimes, who was extremely sympathetic. He was anxious about the Sheriff's decision and agreed to interview Crummer. This he did—and was told that Church 'had nothing to do with the break-in, and nothing to do with me'. Crummer had already served his sentence and had nothing whatsoever to gain by wrongly exculpating Church.

Three weeks later we were back in court. The probation report echoed Church's innocence.

Fiscal Grimes spoke first, 'I wish to indicate to the court' he said 'that I feel some disturbance in this matter. It had become apparent that there is a great difference between the persons of Crummer and Church. There appears to be no connection between them. However, enquiries have been made and it has become even more apparent that Church has a completely clean record and might be put in a position which might totally overwhelm him. There appears to be a chance of a possible error of a kind not usually made.'

Most people hearing phrases like this from the prosecution would, quite properly, take them to mean that there was a chance of a miscarriage of justice. I followed this up. 'I think it is quite clear that there must be doubt about my client's guilt. I was astonished at the verdict of Guilty. Church is in no way connected with the culprit Crummer. I think there is a distinct possibility of a miscarriage of justice in this case. It is, surely, not too late to remedy matters,' I urged.

The case was again continued for several weeks for further consideration by the Sheriff.

At the next—and final—hearing of the case the crown sent the Senior Assistant Fiscal, Mr Russell L J Miln, second-in-command of the Fiscal's Department.

Mr Miln began by criticising certain newspaper reports of the previous hearing.

'The words used by my assistant Mr Grimes, last time, did not at all mean that the Fiscal's Department supported Mr Beltrami's view that this had been a miscarriage of justice. My department does not believe that your Lordship inadvertently committed a miscarriage of justice. My department is satisfied with the result of this case, and believed that the accused was properly convicted.'

More than a little angry by this time, I replied 'My learned friend Mr Miln did not have the opportunity and benefit of hearing Nicholas Church and his witness giving evidence on oath at this trial. At no stage did I go so far as to say that there had been a miscarriage of justice. How could I? I did not witness the break-in and the escape of the two men. At the last hearing I spoke of a *possibility* of a miscarriage of justice—and I rigidly adhere to that view today.'

Sheriff King-Murray, obviously somewhat moved by these unique developments, granted Church an absolute discharge without further ado. Later, a spokesman for the Crown said to the Press that the finding of absolute discharge by the Bench would not be regarded as a conviction against Church.

But next day the Press carried the following comment ' "There appears to be a chance of a possible error of a kind not usually made...." Fiscal Grimes, of 19 December 1961. And.... "My Department is satisfied with the result of this case and believed the accused was properly convicted...." Assistant Procurator Fiscal of Glasgow, Russell L J Miln, 23 January 1962.'

After the final hearing and satisfactory disposal of the case, Nicholas Church said 'Thank goodness it is over. I consider myself cleared—as, indeed, I should be.'

As, indeed, he was—no matter what the disagreement between the Fiscals.

So strong seemed to be the eye-witness evidence in another case that I took the unusual step of subjecting my own client to a lie-detector test!

The polygraph—better known as the lie-detector—is a machine frequently used in the United States in connection with the exposure of criminals, as well as the elimination of suspects. To my knowledge, it has never been invoked in this regard in Scotland—apart, that is, from one notable exception: the strange case of Joe Boyle.

Even in this case, however, we did not produce the conclusive evidence in court. Bearing in mind the decision of three senior judges, who refused an application some years earlier in Patrick Meehan's 'truth-drug' submission, it was probable that a second application before the High Court would have met a similar fate. However, I found the use of the polygraph apparatus extremely useful in helping me to make up my own mind in deciding to defend Boyle against a conviction for attempted murder.

American experts in the field of polygraph tests tell us that, although never one hundred per cent reliable, it can be more than a useful guide in the search for the truth. Their practical experience over many years seems to support that proposition. In the case of Boyle, the test conducted by an American expert who just happened to be over in this country on a lecture tour proved to be 'spot on'.

Fortunately, the convincing result of the experiment—conducted at the *Scottish Daily Record* offices in Glasgow—merely matched additional real and relevant evidence which was submitted to the Court of Criminal Appeal. This resulted in the quashing of a ten-year sentence and conviction in respect of an attempted murder charge imposed some months earlier in the Glasgow High Court.

Boyle had been charged with attempted murder after having been put in an identification parade and identified by two men. One of these witnesses claimed that an attempt had been made to run him down by Boyle, who had been behind the wheel of an old 'banger' outside the 'Plainsman' public house near Airdrie. The other witness was the first man's friend and had been in his company that evening. Both witnesses claimed that they had not known Boyle prior to the incident.

On being charged, Boyle had stressed his complete innocence. He had instructed a local solicitor and had been allowed bail when he appeared at Airdrie Sheriff Court next day. Thereafter it seems that Boyle took matters rather lightly and seldom sought out his lawyer to formulate his defence to the charge. He was pleading alibi. I imagine that he buried his head in the sand in the firm belief that, sooner or later the prosecuting authorities would realise that a monumental error had been made and the matter would inevitably be abandoned. The thought of conviction probably did not enter his mind—after all, he was innocent!

But the shock of receiving the High Court indictment jolted him out of his inertia and he made haste, with his papers, to his lawyer. There were now only weeks before the trial was due to proceed.

At around this time there occurred what can only be described, euphemistically, as a 'breakdown in communications' between solicitor and client. Even at the Pleading Diet in Airdrie the parties were to miss each other.

Although Boyle had not been at the Plainsman that night, his alibi was never properly checked, and he had even missed out on a pre-trial consultation with his counsel, Mr Fairbairn Q C. On the morning of his trial (before Lord Johnston) Boyle duly arrived at 9.30 a.m.—the case was due to start at 10 a.m.—and had time only for a hurried meeting with Mr Fairbairn. Although there have been better prepared defences, no motion was made for an adjournment. In any event, such motions are not all that well received in Scottish courts.

That afternoon Boyle was to find himself convicted by a majority verdict and sentenced to ten years' imprisonment. His demeanour and the way in which he gave his evidence of denial—and probably the utter astonishment with which he accepted the verdict and sentence—had not escaped the notice of the Advocate Depute, Lorne Cowie Q C, and even Lord Johnston himself. The feeling was already about that there had been something dreadfully wrong with this case. Even then the awesome suspicion of a possible, almost certain, miscarriage of justice had reared its head.

A shattered Boyle was detained to serve the first day of an unacceptable prison term. But his luck was to change—it had to—and after four days a most unusual move took place.

The charge to the jury by the judge had been unimpeachable. The only issue that could possibly be left was one of fact only, and there was enough legal evidence in the shape of two positive and unshakeable eyewitnesses. There appeared to be no persuasive ground of appeal—but one was lodged in skeleton form. And, astonishingly, bail of £20 was allowed by the High Court judge, pending the hearing of the appeal. There had seldom been precedent for this. It later became known that the trial judge had been so concerned with the whole pitiful affair that he had taken the step of communicating his doubts to his colleagues. The bail judge had acted upon these—and so Boyle was granted interim liberty.

During all these events I had been cruising abroad on holiday and knew nothing of them. I had never even heard of J J Boyle—who had only one trivial and ancient peccadillo chalked up against him. But only days after my return, Boyle consulted me for his appeal. He explained all the circumstances. He impressed me. So he signed a mandate, which I forwarded to his trial solicitor, indicating that I would assume responsibility for his client and requesting all the relevant papers on the case. These papers were duly sent, and I also considered many Press cuttings of the trial and its aftermath. The fact that bail had been fixed—and at £20—astonished me, and I felt that this must betray feelings of doubt in the minds of those who mattered.

I checked Boyle's alibi, and personally took statements supporting it. Then I went to the Plainsman and interviewed the owner and members of his staff, including the doorman. These made up four witnesses who were all on duty on the night of the offence, and who stated that Boyle had *not* been on the premises that evening. Judging by my experience, I thought they were credible and reliable. Boyle's alibi had been that he was at home with his wife for the whole evening.

The charge against him was one of attempted murder of two pedestrians by driving a car at them and injuring them on the roadway some hundred yards from the Plainsman.

The complainer had said that he and his friend had had an argument in the car park of the Plainsman with two men—one of whom was Boyle, he said. Both men had come from the Plainsman. Minutes later, added the complainer, he was struck by a car and hurled through its windscreen. Lying on his back on the bonnet of the car, and holding the top of the shattered windscreen, he said that he had got a good look at the driver, who was Boyle. His friend had been struck a glancing blow by the car and pushed to one side. He suffered only bruising—but he also identified Boyle as the driver.

It was also stated that the car was a white Cortina, with the registration number NGA 415. Boyle owned a red Corsair. And despite strenuous efforts by the police no link was ever established between a white Cortina, its registration number and the accused. In fact, the registration number proved to be a bogus one that did not relate to anyone.

The police had said that two months after the incident they had received an anonymous phone call saying 'It was a man called Boyle who did it.'

The key Crown witness had been shown a photograph of Boyle one week before eventually identifying him at a parade.

During the trial Detective Inspector Imrie admitted that the car with the smashed windscreen had never been traced, nor were there any traces of old cuts on Boyle when he was first interviewed by the police.

In his charge to the jury Lord Johnston said that the jury must make up its mind that the identification was accurate. He asked them to bear in mind that the incident happened on a dark November night, and that the victims had only a glimpse of the car's occupant. Further, he pointed out, the parade was held more than two months later.

Boyle, as it turned out, was well-known in the Plainsman, as he lived only a few miles away and, on occasions, played the organ there. But he had not been in the Plainsman that night, he said. And we had four witnesses from the pub who were both respectable and impressive.

I decided to go back to the scene, accompanied by my brother, Ray, a photographer with the Glasgow *Evening Times*. I told him what I wanted and he took photographs of the main door to the pub, the car park where the initial confrontation had taken place and the important positioning and strength of the lighting in the car park. We took these pictures as near as possible to the conditions which would have obtained on the night of the offence. I noted that there would have been much shadow, and to identify a stranger accurately after a brief exchange must have been far from easy.

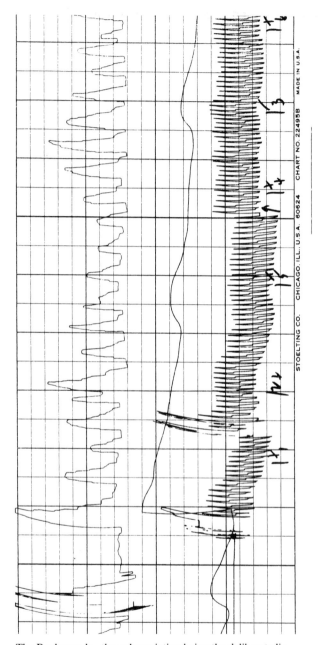

The Boyle graph—the only variation being the deliberate lie

106

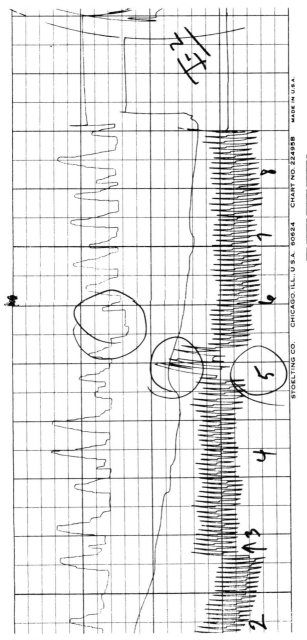

Continuation of the graph

There had been nothing else in the Crown case favourable to the prosecution. I sent copies of the photographs and additional statements to the Clerk of the High Court, and the Lord Advocate's Department. And by this time I had instructed Mr Fairbairn for the appeal—extending the grounds of that appeal to include the introduction of new evidence.

Meanwhile, Boyle had been going around scrapyards in Lanarkshire and elsewhere, trying to trace the car which had been described by the two principal witnesses. It was an unsuccessful quest—it was like looking for a needle in a haystack and even all the resources and manpower of Lanarkshire Constabulary had drawn a blank.

It was at this stage that Arnot McWhinnie, an experienced court reporter with the *Daily Record* who had attended Boyle's trial, told me about the trial—of how he had been impressed by Boyle but far from impressed by the defence preparation. He could remember vividly Boyle sobbing bitterly as he was led downstairs to the cells below the High Court after sentence. Four times he heard him shout 'I didn't do it!' before his protestations faded in the distance.

Through his many contacts, Arnot learned that an acknowledged American expert in the application and administration of the lie-detector, Vic Cochran, was touring this country and giving lectures on the subject.

Arnot arranged to meet Cochran, a Californian who had tested more than 6000 suspects in fifteen years of police work. On Arnot's request he agreed to conduct an experiment with Boyle and was duly informed of the background to the case. Boyle agreed to carry out the experiment, although he knew that it would be of no evidential value. But Arnot and I were interested to know what the polygraph would show. We were sure we had not been misled by Boyle.

The polygraph records breathing, skin resistance and blood pressure in the one graph. In other words, it records the respiratory and pulse rates as well as electrical conductivity over the skin surface. All these aspects vary with the level of a person's anxiety.

Vic Cochran told us of the accepted practice of asking a person during the experiment to tell deliberate lies. And one did see that the graph wavered only at this particular point.

The test took one hour and numerous questions were put to Boyle by Cochran. At its conclusion Cochran said that the man was undoubtedly innocent. 'He did not commit the crime with which he is charged,' he said. 'The polygraph could not be so far out were he a guilty person.'

Reinforced in my belief—indeed, my conviction—that Boyle was innocent, I travelled to Edinburgh for the appeal on 14 December 1973. But I still did not know what the outcome would be.

It was to be all or nothing. If the appeal was unsuccessful, the Court must allow the sentence of ten years, to stand. Given his guilt, the sentence was not in any way excessive—so we could hardly contest that.

I noted with delight that Mr Lorne Cowie Q C—now Lord Cowie, Senator of the College of Justice—was in his place as Crown representative for the appeal. In my many dealings with him in this capacity he had always been the essence of fairness, although a formidable adversary. Although it was not normal practice, Cowie addressed the Court at the outset and clearly indicated what the Crown feelings were on the merits of the appeal. He advised the Court that he had received photographs and statements from the defence, and that these had been carefully checked at his insistence—and he felt that, had these been available to the jury at an earlier stage, acquittal might well have resulted.

We had, I thought at the time, obviously won this appeal without requiring to make any submissions to the bench. With that degree of responsibility and integrity that is inherent in the Crown, it had conceded the controversial matter in the best interests of justice.

The appeal took only seven minutes, and Lord Emslie, Lord Justice-General, said at the conclusion of the hearing 'I am bound to say we feel certain anxiety about the quality and sufficiency of the identification evidence at the trial.'

The conviction was duly quashed and Boyle walked free. His nightmare was to become only a distant, frightening memory.

In this case the Crown, the defence and the Appeal Court judges had combined to erase a blot from our normally reliable and fair system of justice.

Truly, as the eighteenth-century judge Sir William Blackstone said, 'It is better that ten guilty persons escape than one innocent suffer.'

Two, of course, can play the identification game—as I can illustrate with a case concerning that old client of mine, Colin MacLean Beattie, our Glasgow 'hard man'.

It was alleged that 'Big Coalie' had punched a steward in the old Astoria ballroom in Sauchiehall Street, Glasgow. The circumstances were that one of the dancers entering the ballroom had been reluctant to surrender his bottle of whisky and had threatened, on being refused admission by the steward, that he would 'get him later'. The threat had been clearly idle in nature, as the man in no way matched the steward in build and physique. In sobriety he would not have opened his mouth—but on this evening 'Dutch courage' had summoned up the threat.

The man had been unceremoniously ejected from the ballroom by the steward with the minimum of effort. The allegation was that Beattie had then appeared on the scene and said to the attendant 'why wait until later?' It was further alleged that Beattie then punched the attendant, causing him to stagger downstairs.

There was no evidence that Beattie even knew the tipsy customer who had entered the ballroom with his beloved bottle.

At the trial there were three main witnesses for the prosecution—two of them stewards. The complainer positively identified Beattie as being the person who had assaulted him. The second witness, an attendant called McQuade, also identified Beattie as the culprit.

In my own preparation for the case I became aware of the fact that Beattie had been in these premises with several people, one of whom looked remarkably like him. This man, William Hynds, was of similar build and complexion to my client.

In the course of cross-examination of the second witness I introduced Beattie's friend into court, having earlier intimated his name as a defence witness. On being confronted with this man the witness admitted that he could be mistaken as to the identity of the assailant. They were so alike. At the trial Hynds and Beattie wore similar red pullovers and had matching dark suits. Truly, they were like the Toni Twins that morning!

The third witness was a sixteen-year-old pageboy who, on being shown our defence witness, frankly stated that he could not distinguish between them and that the witness Hynds could have been the person who had assaulted the complainer.

After these three witnesses had given evidence for the prosecution, the case came to an abrupt end with the Fiscal, Mr William Morton, rising to tell Sheriff Middleton 'Under the circumstances, I feel I must drop the case against Beattie. The issue of identification is most certainly suspect.' Beattie was accordingly found not guilty and discharged from the dock. Had the trial proceeded, Hynds would have admitted the assault and exonerated Beattie in any event. The young pageboy had been right.

I should point out here that Beattie is about six feet tall, extremely well-built, with a dark complexion. He is the type of person who would stand out in a crowd.

Identification was at issue in another case against Beattie, when he was charged—initially—with murdering a man called Francis Whitelaw in the West End Ballroom at St George's Cross, Glasgow by striking him one blow with his clenched fist and pole-axing him to the floor.

After the incident, Beattie had left the dance-hall before the expected arrival of the police, and later got in touch with me. He told me that there had been an argument between the two of them and that Whitelaw had put his hand into one of his pockets. Beattie had thought Whitelaw was armed and had at once punched him on the jaw in his own defence, thinking that he was about to be seriously attacked.

I took Beattie to police headquarters where he surrendered himself and, on being charged with murder, replied 'Not Guilty' in accordance with my advice. The charge was later reduced by the Crown to the lesser one of culpable homicide (manslaughter in England) and bail was allowed.

In our criminal legal system there must always be incriminating evidence against the accused from at least two separate and independent sources—two separate fingers pointing towards the accused as being the perpetrator of the crime. A single witness can, of course, be corroborated by at least one additional person, or alternatively by facts or circumstances which point unerringly to the accused as the guilty party. Needless to say, these facts and circumstances must be of a cogent nature and should incriminate the accused to the exclusion of all others. This principle was to be well illustrated by Beattie's case. . . .

Shortly after Beattie's arrest, I attended an identification parade at which one witness positively identified Beattie as the assailant. This witness happened to be a friend of the deceased and had been in his company that evening.

Prior to the trial, I lodged a Special Defence of Self-Defence on Beattie's behalf and stated that, without prejudice, although he admitted delivering one punch to the face, he had done so because he genuinely thought that he was about to be attacked by the deceased. It is interesting to note that, in our law, a person can commit an assault without striking the victim—particularly if his actions cause the 'victim' to assume that the attack is imminent.

The circumstances surrounding the Special Defence of Self-Defence cannot, and must not, be weighed in too fine a scale. One must make allowances for the heat of the moment, as opposed to dissecting and analysing the circumstances in the cool, calm atmosphere of a court of law. Even if it is proved that the assailant did not possess a weapon, if his actions caused a person to deduce that he had, then such a Special Defence would be open for the jury's consideration. It is very much a subjective test of the state of mind of the accused, and this is of paramount importance, even if the conclusion he jumped to was an erroneous one.

The trial started before Sheriff H Pirie and a jury, and the Crown case was led by Mr Russell Miln.

A witness—a friend of the deceased Whitelaw, and the one who had identified Beattie at the parade—gave evidence and stated that, for no apparent reason, Beattie had punched Whitelaw on the jaw and caused him to fall heavily to the floor. I hotly disputed this evidence, maintaining that Beattie had been acting in self-defence, having been menaced by the deceased.

Medical evidence from two celebrated pathologists concluded that there was evidence of only one blow to the jaw of the deceased. The cause of death had been cerebral haemorrhage as a result of the single punch. Such a regrettable situation is extremely rare.

Realising that the Crown case rested on the uncorroborated evidence of one witness, I led no evidence for the defence and promptly withdrew the Special Defence of Self-Defence. Try as he might, I felt, the Fiscal would not convince the Sheriff that he had the necessary 'fingers of evidence' in this case.

In the course of the legal argument which followed the evidence (in the absence of the jury) I accepted the statement of the single witness, for the purpose of my submission to the judge, but argued that proper corroboration was non-existent.

The Fiscal argued that there was ample evidence to the effect that Beattie had been in the ballroom that night. (This was never in dispute.) I countered by saying that more than a hundred other people had also been in the same premises on that occasion.

The Fiscal then argued that Beattie had not given evidence in his own defence with a view to explaining why he had felt obliged to punch the deceased. I pointed out that Beattie did not require to prove his innocence as, in the law of Scotland, it was for the Crown to prove guilt beyond reasonable doubt—and to do that by bringing evidence which measured up to the required standard. This could not be done with one witness only.

After lengthy deliberation, the Sheriff decided to withdraw the case from the jury and, on their return, directed them that as a matter of law they must return a verdict of Not Guilty. In such matters, the Sheriff is the master of the *law* appertaining to the case, whereas the jury are always masters of the *facts*. The Sheriff went on to tell the jurors that he was withdrawing the charge from their consideration, even in the knowledge that the principal Crown witness might well have been truthful. He told them briefly that there must be corroboration and that in this respect the Crown case fell short of the legal requirements.

Our legal system, in my view, is very fair in this respect. However serious or trivial the subject-matter of a charge may be, if the prosecution case is based on the evidence of a single eye-witness only, without cogent corroboration from other sources, then no matter what the calibre of the witness—be he the Moderator of the General Assembly of the Church of Scotland or Pope John Paul II—the case could not be considered proved against the accused beyond reasonable doubt.

Conversely, if there were two witnesses of such calibre as the Moderator and the Pope, then it might well be prudent advice to negotiate a speedy and acceptable plea of Guilty to the charge!

A legal friend of mine was somewhat verbose and loquacious. It did not pay to be following him in a case because of the length of time involved in his.

I remember well a case many years ago when his client was arraigned on a matter of an attempt to break into office premises. This had occurred late at night, in the hours of darkness. My friend was cross-examining the first police-officer witness in the case who stated that, from a distance of about fifty yards, he had seen the accused trying to force his way into the premises. As he approached, the accused saw him and ran off.

'How can you be certain that the person whom you saw trying to break into the premises was the accused? After all, it was dark and there was much shadow in the area,' my friend persisted. The policeman maintained his degree of certitude and the cross-examination went on at length. Eventually, trying to assess the distance between the officer's observation point and the accused, my colleague forced him to say that he had been about forty yards away when the accused ran off.

Then the policeman was questioned about the lighting. He said there had been a street lamp directly in the vicinity of the entrance to the office block and that this had illuminated the face of the accused.

Unrelenting, my colleague again tried to show the jury what the distance had been between the officer and the accused at the time.

'Assume, for the moment, that I am the lamp-post,' he said, adding 'Although I am not as tall.'

'And not as bright either!' retorted the officer promptly.

There was really no answer to this remark, and from that stage the defence case deteriorated in no uncertain fashion. . . .

6
The Glasgow Police Murders

Tuesday 30 December 1969 was one of the blackest days in the history of the City of Glasgow Police. That day three Glasgow police officers were shot at point-blank range in a house in Allison Street, Glasgow. One died almost immediately, another was to die some five days later and the third was so seriously injured that his life hung in the balance for several days.

The man who did the shooting was himself an ex-Glasgow police officer.

I first heard about this tragedy in a television news bulletin during the late afternoon of 30 December. At about 11 p.m. that same day I received a telephone call at my home in Bothwell. It was the police. Three men, who had been arrested and charged with murder, wanted to see me urgently. I picked up my erstwhile partner, Willie McGlynn, at his King's Park home and we hurried to the Southern Police Office. There we were received by Detective Superintendent James Binnie of the C I D. His room was packed with C I D men and I could see that he was extremely upset, as were all his colleagues. The room was a hive of activity and the floor was littered with productions. Mr Binnie quickly gave me a résumé of the events of that day. As I was about to leave him to see my clients in the cells, he shocked me further by saying that two of the three accused were ex-members of the City of Glasgow force.

I could well understand why the tears were not far from his eyes. Clearly the background of these two exacerbated the whole calamitous situation. The third person charged, I was told, was a garage proprietor.

In the cells I saw my clients for the first time. All three were very agitated. The enormity of what had happened had well and truly sunk in.

I learned speedily that the actual shootings had been carried out by only one of them—Howard Wilson, an articulate, well-spoken, smart and clean-cut individual. He appeared to be a man of considerable intelligence. It turned out that he came from a respectable family and had been a member of Glasgow police for ten years— being nine times commended for efficiency during his police service. He was then aged thirty-one and was happily married, with a young family. As I listened to him, and tried to sort matters out in my own mind, I kept asking myself what had possessed him. He looked more like a businessman than a criminal. And the same could be said of his two co-accused.

One of the co-accused was also aged thirty-one and was also married with a family. The other—only twenty-two years old—had been, like Wilson, a member of Glasgow police force. He had been required to resign, as it was thought he was unlikely to become an efficient officer.

Gradually, the full story of that terrible day—and the events leading up to it—unfolded. On 16 July 1969 all three accused—assisted by another man—had successfully robbed a bank in Williamwood, Renfrewshire. The fourth man has never been traced by the police and is now presumed dead.

Dressed like businessmen, the thieves had arrived at the bank, each carrying a briefcase. One of them was armed with a pistol while the others carried plastic containers filled with ammonia. With nylon stockings pulled over their faces, they held up the British Linen Bank staff of three men and two women at gunpoint.

One of them was heard to say to the staff 'This will only take a few minutes. If no-one does anything silly, no-one will get hurt.'

The telephone was wrenched from the wall and the staff were forced into the manager's office. All except the manager were blindfolded and bound. The manager was forced to open the safe, from which the raiders took £21 000. They then made good their escape.

Not one of the robbers had a criminal record—so their fingerprints and photographs were not in police files. Despite an extensive hunt, weeks passed without any real progress in the case. The raiders were unknown to the 'underworld' and so no information could be got from that valuable source. There were simply no leads, no breaks for the police. The file on the case, however, was never closed.

On 30 December 1969 the three accused—flushed, no doubt, with their success five months earlier—entered the Clydesdale Bank in Bridge Street, Linwood, in Renfrewshire, at precisely 3.15 p.m.

This time they were not masked, although they were armed with the same pistol as well as with a dagger and a knife. They also had a number of pillowcases, some string and two suitcases.

In the absence of the manager, his assistant, Mr Mackin, showed them into his superior's office, having been told that they wished to open an account in connection with a successful plant-hire business. Once inside, however, Mr Mackin was pushed aside and the door closed. The pistol was pressed against his temple and he was told 'If we have full co-operation, no member of the staff will be harmed.' A pillowcase was put over Mackin's head and his wrists were tied together.

When the manager, Mr Fleming, arrived the pistol was placed against his neck, with the instruction that he should remain silent. A pillowcase was put over his head and he was also bound. The other staff members, and an unfortunate customer, were also thrust into the room and tied up in the same manner.

The bank's safe was opened and the sum of £14 212 was put into two suitcases. The robbers also took a large quantity of silver coin, which was put into a black metal box and some canvas bags. As it turned out, this was to prove their undoing. . . .

The bank staff and the customer were left locked in the bank and the robbers drove off swiftly. They proceeded to Allison Street, in Glasgow, where Wilson owned a flat, arrived there at 4 p.m. and parked their car within a stone's throw of the headquarters of the Southern Police Division at Craigie Street.

The three men then began carrying the suitcases and the metal box into the tenement close at No 51, where Wilson had his flat. They made two journeys—and it was during the second journey that they were spotted by Police Inspector Andrew Hyslop, who was in a police Panda car with Constable John Sellars as it emerged from the rear of the police office.

One of the men was carrying a black metal box and the other two were struggling with what looked like an extremely heavy suitcase. Hyslop saw all three enter the close at No 51.

Hyslop recognised one of the men as an ex-policeman, Howard Wilson, and decided to investigate the matter. Hyslop and Sellars went into the close and stopped outside the door of a ground-floor flat. Then they went through into the back court and looked through the kitchen window of the flat. But they could see no-one.

Leaving Sellars in the back court, Inspector Hyslop returned to the police station across the road for assistance. He came back with Detective Constable John Campbell, Acting Detective Constable Angus McKenzie and Constable Edward Barnett.

As they crossed Allison Street they were met by Howard Wilson, who asked Hyslop how he was getting on. Hyslop replied that he was all right, but said he wanted to speak to Wilson because he had seen Wilson and two others carrying a heavy suitcase and a black box into the close a few minutes earlier. What was in them? Wilson denied that he had been carrying anything, whereupon Hyslop said he would like to look at Wilson's flat. Wilson agreed that he could search it if he wished.

The officers found the two suitcases on the living-room floor of Wilson's house. The two other men were also in that room. When opened, the cases revealed the loot— several canvas bags full of silver coin and a substantial number of banknotes. The officers realised that a routine investigation had developed into something much more important.

Hyslop asked to see the metal box which he had seen carried into the house. The existence of such a box was strenuously denied and Hyslop and Sellars left the room to look elsewhere in the house for it. Not finding it, Hyslop returned to the hall. He saw Wilson standing a few feet away from him, carefully taking aim at his head with a pistol. Hyslop said 'Don't be a bloody fool, man!'

The trigger was pulled, but there was only a click. The gun had jammed. Wilson cleared an obstruction in the pistol, took aim and pulled the trigger again. A bullet shattered the left-hand side of Hyslop's face. Hyslop collapsed, bleeding profusely.

As the shot was fired, one of the other two men in the house ran off. The sound of the shot brought Constable Barnett into the hall, where he was shot through the head and fell to the floor. Then Detective Constable McKenzie was also shot in the head, and was shot again as he lay on the floor.

Of the five police officers in the house only two remained unharmed—Detective Constable Campbell and Constable Sellars. Sellars ran into the bathroom, locked himself in and began calling on his radio for assistance. Wilson tried to get into the bathroom to stop Sellars, but failed. At that stage Detective Constable Campbell, showing tremendous courage, launched himself at Wilson and knocked him to the floor. A struggle took place, in which Campbell managed to get hold of the pistol.

During the struggle Wilson called upon his twenty-two-year-old accomplice to assist him, but the young man did not intervene. When Campbell got the pistol he covered both robbers with it until two police sergeants arrived in the flat in response to the radio call, and both men were arrested.

The third robber, who had fled on hearing the first shot fired, was later arrested at his home.

On my first meeting with the three accused at Craigie Street, Wilson—to his credit—immediately accepted full responsibility for the shootings. It is true that the other two knew that he had been armed—having seen him with the pistol at the Clydesdale Bank earlier—but they did not anticipate that he would use the loaded weapon in Allison Street.

It is interesting to note that, in law, had Wilson shot someone at the bank the other two would also have been guilty on the basis of the Scots law of concert. After all, they had all set out to rob the bank—there was a 'common plan or purpose'—and all knew that a pistol was part of their weaponry. In that situation, each one of the participants would have been deemed guilty if a confederate had used one of the weapons.

This common purpose, however, did not encompass the later situation, when all three found themselves trapped in Wilson's flat. In that situation my other two clients could not reasonably have anticipated Wilson's foolhardy and dastardly actions. There was no evidence of either of them inciting or encouraging Wilson to produce and fire the pistol. Had there been we would have had a situation similar to that of Craig and Bentley in the celebrated London case some years before.

Not only had Wilson accepted full responsibility at the police station, he continued to do so while all three accused were in the untried block at Barlinnie prison. At no time did he deviate from this—as others might well have done. There was never any question of Wilson endeavouring to drag the other two down with him in the hope that this factor might affect his ultimate sentence.

My clients appeared the following day at Glasgow Sheriff Court on Petition before Sheriff A C Horsfall, all three charged with the murder of a policeman and the attempted murder of two other officers. A fourth charge alleged that they had assaulted Constable Sellars by presenting a firearm at him and threatening to shoot him. No plea was taken from them and, after a brief appearance lasting only a minute, they were remanded to Barlinnie Prison.

On 9 January 1970 I again represented my clients when they appeared at Glasgow Sheriff Court on Petition before Sheriff H Pirie. Each was handcuffed to a police escort.

All three were charged with the murder of Constable Edward Barnett, who had died in the Victoria Infirmary since their earlier appearance. They were further charged with the two armed bank robberies at Williamwood and Linwood, and with stealing a total of almost £35000. There were charges of assaulting various persons—employees of the banks and a customer. A pistol, ammonia, a dagger and pillowcases were mentioned in these assault charges.

On this occasion, Wilson emitted a judicial declaration before Sheriff Pirie, in which he accepted full and complete responsibility for the murder and attempted murder charges. In this declaration he emphasised that his two co-accused had not been in any way involved with him. Such a declaration before the Sheriff is a rare occurrence and is purely voluntary in nature.

After this second appearance all three were again remanded to Barlinnie.

Within days of this appearance I attended the annual Police Guild dance at the Ca'dora Restaurant in Union Street, Glasgow. Naturally, the case was very much in the minds of the numerous policemen who were there. Indeed, the Chief Constable, Sir James Robertson C B E B L made reference to the case in the course of his after-dinner speech.

Both my wife and myself were extremely conscious of the fact that heads were constantly being turned in my direction. I suppose the attitude of the officers was understandable. How dare I represent, as they all knew I did, the men charged with this ghastly crime of murdering police officers?

I remember that we left the dance fairly early on, as I felt that the time was inappropriate for such a normally festive occasion.

Shortly after the second appearance of my clients, I was given specific instructions by all three accused—and in particular by Howard Wilson. As a result, I made an appointment with the Procurator Fiscal of Glasgow, Mr Henry Herron. I told him that Wilson would plead Guilty to all the police charges, provided that his two co-accused should plead Guilty only to the two bank robberies.

No decision could be taken then, as I knew. This was a mammoth case, attended by tremendous publicity, as one might expect. The Crown Office in Edinburgh, and the Lord Advocate, would require to be consulted for their final say. However, I put my offer in writing to the Procurator Fiscal. Under Section 31 of the Criminal Procedure (Scotland) Act 1887, this was done on a special printed document, which I signed on behalf of my clients. That document was transmitted by the Fiscal to Edinburgh without delay.

At this meeting I pointed out to Mr Herron that there was simply no evidence to tie the two other accused to Wilson on the shooting charges—and that nothing incriminating could be inferred from their actions in Wilson's house, where all three had reached the very end of their bank-robbery line and had been caught red-handed with the loot.

It might be illuminating at this juncture to say something about the law relating to concert—that is, the position of an accessory in Scots Law.

A basic principle of Scots Law is that all persons who are concerned in the commission of a crime are equally guilty and that each is responsible for the whole actings. If a number of men form a common plan whereby some are to commit the seizure of property which is not their own and some, agreeing to the scheme, keep watch for the police or other persons who might thwart the plan while others—again in accordance with the general agreement—are to help to carry off the loot, then, although the actual robbery may only have been committed by one or two of them, everyone is guilty of the crime because they joined together in a common plan to commit the robbery, each with a relevant part to play.

This maxim applies when it has been properly and legally established by the Crown that there was such a common plan, and that the accused were parties thereto. Without such proof, each accused is only responsible for what he himself did and bears no responsibility whatever for what any of the other accused may have done. Conversely, if an accused can be convicted of a crime only on the assumption that he was acting in concert with the principal—his co-accused—he cannot be convicted if the principal is acquitted.

Thus if six persons agree to rob certain premises in the knowledge that guns will be carried by some of them, and one of them discharges a gun and kills a guard, then all six would be guilty of murder and robbery. If, however, at the material time one of the six tried to stop his confederate from firing the gun, it can—and would—be argued by the defence that he had dissociated himself from the consequences of the shot—and it might be that the chain of concert had been broken by his proven actions.

Each individual case must be regarded on its merits, and seldom are the circumstances of any two entirely identical. Perhaps this is one of the reasons why criminal law is so interesting.

In the present case, the common criminal purpose of robbing the bank at Linwood had been achieved—and there had been no opportunity to form a murderous plot at 51 Allison Street. That being so, in the absence of concert, Wilson and Wilson only was responsible for the shootings there. No assistance whatsoever was afforded him by his two friends—indeed, the younger of his associates declined to assist him during his frantic struggle with Campbell and so clearly dissociated himself from the actions of the berserk gunman . . . while the other co-accused had bolted on hearing the first shot.

Concert could not be inferred by mere presence at the material time in Wilson's flat. There would have to be evidence of participation—or of planning beforehand. And one cannot be an accessory after the fact in Scotland. The Crown case fell far short of the degree of proof required for conviction of the two associates of Wilson, and was totally devoid of the necessary ingredients for accessory involvement.

Several days after my meeting with Mr Herron, he sent for me and told me that my qualified offer was acceptable to the authorities. I must confess that I was a little surprised and had thought that, following the enormous publicity the case had received, the whole matter of concert—or the lack of it—would require to be ventilated in the High Court, at a trial.

I hurried to Barlinnie Prison to advise my clients of the situation. All three were relieved. So far as Wilson's associates were concerned, their relief was understandable. But even Wilson was pleased, such were his feelings regarding the plight of his two friends—their nightmare being attributable to his own panic-stricken actions. All three, I remember, thanked me for my efforts thus far.

On 6 February the three accused appeared before Sheriff Middleton, with Wilson charged with the double murder of McKenzie and Barnett, the attempted murder of Hyslop and threatening to shoot Sellars, as well as both bank robberies. His two co-accused were arraigned on the same indictment, but only in respect of the two bank robberies.

The packed court was totally silent as the three took their places in the dock. Pleas of Guilty to the respective charges were intimated by me to a hushed court. There was little that one could say at that stage by way of mitigation, in view of the fact that the charges required to be remitted by Sheriff Middleton to the High Court of Justiciary in Edinburgh in view of their gravity. The Sheriff's powers of sentence are restricted to a term of two years' imprisonment—and clearly that was inadequate in our case.

I did say, however, that the two persons charged along with Wilson had repeatedly protested their innocence of the shootings and yet had been held in prison for some five weeks charged with these dreadful crimes.

I added 'The Crown Office in Edinburgh is now in full agreement with their protestations, and as a result the murder and attempted murder charges have been very properly abandoned for all time against them.'

My clients were duly remitted to the High Court, where they appeared on 13 February 1970 before the Lord Justice Clerk, Lord Grant. Wilson was sentenced to life imprisonment, with a recommendation that he should serve a minimum period of twenty-five years' imprisonment. The two others were each sentenced to twelve years' imprisonment for the two bank robberies.

I have asked myself—as others have asked—why did an intelligent man like Howard Wilson, an ex-police officer, shoot his former colleagues and try to kill them all?

My own view of what happened on that fateful day is this. Wilson, an ex-policeman with no previous convictions, was suddenly—all within a minute or so—caught red-handed by the police. Regrettably, of the three he was the one with the loaded revolver which he had taken to the bank earlier— and he clearly panicked when he saw his whole world on the point of collapsing about him.

The indictment to which Howard Wilson pled Guilty was the most serious in the history of Scots Law short of a trial. Prior to 1965, when the Homicide Act was repealed, Wilson would have been guilty of capital murder on four counts—using a firearm, killing a policeman in the execution of his duty, resisting arrest and double murder. It was not, however, possible to plead Guilty to such a charge. This was because—the penalty being death—it was felt that the Crown must really be put to the test, must be made to prove its case beyond all reasonable doubt. There was always the chance, too, of some crank 'confessing' to the murder—and there had to be some safeguard against that.

Looking back over a quarter of a century I still maintain that there is some merit in the death sentence for cold, callous and premeditated crimes of murder. One must make a distinction, and I feel that the ultimate crime

126

should be categorised—as it is in some states of the USA.

Cases which I would place in this category are the 'contract killing' by the 'hit man'—there can be nothing more callous than that—and murder by poisoning. It is worth noting that poisoning was not even mentioned in the Homicide Act, yet it seems to me one of the most abhorrent of all crimes. I consider that indiscriminate killings by terrorists, through public-house bombings and the like, should also be considered as capital matters—in short, all murders in cold blood.

My views are not based on the principle of retribution—an eye for an eye—but on the question of deterrent. Whereas I feel that the death penalty would be of little deterrent value in murders carried out in hot blood (where the culprit usually takes little time to think of the possible consequences), I am genuinely of the view that with the type of premeditated murder I have just specified the fact that the murderer would, if convicted, be sentenced to death must cause such a person to do more than hesitate before proceeding with his planned enterprise.

However, my experience tells me that most murders are committed without premeditation and I feel it would be wrong to classify this type as capital. Indeed, I would find it difficult to categorise capital murder absolutely at the present day, although policemen and prison officers in the course of their duties would certainly require to be protected.

But a word of warning here—although the Police Federation is staunchly behind the reintroduction of capital punishment, as also are persons like Teddy Taylor and many others, the Crown always required to prove a capital charge 'up to the hilt', and the death sentence would, naturally, be subject to proper and cogent proof of guilt.

One has then to ask oneself 'How cogent is cogent?' One remembers, as one must, the case of Patrick Meehan, who was wrongly convicted of the dastardly murder of an aged lady just over a decade ago. Had capital punishment been apposite at that time for that particular type of killing, he would certainly, once convicted, have been hanged. That thought would probably put most of us against the ultimate penalty. I do feel, however, that the Meehan case was fortunately highly exceptional—perhaps even unique. I think it would be wrong to rule out the death sentence because of one isolated case—never, I hope, to be repeated.

Perhaps more importantly, I feel that Meehan would not have been convicted by the jury had the charge been a capital one. The Crown case was far too loose and indecisive—it had to be, in view of his now accepted innocence. I believe that his jury would have returned a verdict of culpable homicide and robbery.

It is my opinion that many convictions which have followed since abolition in what would have been capital charges would not have reached first base had the old penalty still been in existence. Evidence of guilt had to be extremely clear-cut then, and very often this cannot in practice be the case. Murders are seldom committed in the presence of an abundance of reliable and credible witnesses. By their nature, they are often extremely clandestine. More often than not, inferences have to be drawn from ambivalent facts, and juries might well be less likely to draw Crown deductions from these facts were the life of the accused at issue. After all, jurors are human, and there is a world of difference between a sentence involving the death of the accused and a period, albeit lengthy, of imprisonment.

In short, I feel that if the Police Federation and its allies have their way in connection with the reintroduction of the death penalty for murder—premeditated or unpremeditated—the incidence of convictions would be greatly reduced. Would this not then lead to further clamour?

My opinions are based on considerable experience of murder trials. I defended in ten capital murder cases—and lost not one client to the hangman. And at the time of writing I have represented accused in 250 non-capital murder cases.

The man in the dock listened intently to his lawyer as he told the jury, somewhat impassionedly, that his client was entirely innocent of the monstrously unwarranted charge levelled at him. Tight-lipped he followed the many points so ably argued on his behalf.

There he was, ensconced between two dutiful police officers—resplendent in their tailored uniforms, spotless white gloves to the fore and each with baton discreetly drawn—more than a little ashen and ill at ease.

Consequent upon the Not Proven verdict he spoke to his Counsel in the privacy of the nearby interview room:—

'The more ah listened to you, the more ah began to think that ah didnae dae it masel, by the way.'

The Rev. Alan Hasson on a Twelfth of July parade

7
A Hint of Orange

The Rev. Alan G Hasson, Church of Scotland minister and Grand Master of the Grand Orange Lodge of Scotland, did not suffer Catholics gladly, if at all.

In his wildest dreams I would wager that at no time did he envisage a situation whereby a Roman Catholic—myself, in fact—would hand him a lifeline, and where he would seize it gladly.

The hour of need came to Alan Hasson in the year 1971. But our story begins long before that. . . .

Away back in the late nineteen fifties, Alan Hasson was a Grand Master in the Orange Order, and a popular one at that. He was a kenspeckle figure, his name seldom out of the Press, and he seemed to symbolise the Protestant cause in Scotland and Northern Ireland. It was from the Bonhill Manse in Dunbartonshire that he set out, each Twelfth of July, to lead the Orange parades, ensconced on a powerful white charger suitably bedecked for the occasion.

There was one notable year when, on the night before such a parade, the same white charger was surreptitiously daubed with green stripes. One can imagine the consternation the following morning—this was nothing short of heresy! But, undaunted and seemingly unmoved at this dastardly outrage, Grand Master Hasson went on to lead the parade as usual—on a hurriedly-found dapple-grey. . . .

Having come to know Alan Hasson since, I should imagine that he appreciated the endemic humour of this near-catastrophic piece of sabotage. He was the essence of confidence and had a good sense of humour—a man who was not easily knocked off his stride.

However in 1960, suddenly and unexpectedly, Alan Hasson deserted his flock at Bonhill and was next heard of in Canada. For some ten years he found remunerative work there on radio and television—running quiz shows, presiding at panel games, covering and commenting on sports of various types. He was soon a popular figure. Shortly after his unheralded departure it came to light that the sum of £10 300 had disappeared from the coffers of the Grand Lodge. The police were brought into the affair, and the mysterious 'flight of the Hasson' no doubt contributed to the decision to issue a warrant for his arrest on a charge of embezzling the missing funds. There were also other ancillary and connected charges.

It would appear that only Hasson and the Lodge Treasurer had had full access to the bank accounts where the funds were lodged.

The authorities knew full well where Alan Hasson was—but no extradition proceedings were started. They decided to wait—and this they did for eleven long years. Then the C I D got a tip-off: Hasson was leaving Canada to travel to the Middle East, for some obscure and complicated reason which no-one has yet been able to determine satisfactorily. The reason did not matter anyway. He would break his journey at Heathrow Airport—and Scotland Yard was immediately warned. Several senior members of Glasgow C I D travelled south and, with the assistance of their English colleagues, intercepted Hasson in the process of changing aircraft.

Even Alan Hasson must have been more than taken aback at the precision and timing of this successful operation—and before long he was being bundled on to the Glasgow plane, by virtue of the old warrant. He duly appeared at Glasgow Sheriff Court on the following day, when he was represented by a local solicitor, Benny Heslin. Several applications for bail were promptly made—but just as promptly refused—and he was committed to Barlinnie Prison for his long-awaited trial.

Months later, Hasson was indicted before the High Court in Glasgow, and by that time Mr Heslin had instructed a young advocate, Colin McEachran, to act along with him. At the Pleading Diet, Hasson's plea of Not Guilty was tendered by his solicitor and intimation was made of a Special Defence of Incrimination—sometimes known as Impeachment—which outlined the defence's intention to blame the former Treasurer of the Lodge for the crime with which Hasson was charged.

On the morning of the first day of the trial, and before starting time, Messrs Heslin and McEachran appeared with mountains of documents and paperwork—clear evidence that an inordinate period of their time had been devoted to this case. The trial began with a sensation. When the Diet was called Hasson told the court that he wished to dispense with the services of his solicitor and advocate—although, he said, he appreciated the work put in by them on his behalf. He was going to defend himself, he said. Messrs Heslin and McEachran were duly excused by the trial judge, Lord Johnston, and both left the court-room. Hasson was on his own.

The evidence lasted seven days, and Hasson closely cross-examined the former Treasurer in particular when he was called by the prosecution. Hasson put it to the Treasurer that he, not Hasson, must have embezzled the Lodge funds, as only the two of them had had the right to sign cheques as well as having access to the bank accounts. This allegation was staunchly denied.

In the course of the trial I had spent several hours listening to the way in which Hasson conducted his defence. I formed the view that, for a layman, he was performing his task particularly well—and seemed to be enjoying the attendant publicity. Then, right out of the blue and two days before the evidence was due to be concluded, I received a letter from Hasson requesting me to see him at once at the prison.

He wanted me to assist him in preparing his jury speech, as he was not possessed of that knowledge of law which he considered to be necessary for the purpose of his summing-up.

I am never happy in a situation where the accused, for good reasons or bad, represents himself before the High Court—so I saw him that same evening in the prison. He went over all the preceding evidence with me and filled me in as best he could with regard to the whole background. Throughout that evening and the following one I did my utmost to assist him to prepare his summing-up for the jury, and pointed out some of the relevant legal concepts which applied. I had armed myself with back numbers of newspapers which had carried the main evidence in the case.

Eventually the prototype of the jury speech was formed, and thereafter the polishing-up process began. At this time I was amazed at the extent of Hasson's memory, which was photographic, and at the way he could reel off lengthy passages of the earlier evidence. He made a succession of points which—to me—seemed impressive and without referring to notes could quote lengthy extracts from some of the Crown productions, such as the bank statements.

I sat in court throughout his long address to the jury. I noticed that many lawyers had taken time off to come and listen to him as his trial was reaching its conclusion. Most of them were more than impressed at the way in which he tackled his speech. He had little recourse to notes, and his summing-up was done dramatically. Towards the end of his speech, as he was building up to the climax, he took hold of a number of notes from the table beside him and, as he finished, purposely allowed these notes to flutter to the floor. This seemed to emphasise the points he had been making at the close of his speech. Hasson seemed to have most of the qualities which would have made him, had he wished, a successful actor!

The judge's charge to the jury, summing up the evidence and the law applicable to the facts, was lengthy and comprehensive. He pointed out that, although the trial had lasted some considerable time, the nub of it was fairly simple and straightforward. He referred to the Special Defence of Incrimination and expanded on this matter.

Issues of credibility, said the judge, were for the jury to decide and if they believed Hasson, in his own evidence, then he must be acquitted. Hasson, he said, stated that the former Treasurer must have been responsible for the missing funds. On the other hand he quoted the evidence given by the former Treasurer, who had denied any possible involvement. If the jury accepted the former Treasurer's evidence as being truthful, guilt must be established against Hasson. In view of the backgrounds of both men—neither had had any previous court experience—the issues seemed to be black and white and there was no room for grey. He thought that in fairness to both principal parties, Hasson and the ex-Treasurer, the verdicts open to the jury were those of Guilty and Not Guilty.

'The verdict of Not Proven, in the special circumstances of this case, would appear to me to be inappropriate and unsatisfactory,' said Lord Johnston.

That comment was made towards the conclusion of the charge, and I immediately sat up and made a special note of what had just been said.

At this stage coincidence was to play a major part in Hasson's predicament. I could hardly believe what I had just heard—it brought back to me, as I sat there, a previous case in which I was involved, which had gone to the Court of Criminal Appeal in January 1964. . . .

On 12 September 1963 an ex-boxer client, Hugh T McNicol, had been charged with murdering a man called Whyte in a common court in Glasgow. The case went for trial before the High Court, and I had instructed Mr C R McArthur Q C to represent my client. We had lodged a special plea of Self-Defence in answer to the charge. In process of the trial the Crown saw fit to reduce the charge to one of culpable homicide.

Towards the end of the trial, during the trial judge's charge to the jury, Lord Cameron told them 'There are three possible verdicts which you can return on this indictment. You can return a verdict of Guilty to culpable homicide, as the charge is now restricted. You can return a verdict of Not Guilty, according as you think to the special plea of Self-Defence which has been made out, or if you think that the Crown has failed to prove its case against the accused.

You are also entitled, if that is the view you take, to return a verdict of Not Proven. I confess to you, quite openly and publicly, that I do not ever feel happy about verdicts of Not Proven because although these are, strictly speaking, acquittal and can be logically justified, it seems to me an honest and proper thing to do is either find a person Guilty or, if the Crown has failed, to acquit him with a verdict of Not Guilty. But that verdict of Not Proven lies open to you and you can use it if you so wish.'

The jury in this case had returned a verdict of Guilty of culpable homicide against McNicol, and he was sentenced to six years' imprisonment.

In view of the unusual remarks made by the trial judge relative to the Not Proven verdict, and in view of the fact that he seemed to be fettering that verdict, an appeal was marked and decided in the High Court in January 1964. The presiding judge of the Appeal Court was the late Lord Justice General Clyde, and in the judgment which followed legal arguments he made the following statement:

'The trial judge, after telling the jury that there were three possible verdicts—Guilty, Not Guilty and Not Proven—went on to say to them "I confess to you quite openly and publicly that I do not ever feel happy about verdicts of Not Proven. . . ."

The verdict of Not Proven is well-established in the law of Scotland. It has for some centuries proved a useful part of our criminal law and in practice it has worked well. In our view it ought to be left completely open and free to a jury to return a verdict of Not Proven if they so decide, after hearing the evidence and speeches at a trial—but, with the explicit and pointed criticism which was made by the presiding judge in the present case of this well-established Scottish rule, it is quite obvious that the jury was strongly discouraged from bringing in a verdict of Not Proven. They were in fact left with only two possible choices when in fact they should have had three. For they were told that the honest and proper thing was either to find the appellant McNicol Guilty or Not Guilty.

It is, of course, quite true that in the English system there are only two verdicts, and periodically a cry is raised from across the Border that we in Scotland should tamely accept the rule established in the law and practice of England. But for upwards of two hundred years a Not Proven verdict has been available as a third choice in the law of Scotland, and no convincing argument has been advanced to justify its elimination from the law.

It is unnecessary to consider all the reasons in its favour, but perhaps I might just mention two. Its inclusion in the list of possible verdicts is much more humane and more advantageous to an accused than if it were not so included. It gives a jury who have some lingering doubts as to the guilt of the accused—and who are certainly, on the evidence, not prepared to say that he is innocent—the chance to find the charge against him Not Proven. If that third choice were eliminated and if the jury had only two alternatives left, it is almost inevitable that in the situation I have just envisaged they would hold that their doubts of Guilty were not enough to amount to reasonable doubt, and he would be convicted.

In the experience of all of us there are many cases where a verdict of Not Proven has been reached and where, had that verdict not been available, the jury would have found the accused Guilty; and there are many men and women today in Scotland who have been acquitted on a Not Proven verdict and who, had it not been available to them, would have been in prison.

I do not agree with the trial judge that the only honest and proper thing to do was to adopt the system which operates in England, with only two choices. But apart from this aspect of the matter, the three choices are in fact much more logical and in accordance with principle than merely to give the jury two. Juries are not all-seeing and all-knowing. They are merely human beings and they can never know with certainty that a man is guilty. The furthest they can go against him is to hold that, on the evidence laid before them, it is proved beyond reasonable doubt that the accused did commit the crime. That, after all, is all that a verdict of Guilty means. The true alternative to that verdict is that the Crown has not proved its case beyond reasonable doubt and the truly logical alternative, therefore, is a verdict of Not Proven.

But there are cases where a jury can go further in the accused's favour. The crucial Crown witnesses may be disbelieved or may be proved discreditable, and the defence may be shown to be a true defence, which they accept. In that case a jury may well be prepared to hold it positively established by the evidence that the accused did not commit the crime, and the appropriate verdict would then be one of Not Guilty.

In the present case all three choices were not left freely available to the jury. The jury had been pointedly discouraged from considering a verdict of Not Proven. In this situation, in our view, there was a misdirection by the trial judge, and it follows that the conviction cannot stand.'

In accordance with this interesting judgment by the Court of Criminal Appeal, McNicol's conviction and sentence were quashed and he walked free from court. . . .

By the time my thoughts about this case seven years earlier had been exhausted, Lord Johnston had terminated his address and the members of the jury were filing out of the court. The court was adjourned and I went downstairs to confer with Hasson. I mentioned the McNicol case to him and told him that in the event of a conviction I would certainly mark an appeal next day based on the previous case, which was binding on the law of Scotland.

My impression was that Hasson was somewhat diffident about my enthusiasm and the confidence of my views. He merely said that he would await the verdict of the jury and hope that he would be acquitted in any event.

After a delay of more than an hour, the bell was rung to signal the return of the jury and we took our place in that trial court for the last time. The foreman of the jury was asked by the Clerk of Court for his verdict and replied that it was one of Guilty to the charge. In due course Hasson was asked to speak on his own behalf in mitigation of penalty, and was then duly sentenced to a period of three years' imprisonment.

Next morning I obtained a photostat copy of the judgment in the earlier case of McNicol from my files and took this with me to Barlinnie, where I interviewed Hasson and allowed him to read the relevant passages of the previous case. The despondency which had greeted me at this meeting was immediately lifted when Hasson had studied the judgment. He became buoyant once more and expressed the view that his own situation was very much akin to that of McNicol.

I pointed out to him that he should not be over-confident: that the wording by the two judges in their summing-up had been slightly different. I followed this up, however, by saying that the principle seemed to be identical and that in each case there had been a cloud cast over the Not Proven verdict by the presiding Judge.

I obtained the appeal papers and drafted the grounds of appeal against conviction, making reference to the previous case and to the important parts of the earlier judgment. I did not mark an appeal against sentence.

In the very short space of three weeks Hasson's case was before the Court of Criminal Appeal in Edinburgh. I took the precaution of instructing the same Counsel as I had instructed seven years earlier, Mr C R McArthur Q C. In the intervening period between trial and appeal, counsel and myself had had several meetings and each believed, from first-hand knowledge of the McNicol case, that the prospects of success were bright indeed.

At the appeal hearing Mr McArthur outlined in

139

The late Rt Hon Lord Wheatley in the robes of the Lord Justice Clerk

detail the circumstances of the previous judgment and applied these to the present case.

By this time we had received a transcript of the judge's charge to the jury in Hasson's case and, although this was lengthy, the substance of the appeal was based virtually on one sentence which we had well and truly underlined in red ink. *'In the special circumstances of this case I consider that the verdict of Not Proven is both inappropriate and unsatisfactory.'*

The trial judge had gone on to say that notwithstanding his remarks the Not Proven verdict was still available to the jury. Our argument, in a nutshell, was that despite this the verdict had been clearly hampered and fettered, as well as qualified, to an inexcusable extent.

The hearing lasted not more than thirty minutes and the presiding judge, Lord Wheatley, made the following remarks, after arguments had been heard:

'I am of the opinion that this ground of appeal is well-founded and the result must lead to a quashing of the convictions on all five charges of which Hasson was found Guilty.

'This was undoubtedly a case where the three verdicts should have been left open to the jury, including the verdict of Not Proven. A number of grounds of appeal have been tabled, but it is accepted that if the first ground is substantiated it vitiated the whole conviction.'

Lord Wheatley referred to the McNicol case and the opinion of the court, and to the fact that the jury had been left with only two possible choices. He went on to say 'Whether in any particular case that situation had been created would depend on the words used by the judge. It was true that, in the McNicol case, in effect the condemnation of the Not Proven verdict was a general condemnation and was not related to the circumstances of the particular case—whereas in the present case the views expressed by Lord Johnston on the unsuitability of the Not Proven verdict were related to the facts of the case.

I do not think that necessarily makes any difference

if, in point of fact, the result of the judge's charge in the case of Hasson was to prevent a reasonable jury from considering a Not Proven verdict as a proper option left to them.'

Another appeal judge, the late Lord Walker, agreed with Lord Wheatley and stated that it was unfortunate that the conviction must be quashed. The jury had been left with only two possible choices as to the verdict, when they should have had three. The trial judge had said that if the jury did not believe the main witnesses, including the former Treasurer, then the proper verdict was Not Guilty. If they believed the main witnesses, then their verdict was Guilty. In that situation, he said, the trial judge made no reference to the intermediate position where, without believing or disbelieving the main witnesses, they might have reasonable doubt.

The third appeal judge, the late Lord Milligan, also agreed that the conviction of Hasson must be quashed—and so the decision was unanimous.

Hasson had spent exactly twenty-one days in prison since sentence had been passed and, on hearing the foregoing remarks made by the presiding judge, he beamed with delight. Afterwards, he strode jauntily through the corridors of the court building with me. When we reached the court exit Hasson was heard to whisper a brief prayer on the steps and then, hands still clasped, he walked into the afternoon sunshine. He told waiting pressmen 'I prayed. My God, how I prayed! Now my prayers have been answered. I think there will be convulsions within the Orange Order as a result of the verdict. Some of them will be standing on their heads. I am now going back to be a spy for the Arabs—if they want me. It is a great day.'

And he described the verdict as being 'dandy'.

After the appeal I agreed to drive him back to Glasgow—and decided to stop at my home in Bothwell on the way. We had tea and biscuits. I was amused to notice that the napkins put out were orange in colour!

The woman who helped my wife at that time in the

house was a devout Roman Catholic, and she did not take too kindly to preparing a snack for my client! I could see from her facial expressions that she had gone about this chore somewhat grudgingly, and she made a point of having no conversation whatsoever with the ex-Grand Master. Hasson clearly realised what was going on and, possibly to put her at her ease, jocularly remarked that he thought that I had sown the seeds of religious conversion in his mind.

His remark fell on stony ground—the good woman simply turned and abruptly left the room. It may have been coincidence, but she gave us notice some time later.

Some readers might find the background to the 'Not Proven' verdict interesting. The verdict is peculiar to Scotland, and the logic behind it seems to be quite clear in present practice.

There may well today be a situation where the Crown has fallen short of establishing guilt beyond reasonable doubt. This could, for instance, be due to difficulties with regard to corroboration. In that case it may be that a jury would appreciate that the Crown case has not been established to the required standard, but might not wish to return a verdict of Not Guilty as this might be contrary to their views with regard to the position of the accused. A verdict of Not Guilty might then appear to the jury to be a misnomer, whereas Not Proven does not necessarily affirm or rubber-stamp the fact that the pannel (accused) is Not Guilty. The practical effect of both verdicts is the same: the accused is cleared for all time of involvement in the alleged offence and cannot be re-tried, despite the possibility of fresh evidence coming to light at a later stage.

In short, juries may wish to distinguish between legal proof and their factual views on the question of possible perpetration by the accused.

The actual origin of the Not Proven verdict in Scots Law is to be traced to the recognition of the inability of an unskilled jury to interpret the significance of particular facts, and to the reluctance of Scottish jurors to assist the government of Charles II in its repressive religious practices.

In early practice the determination of the guilt or innocence of an accused was left to the jury, and indictments were framed in general terms. After a 1662 case, however, the practice arose of drafting indictments specifying in detail all the circumstances of the crime. The judgment or order of the Court sending the case to the jury declared that the facts set forth in the indictment would, if found proven, amount to evidence of the commission of the crime.

The practice thus arose of the jury finding merely that certain facts had been proven and others not proven, according to its view of the evidence. This was encouraged for political reasons when juries between 1662 and 1689 refused to convict on prosecutions brought under unpopular and repressive statutes. The jury would be asked to return what was called a 'special verdict'—not of Guilty or Not Guilty but stating which of the facts set forth in the indictment were proved.

Originally, therefore, in the case of a man charged with murdering his wife the jury would be asked to say whether they thought he had done it or not. Subsequently, the indictment would specify that he had struck her on the head with a blunt instrument, and the jury would be asked to decide whether or not the Crown had proved that that was indeed what he did. It was then for the Court to say whether, on the facts found 'proven', the verdict should be Guilty or Not Guilty, thereby depriving the jury of the last word.

The practice of returning a special verdict, finding certain facts proven and leaving their interpretation to the Court was usual until 1728, and in some cases was still found in the later part of the eighteenth century. In a case in 1728 the jurors—in response to an appeal by the defence—returned general verdicts of Not Guilty. Thereafter the Not Proven verdict was generally retained for those cases in which, as I have explained, there was insufficient lawful evidence to convict, but in which suspicion attached to the prisoner.

Sheriff Langmuir was addressing three youths charged with breach of the peace. One of them had an inordinate mass of hair. They had all pled Guilty to the charge.

The Sheriff sentenced his two companions to a fine of £10 and then said—rather rashly—to the third, hairy, accused 'Look at you—you are like a relic from the time of Charles the First!'

Quick as a flash, the accused countered. 'I hope you are not considering the same sentence?'

8
The Three-in-a-Bed Case

In September 1978 I was in New Orleans for the Ali-Spinks world heavyweight title fight.

While I was there, a dentist called at the hotel where I was staying and asked to see me. He told me that he had been reading about a trial in which I had defended a young schoolteacher, John Adamson, accused of having sex with two thirteen-year-old schoolgirls.

The trial had ended two weeks before my American visit and had received wide publicity—although I had not realised that it had travelled as far as the United States. However, the dentist told me that it had been fully reported in the American Press—as the 'Three-in-a-Bed' case—and that he had followed the trial with special interest. As he pointed out, what had happened to Adamson could have happened to any professional man who meets members of the public in the privacy of his chambers—which includes lawyers, doctors, dentists, for example.

He went on to say that a person in his profession could be vulnerable to highly imaginative female patients, who need only make a complaint involving some measure of indecency to cause untold anxiety and strain to such a man—coupled with the possibility of legal proceedings and harmful publicity. Indeed, in America—he told me—meetings had been arranged by just such professional men to consider safeguards against such action, and guidelines had been laid down for their protection.

I had not known that professional men in the United States had taken their concern to such lengths—but I was not surprised. I recalled saying to the jury in the

Adamson case 'There is no hiding place for this man, irrespective of the verdict which you will return, in view of the fact that the whole case has been ventilated very much in public and carried by every newspaper in the land, as well as other lands.'

Perhaps because it carries such a clear salutary message for all professional men who have contact with adolescent girls, the case has much piquancy still. Goodness knows, John Michael Adamson, the young Catholic schoolmaster, flirted with professional disaster—if not with the little Lolitas among his pupils. . . .

John Adamson was a twenty-five-year-old teacher of English at Holy Cross Comprehensive Secondary School in Hamilton, Lanarkshire. His pupils were both boys and girls, ranging in age from twelve to sixteen. He was inexperienced as a teacher and rather handsome.

I suppose it was because of his youth and natural good looks, as well as his easy, friendly disposition, that he was singled out by a number of girl pupils for special attention and adulation. As they were to admit later in the witness box, a number of them developed a 'crush' on him. This manifested itself by their following him around the school, sending him gifts for Christmas and birthdays, volunteering to run errands and hanging about the masters' common room during school breaks, merely to hear him conversing with other masters. These events covered a period of over a year, and at his trial I was to refer to him as the 'Pied Piper of Hamilton', with numerous young girls following in his wake!

There is no doubt that his inexperience as a teacher contributed greatly to the fact that he was eventually charged. He should have realised the danger he was putting himself in, and should have chastised these girls—especially for following him around the school, as he knew they did. He was also asked for locks of his hair—and at this stage one would have thought that the red danger light would have flickered in his mind. On the other hand, he was a pleasant, quiet person who would have found it difficult to rebuke anyone.

147

It was argued by the prosecutor at his trial, and also mentioned by the trial judge, Sheriff Leonard Lovat, that there must have come a stage when Adamson should have sought the guidance and advice of his more experienced professional colleagues, or even the Headmaster.

Alas, this is hindsight and we can all be very much wiser after the event. Adamson did nothing along these lines. In fact, he said to me on many occasions before the trial, when I put these points to him, that he felt that these 'crushes' would disappear naturally, without requiring him to reprimand the infatuated schoolgirls.

One can imagine his shock when, on 16 March 1978, police officers called at his home and charged him as follows:

'That [he] did between 19 September 1977 and 9 March 1978 on three occasions in the house occupied by [him] have unlawful sexual intercourse with two pupils, both girls being at the time between the age of 13 years and under the age of 16 years, contrary to the Sexual Offences (Scotland) Act 1976, Section 4.'

The allegations, in more detail, were that on 19 September and 16 December 1977 Adamson had had intercourse with both girls at his home. In addition, it was alleged that on 9 March 1978 he had intercourse with one of the same girls in his home.

His immediate reply to the charge was 'No girls from the school have ever been in this house.'

Adamson was not detained in custody, but was arraigned to appear in court on Petition in May of the same year. He was allowed bail at once, and was later indicted for trial by jury in Hamilton Sheriff Court for a date in late August of that year.

Before the trial, I saw my client on numerous occasions and some of the meetings were extremely long and tiring. I acted, as I often do with clients, devil's advocate with him, and pressed him hard on the telling prosecution points. Indeed, I am sure he would agree that I grilled him thoroughly, and on occasions would appear to be extremely hostile in my endeavour to satisfy myself that he was entirely innocent, despite the formidable evidence against him.

We had obtained full statements from the Crown witnesses, with the exception of one of the complainers—whom we shall call Miss X—who had refused to cooperate with us, as she was of course entitled to do. It is somewhat unusual, however, for a vital prosecution witness to refuse to give a statement to the defence. Normally, before a trial, both defence and prosecution know the case they have to meet and can prepare accordingly, but in this particular case, which was of so much importance, I had to go in 'blind' so far as the first and most material witness was concerned. I had to anticipate what she might or would say, having had the benefit of a full statement made by her friend, the second complainer—whom we shall call Miss Y.

Numerous productions were lodged by the prosecution and a number by the defence. On my client's behalf, I lodged a Special Defence of Alibi—claiming that on 19 September 1977 and 16 December 1977, the dates on which it was alleged that my client had intercourse with both girls at the same time, Adamson had an alibi, because he was elsewhere at the material times, and was certainly *not* at his home.

Among the prosecution productions was a most interesting document—a diary compiled by Miss X. This, incidentally, was not found by the police when they first questioned Miss X, but was freely volunteered and handed over by her later. Her parents did not know of its existence; nor did anyone else. This diary was well-filled, and we took photostat copies of its many pages. There was much graphic detail of the alleged sexual activities between herself, her school friend and my client.

In many ways, to my mind, the diary—albeit a prosecution production—worked in favour of the defence. Later, I was to say to the jury 'It reads like a fairy-tale, with numerous figments of a somewhat active imagination.' But I also argued that it supplied a vital link in the case—motive.

I had to consider what the jury's reaction would be to the evidence they would hear. In particular, they would be asking themselves, why should two young girls invent and concoct an evil story to ruin the career and reputation of a master they so dearly liked and with whom, indeed, they were infatuated? Many an hour I spent contemplating this question of motive.

The diary had not come into the possession of the prosecution until after Adamson had been charged, and on page 31 there was a passage which read 'My friend told her parents and big sister. There is now going to be a court case unless he says he is guilty. I still love him very much, even after all he's put me through. When he's found guilty and after everyone deserts him, there is one thing I'll promise, i.e. to wait for him no matter how long.'

Miss X went on to say 'I have now no doubt about Addie's love for me. It is me he loves. I think I am pregnant, and I love him very much.'

It should be pointed out that the girl was not pregnant.

In another part of the diary there was the statement 'I hope his wife gets off the scene—and I will marry him.'

It was clearly arguable that this unfortunate young girl had been jealous of Adamson's marriage and was trying to break it up, in the hope that she could win the favours of her schoolmaster. Was not this motive, indeed?

Still on this question of motive, I studied page 32 of the diary, which stated 'I'll always love him. With everyone trying to pry us apart, I am even more determined to love him. I know now that it must have been God's plans for me and him. I cannot tell anyone these feelings but this little book. I hope they are very lenient on him and when I hear his sentence, and if I can lower it, or help him in any way, I will, but I don't think he'll bother about me, in fact I thinks he hates me. But I will never hate him.'

150

One of the problems to be resolved before the trial was the tactics to be followed by me for conducting the defence. I had decided that our case was that this was a wicked and diabolical conspiracy by two girls to involve the accused, with whom they were both infatuated, and that this conspiracy had developed from earlier fantasies nursed by them. Long before my client was charged, there was evidence from other schoolgirls that these two had been boasting about their friendship with Adamson and I had put that down to wishful thinking on their part.

It will be obvious that this type of case raises special problems for the defending lawyer, who must be conscious at all times that there is present in the courtroom a jury of fifteen ordinary men and women, who have no knowledge of the underlying background and who are seeing the accused for the first time at the beginning of his trial. It would be suicidal to antagonise such a jury by appearing to take advantage of the obvious shortcomings of young, inexperienced girls, who are probably giving evidence for the first time in their lives. An experienced lawyer attempting to bully teenage girls can have disastrous consequences for the accused.

At the same time, when the case is one of a head-on collision between Crown witnesses and those of the defence, when there is no half-way house, a measure of tactful firmness must be exerted by the defence— who have, after all, a duty to both the court and their client.

Another pre-trial difficulty, with which I wrestled for some months, was that both girls could describe my client's home to a T. They had, as I learned from police statements, mentioned such details as a map of Dundee on the wall of the lounge, a guitar in the living room— and even a mug with Adamson's zodiac sign imprinted on it.

They could also describe a number of model soldiers on a table in the lounge, and give a vivid description of the bedroom, lounge, and dining room.

When first charged, Adamson had steadfastly denied that either girl had ever been in his house *at any time*. He was resolute about this throughout. The girls, I reasoned, could have followed Adamson to his home without his realising that he had been followed. However, his house was one storey up, and they could not easily have looked through the windows.

If they had not been in the house prior to police involvement, then how could one account for such detail in their description? This was puzzling in the extreme, and was obviously the prosecutor's long suit.

Adamson had explained to me that these girls followed him about the school, listening in to his many conversations with others. He said that his interest in war games was well known, and that they had even tried to start such a club in the school. That might account for this piece of knowledge. He had also played guitar at a number of school concerts, so one might assume that he had a guitar at his home—indeed, he had several!

Naturally, Adamson could not remember the details of the many personal conversations he had had over such a lengthy period of time, and could not say whether or not he had mentioned to anyone the fact that he had a Dundee map or a zodiac mug in his home. Nor could he remember telling anyone about the layout of his home.

Both girls told the police about the graduation photograph in his living room, which had been inscribed—but then, he had on one occasion taken this photograph to the school to try to encourage pupils to develop their descriptive powers.

Many of the details could be thus individually explained, but the combination was a worrying factor. There must be something else, I thought. . . .

Had he taken two young schoolgirls to his house, both wearing the Holy Cross uniform, would not this have been noticed by some of the neighbours, who all knew that Adamson was a married man? I checked with all the neighbours and learned that no-one had seen one—far less two—girls in school uniform going into or leaving his house.

In any event, would it be likely that a teacher who had girls falling all over him would take two of them on two different occasions to his home—when anyone with

152

any sense knows that with two witnesses the Crown has that often difficult-to-establish factor, corroboration?

In the course of our many discussions, however, Adamson volunteered the information that months before he was charged he had gone with his wife to the County Bar in Hamilton where he had met a male pupil, whose sister was a close friend and classmate of one of the complainers.

This lad had been drinking too much and had missed his bus home. Adamson took him to his own house, where he stayed the night—but not before being given a substantial quantity of coffee to help him sober up. Before going to bed he had had a good look at the house and had even questioned Adamson about the Dundee map. He had also seen an ornamental nineteenth-century Greek knife, which he had been curious about. This knife was mentioned by one of the complainers to the police.

Now, this lad would have seen the layout of the house, graduation photograph, model soldiers, guitars and other details. He was, after all, at the same school as the complainers, and his sister was a close friend of one of them. He would know of his sister's friend's 'crush' on Adamson, and might well tease her about it. Would he also boast about being in Adamson's house, and to support his boast would he give graphic details of the interior? Alternatively, could these girls have found out that this lad had spent the night in Adamson's house and could they have asked him for details, in order to add fuel to the fairy-tale which they had spun around the master?

The lad was questioned by us and denied telling anyone about the details of the house, although he did admit that he told some people that he had been in the house. We decided to call him as witness, in fairness both to the prosecution and to the defence, and we would explain to the jury that it might be difficult for this youth to cast his mind back to a period months earlier and to remember everything he had said about his visit to Adamson's home.

Perhaps he had forgotten some of the conversations he had had about this matter. . . .but it was only reasonable to assume that he would have told his schoolmates about this trip to the teacher's house. After all, it is not every day that a pupil spends a night in the home of one of his masters!

Yes, it was felt that this line of evidence had borne fruit and would help us to explain away what was otherwise rather a predicament for the defence.

Our investigation also established that, after the charge was preferred against Adamson in March, police photographers had gone to his house and had taken numerous coloured photographs of the interior, which—suitably enlarged—showed many details, including the graduation photograph, the guitars and other objects.

It further emerged that when the girls were being precognosced by the prosecutor they had been shown these detailed enlarged photographs of the various items, and were in a position to study them and speak to them in the witness box.

I felt that it had been a mistaken tactic on the part of the prosecution to show these photographs to the girls— as I felt it undermined their long suit. It gave me the opportunity, when addressing the jury, to say that, after all, the girls had seen all these details long before they were asked to give evidence at Adamson's trial.

As the trial approached, my meetings with Adamson became lengthier. I was disturbed to learn that he had accepted gifts from the girls—such as a shirt and tie—but was relieved to find out from his wife that he had immediately taken the gifts home and shown them to her, and told her exactly how he had come into possession of them.

Indeed, it turned out that he had told his wife almost everything about the girls, and how they seemed to be infatuated with him. I felt that this would make his having had intercourse with these girls even more unbelievable. As often happens in a trial, the Crown evidence of the gifts given to Adamson—which seemed to be, on the face of it, damaging evidence—turned out to be favourable, in that Mrs Adamson knew all about them and gave evidence to that effect. In a court of law many points can be double-edged—they may look favourable to one side at first, but on closer scrutiny prove to be in favour of the other.

The preparations having been completed, and my being entirely satisfied as to the total innocence of my client, I looked forward to the trial. . . .

The first witness, Miss X, was in the witness box for most of the first day, and was cross-examined by me for several hours. She was a tall, well-built girl with a strong, determined face. She was quite attractive and looked older than her years.

Miss X gave the prosecutor many details which supported the charges against my client. However, she also said that on the first occasion Adamson had taken them to the house in September, he had had intercourse first with her friend, Miss Y—and then herself.

I knew from the statement that I had taken from Miss Y that *her* recollection of the events was that Adamson had had intercourse with *Miss X* first. I questioned Miss X about the order and she stuck to her story. She said she was in no doubt, as it was vivid in her recollection; Adamson had had intercourse with her friend first.

Basically, the evidence given by both girls was that in September 1977 they were at school when they were approached by Adamson and asked to follow him home that day after school. This was on Monday 19 September, according to the diary. Both girls claimed they agreed to do so because each had a considerable 'crush' on Adamson at the time.

They said they followed Adamson, walking a short distance behind him, from Hamilton to the Burnbank area where he lived. When they arrived at the door of his house he asked them in for coffee. They both went into the living room and Adamson then made coffee, which they sat drinking.

At first, conversaiton was quite casual and they said that he mentioned that his wife was away in Dundee, visiting relatives.

The girls were sitting on the settee in the living room when Adamson came over and sat between them and began kissing them. They did not attempt to move away from him. After the kissing session, which lasted several minutes, they claimed that he asked them into the bedroom and they agreed to go. In the bedroom all three got undressed. The three of them then got into the double bed and Adamson lay between the girls. It was then claimed that intercourse took place with each girl, and that they were in bed about fifteen to twenty minutes.

Afterwards they got up, dressed, and went back into the living room and finished the coffee. The girls then left the house. While they were drinking, the girls said the conversation was casual and there was no arrangement made at that time for their return to the house.

It was about a month after this 'visit' that Miss X, in the presence of Miss Y, told three schoolgirls about it. This was hearsay evidence, of course, and had no value in law.

On 15 December it was claimed that Adamson again asked the girls to come to his house on the following afternoon—a Friday—after school. The girls claimed that they readily agreed. They made their way to the house, knocked on the door, and Adamson opened it and invited them into the living room.

Almost at once, they said, he started to kiss both of them, and again asked them to go into the bedroom, which they both did. In the bedroom all three undressed and then got into bed in the same positions as the first time. Intercourse again took place and it was stated that, after they got out of bed and had dressed, Adamson made a comment about having soon to go to the Scout group. He told them not to tell anyone about the two visits to the house. The girls then left, claiming to have been in the house for about forty-five minutes on this occasion.

When she got home, Miss X said she told her mother that she had been to the swimming baths to account for her lateness.

After the second visit Miss Y told a schoolfriend about both visits and was present when Miss X told another schoolgirl about them.

Miss X said that on the second visit she was having her menstrual period, and she claimed that Adamson put a sheet of polythene on the bed and that there was a considerable amount of blood on the bed. On that occasion, according to Miss X's evidence, she left her underskirt and an ornamental chain at the house.

Shortly after the second visit, the girls fell out and stopped going around with each other at school.

Miss X claimed that on 9 March Adamson asked her to come to the house alone after school, and this she did. The procedure was similar: they both undressed and went to bed. Miss X stated that at that stage Adamson said that the whole business was becoming too dangerous. Miss X described how Adamson turned her on her stomach and had unnatural intercourse with her, after which the sheets were very messy indeed. As had happened before, Miss X then dressed, left the house and made her way home.

Once again, Miss X's diary helped to show up another serious discrepancy between the stories of the two girls. It concerned the incident on 16 December. In the diary Miss X said that on that occasion Adamson must only have kissed Miss Y—'for I had my hands on his IT all that time.'

Miss X said that Miss Y was also on the bed on that occasion and under the covers—but on the other side of Adamson from her. Miss Y, of course, said in evidence that she had had intercourse with Adamson after Miss X.

Where there are discrepancies or disparities in the evidence given by Crown witnesses, the prosecutor will argue that if there were no discrepancies, and so complete and total agreement, then it would be clear that witnesses had put their heads together. Complete agreement, so the theory goes, smacks of concoction, fabrication and collusion, particularly when the evidence covers a lengthy period of time and a number of incidents. Accordingly, the young prosecutor, Mr David Wilson, argued that on this occasion discrepancies, albeit material ones, were more consistent with the truth. As against that, I argued that the purpose of cross-examination is to test the reliability and credibility of witnesses. There must surely be a line drawn; and whereas some points of disagreement are expected, there should not be too many material differences. After all, witnesses were merely being asked to cast their minds back some months and recall truthfully what happened.

This line between acceptable and unacceptable divergence of evidence must be drawn by the jury, too. They must take into account the demeanour of witnesses, their reaction to hostile questioning and their attitudes to points put to them which clearly could not have been anticipated by them in advance.

Throughout the trial the defence contended that Miss Y was very much under the influence of Miss X—although they were both thirteen years old at the time of the charge—and felt constrained to support her. I felt that this did emerge in the course of the proceedings, because Miss X was extremely mature for her years, ice-cool and confident—even in the face of lengthy and, I hope, searching cross-examination by me. There were occasions when she gave the impression of being cheeky and forward: sometimes, instead of answering questions, she would try to interrogate me. My view was that she seemed to enjoy the trial and her particular part in it. She tried to put the defence on the defensive—and I accepted her attitude as manna from heaven. I knew that her attitude could not be helping her case one little bit.

Miss Y, on the other hand, was much quieter, almost subservient—although sticking to her guns, she did not overplay her part and proved to be much more difficult to cross-examine. She was much smaller and plainer in appearance than her friend and looked younger than her years. My estimate of which was the more dominant personality of the two, and who was capable of leading the other, was clearly established out of their own mouths.

I asked Miss X if, as a Catholic girl, she knew about the Commandments of God—and in particular the Sixth Commandment, which concerned the matter of adultery. She said she did. I asked her how she felt about her obvious wrong-doing—were her evidence correct—with the teacher, and she replied, quick as a flash, 'I did not think it was wrong—I did not think about the Commandments!'

This reply brought some hostile questioning from the Bench, as it clearly seemed to be a lie.

All along it had seemed to me that the seeds of the girls' fantasy had been sown long before the alleged visits to Adamson's home.

One witness, Mr George Muir, Principal Teacher of English at Holy Cross, stated in evidence for the prosecution that as far back as April 1977 he was English teacher to the Misses X and Y, when they were in their first year at the school. At one time he instructed the girls in his class to prepare an essay, which they had to write in their classroom. Another teacher, Mrs Curran, was to mark these compositions, the topic of which was 'A Camping Holiday'.

Mrs Curran, after marking an essay by Miss Y, had approached him and asked him to read it. He found that the theme for the essay was that Miss Y had been away on a camping holiday and her tent had blown down. Her English teacher, a 'Mr Adams'—who stayed in a rural cottage nearby—had invited herself and her girlfriend to come and stay overnight with him. While staying overnight, she wrote, both she and her friend had slept with Mr Adams as there had only been one bed in the cottage.

After reading the essay, and being well aware of the fact that there was a young English teacher in the school called Adamson, Mr Muir decided to speak to Miss Y about the matter. He called her out and asked her if she had shown the essay to anyone else. She had told him that Miss X had read it. Mr Muir then spoke to both girls together, and asked Miss Y what her parents would think if they were shown the essay.

She said that her parents would be very upset.

When Miss X was asked the same question, she said, according to Mr Muir, that her parents would not care and that they would not think anything of it.

Mr Muir then told Miss Y that he was very disappointed with her and tore up the essay.

At the beginning of the new session in August 1977, Mr Muir noticed that Miss X and Miss Y were both hanging around the staff room and the older part of the building used by Mr Adamson.

A number of schoolgirls stated that both girls had told them about some of their 'experiences' with Mr Adamson. Other girls did not fully accept the stories they told, considering that these owed much to the vivid imagination of Miss X. I felt that there came a stage when the two girls found it difficult to distinguish fantasy from fact and make believe from reality—as I was to argue to the jury later.

Another schoolgirl friend gave evidence that before the 1977 summer holidays she was standing outside Mr Adamson's classroom with Miss X. Mr Adamson came out and asked them both to come into the classroom. When Miss X asked Mr Adamson why he must get married, Adamson said that no-one *had* to get married—but that he would not be married on 8 July and could make accommodation for both of them.

When I cross-examined this schoolgirl witness she agreed that this was said by Adamson in the presence of other pupils, and that he was smiling when he said it. He had then said that he was being married on 9 July. On another occasion, this witness said, she had been with Miss X when she asked Adamson for a lock of his hair. According to her, Adamson said 'No'—but went on to say 'I've got something else to give you.' She said that while he was saying this he had raised his eyebrows. This witness also admitted that she had a 'crush' on Adamson.

So far as the lock of hair was concerned, once again the diary was helpful to the defence. Under 9 January 1977—and this date was in the handwriting of Miss X—was the entry 'Today, I asked Addie for my lock of his hair and he said he had still to give it to me, and something else. When I asked what he meant by something else, he had raised his eyebrows.' 9 January was a Sunday, and even Miss X conceded that she had never spoken to Adamson on such a day. Either the date in the diary was wrong, although it was in her own handwriting, or else she chose random dates which had no relationship to the truth in the course of her fantasy.

Another reference in the diary was useful. On page 22, when the 'events' of 16 December were being entered, Miss X had written 'After we had left the house I said to my friend, I have left my chain, and I suddenly felt a draught and I said, Oh, worse than that—I have left my underskirt. Both of us were laughing. The End.' I later suggested to the jury that this read like the conclusion of a fairy-tale.

Needless to say, the police thoroughly searched Adamson's house after they had charged him and found neither a chain nor a child's underskirt. What is more important neither did Mrs Adamson.

Miss X had said that during the visit on 9 March unnatural intercourse had taken place. The sheets, she said, were very messy. On the previous occasion, 16 December, both girls spoke about Miss X having had her period and the bed being consequently heavily blood-stained. However, it was of some significance that there was no evidence from the police, who had examined the bed, clothing and mattress, that they had found traces of blood on any item of bedding. This was a negative point, but still of value.

At the same time I wondered if Miss X had told the police about the unnatural offence—or even the police surgeon who had examined her a week later? Significantly, there was no medical evidence which might indicate that unnatural intercourse had taken place.

Perhaps she had not told the police or the surgeon, and perhaps this was a facet of the fantasy which had developed during the time between my client's arrest and his eventual trial!

Here I must refer to the medical evidence adduced by the prosecution, which I felt was of vital importance to the case. . . .

The police casualty surgeon, Dr Brown, examined both girls on 16 and 17 March at Hamilton Police Office. His evidence was not in entire agreement with that of the Strathclyde Police forensic expert, Dr McLay, who also examined the girls at about the same time. Both gave evidence for the Crown.

In respect of Miss X, Dr Brown said that the hymen was not intact, and that it was possible that she was not a virgin at the time of his examination. Equally, he said, it was possible that she *was* a virgin! In the case of Miss Y, he said, the hymen was torn and she was capable of having, and having had, sexual intercourse. However, he went on to say that she could be a virgin and may never have had intercourse! Both girls had, of course, claimed to have had normal intercourse on at least two occasions with Adamson.

Dr McLay's evidence was that Miss X was not a virgin and had had intercourse. As to Miss Y, he found that the hymen was intact, and was not torn. He said that he could not be certain about Miss Y, and so could not say positively on oath whether or not she had had intercourse at any time.

The discrepancies in the evidence of the two medical experts were striking. I felt that they merely added to the general confusion surrounding the case. Whether or not either girl had had intercourse in the past did not prove anything of a conclusive nature against Adamson in particular—but clearly, if there was a medical doubt as to their ever having had intercourse, this must be a telling factor for the defence.

Perhaps my cross-examination of these two medical witnesses was best summoned up in a droll paragraph in *Punch* at the time:

'Both girls, now aged 14, were examined after the alleged incidents came to light, by Dr Robert Brown, a Hamilton police surgeon. He said about the first girl: 'I feel it was quite possible that she was not a virgin. She could have had possible intercourse.' But when cross-examined by defence agent Joe Beltrami he agreed it was equally possible that she was a virgin. The second girl, Dr Brown thought, could equally have had sexual intercourse, but, at the same time, he agreed that it was possible she was a virgin.'

Mr William Dornan, Assistant Headmaster of the Lower School at Holy Cross, said in his evidence that towards the beginning of February 1978 he was given information by a form mistress about a complaint some schoolgirls in her form had made concerning Miss X, who had allegedly been talking about an affair between herself and Adamson.

Mr Dornan agreed to speak to Adamson, and later told him about rumours being spread about him by Miss X among her friends. Adamson, he said, told him that Miss X had been hanging around the staff room that he used, and had offered to go messages for him. He advised Adamson to be careful, and said his best course of action would be either to ignore Miss X completely and have nothing at all to do with her or to draw it to the attention of other members of the staff on the occasions when she came into the staff room, offering to run errands for him.

Adamson, said Dornan, appeared to be slightly embarrassed by the situation. One could not wonder at this. However, he did say to Dornan that he believed that it was just a schoolgirl 'crush'.

It should be noted that this exchange took place several weeks before the alleged third incident. I felt it was unlikely that after such a conversation the third incident would ever have happened.

Some weeks later, said Mr Dornan, he was called to the Headmaster's room and informed that a formal complaint had been made against Mr Adamson. Shortly after this Mr Dornan was interviewed by the police.

The police evidence which closed the Crown case was hardly in dispute.

Detective Constable Campbell stated that after having interveiwed the two girls X and Y he went to Adamson's home, saw Adamson and told him of the nature of his enquiries. He then cautioned Adamson, who replied 'No girls from the school have ever been in this house.'

In the living room, Campbell saw an old map of Dundee and took possession of this, along with some bedding which was subsequently handed to the police forensic department. Later, he had again called at Adamson's home and had a series of photographs taken of the interior.

In cross-examination, I elicited from Campbell that he had been looking, in particular, for blood stains on the bedding. He admitted that there were no blood stains to be seen, despite careful examination.

This was to be a typical 'jury case.' A 'jury case' is a situation wherein there are no legal niceties and the Crown case, if accepted, is more than adequate with regard to sufficiency in law. In short, the issue is purely one of fact and so very much a matter for the consideration of the lay members of the jury, on whose verdict everything depends. It would be extremely unusual to overturn such a verdict in the Court of Criminal Appeal. This has been done in two cases mentioned in this book (Joe Boyle and Maurice Swanson), but these are rare situations indeed.

In the case of Adamson, the question for the jury to decide was basically a fairly straightforward one. Would, or could, two schoolgirls invent such a wicked and heinous story to crucify an innocent English teacher, of whom they were so clearly fond? It was a formidable prosecution case, and so much depended on the reaction of the jury to the two girls on the one hand and to Adamson and his witnesses on the other.

The tender ages of their two main witnesses would mean points scored for the prosecution. Equally, points would be scored for the defence because of the position held by the accused and the improbability of the whole situation.

And so to the defence. . . .

When Adamson first consulted me in March 1978—the day after he had been charged—I remember saying to him 'How could this happen? Where was your wife at these times?'

It turned out that from 7 September until 28 September she had been in Dundee—where she came from originally—on a teacher-training course, and had been living with her parents there. The Adamsons had received the keys of their council house only in August of that year, and in September it was only partially furnished and hardly habitable. In fact, there had been four large packing cases in the lounge at the time—and yet at the trial neither girl made mention of these!

Adamson was staying with his parents at this period at their home in Glasgow, although he visited his own home to make improvements there. It was known to many of the pupils that his wife was in Dundee.

On the next occasion libelled against him, 16 December, Adamson and his wife were living at their own house, but the 16th was a Friday—and on Fridays Adamson travelled to his parents' home, where he ate and changed into Scout uniform. He was second-in-command of the local Scout troop.

That Friday was to be the last Scout meeting before the Christmas break. Adamson arrived at his father's home by school bus shortly after 4 p.m., and let in his sister at about 4.20 p.m. His wife had arrived shortly afterwards.

In the case of the first and second incidents the girls claimed to have walked to Adamson's house from school. At normal walking rate they should have been there by about 4.30 p.m.

Yet again Crown Production No 2—the dairy—assisted me, because it pinpointed the dates of the alleged offences. According to the diary, the three dates and times were clear—and the Crown was committed to these. The defence, therefore, was able to plead alibi to the first two dates, which were those involving both girls. Very often, in similar cases, one cannot be certain of dates, particularly when they are spread over a period of six months, as they were in this case, and it is usually impossible, as a consequence, to plead alibi because the dates are flexible.

There was no such Special Defence of Alibi for the third incident, as Adamson admitted being in his house *alone* at the time of Miss X's complaint—about 4.30 p.m.

My key witness, I felt, was to be Adamson himself.

I had seen him repeatedly in my office before the trial and had come to know him fairly well. The jury, of course, would get to know him only during the course of the trial. I impressed upon him that, if I were a member of the jury, I would expect him to be indignant—bitter, even—reeking of resentment in the witness box. One might even expect feelings bordering on hatred for the two girls, considering what they had put him through.

By this time I was satisfied that Adamson was completely innocent, and convinced that something diabolical had been concocted by the two girls, for reasons which were difficult—although not impossible—to explain. I have interviewed thousands of clients over the years, most of them charged with serious offences, and after the time I had spent with Adamson I felt that he did not have the ability or acting acumen to pull the wool over my eyes.

Within myself, however, deep down, I knew that the expected feelings of indignation and bitterness would not be conveyed to the jury by Adamson. He was quiet, unassuming, and to some extent rather soft. He was that seldom-met individual, someone it is impossible to rile. He was easy-going, seeing the best side of everyone, no matter what. More than that, his failure to act upon the various warning lights that constantly flickered before his arrest was an indication of a naïvety which one did not associate with a graduate teacher.

I emphasised time and again how important his evidence would be, and that I would achieve only so much in my cross-examination of these well-rehearsed girls. He seemed to understand what I wanted, as I barked Crown points and questions at him one after another, in my endeavours to see him moved and stung into fiery response. I never succeeded alas! And I was not at all surprised to hear him express sorrow and sympathy for the youngsters when he got into the witness box. In answer to the very pertinent and perspicacious questions put to him by the Crown, he never even raised his voice!

It reminded me, at the time, of watching the heavy-weight boxer Joe Bugner—who seemed to fight at the same lethargic pace, unable to 'up' his performance when situations seemed to demand it. And I felt that in the case of Adamson his amazing good nature would tell against him in due course.

I opened the defence—in a crowded, emotion-charged courtroom—by putting Adamson in the witness box and establishing his name, address and teaching qualifications. I did not dare refer to his degree in an abbreviated form—B Ed—for fear of possible laughter in the court. This was always an extremely solemn and anxious case, with far-reaching implications either way.

Then I asked him if he had ever had sex with Miss X and Miss Y.

'No,' he stated, firmly.

I asked him if he could in any way account for their damning evidence against him. He said that he had listened intently to their evidence and felt that they obviously had fertile and vivid imaginations, in addition to their clear feelings for him.

In order to represent this imagination, I referred him to passages from Miss X's diary—which was, by now, fast becoming a godsend to the defence.

On page 24 Adamson read 'After what he did to me I am wondering if I am pregnant. It is quite possible I am. If so, I won't abort the baby, but look after it myself; if not, well, there is always another time. I didn't know whether to wish I was pregnant or not.'

On page 25: 'Last night I had a funny dream. I was standing in a white dress and he was at my feet crying and begging me not to do it. I don't know whether I was getting married or becoming a nun.'

On page 26: 'I sometimes feel like committing suicide but if he does love me I could never hurt him so much by killing myself.'

On page 27: 'It's not fair. All the people who really love somebody can never have him. I love him more than anything. And if it's the last thing I do, I'll be pregnant by him. And he will deliver my baby. But I won't make him stand by me, because I wouldn't ruin his life. I don't care about me. I'm not important.'

After these references to the diary Adamson went on to say that in the last few weeks of May 1977 he realised that a number of girls, including X and Y—although he did not know their names at the time—had developed some kind of 'crush' on him. At this time another teacher had even mentioned the fact to him.

During the summer months a number of telephone calls were made to his parents' home. These calls were frequent, and were made by young girls. At this period, Adamson said, he was often in Dundee and did not answer any of these calls. His parents and sister had taken a number of calls from persons who asked to speak to 'John' or 'Mr Adamson'. His parents regarded these calls as of nuisance value only, and frequently said that he was no longer living with them. Requests were made for his new address and telephone number, and on one occasion Miss Y identified herself as one of the callers. The phone calls ceased at the beginning of the autumn term.

He had had love notes, presents, and Christmas and Valentine cards from female pupils, Adamson said—but he had attached no special significance to these.

I referred him to Defence Production No 4—a letter, which he read out. 'I am writing this letter because I like you. I think you are very nice-looking.' The letter went on to invite Adamson to telephone the writer. On my asking him about this letter, he said, 'I could not take it seriously. I thought it was funny. I have received some worse Valentines from girls.' He went on to speak of presents, including a shirt and tie from X and Y as a wedding present, and of demands for locks of his hair. He had not, of course, either telephoned the writer of the letter nor did he give out locks of his hair.

He said he had noticed as far back as May 1977 that young girls were following him around the school. In particular, he said, X and Y occasionally followed him from the school to the bank—always on the opposite side of the road and a few paces behind him. 'I decided that ignoring it was the best policy, in the hope that they would get fed up and go away.' He agreed, on reflection, that he had been wrong in not taking a more positive step.

I referred him to yet another letter—from X and Y—in which they asked if they could call at his home. Both of the letters, he said, were shown by him to his colleagues and also to his wife. There was a boxed Christmas card, too, couched in somewhat affectionate terms and signed by X and Y.

I felt that had there been anything at all by way of an association then these letters and Christmas card, as well as the gifts, would have been quickly destroyed by him and not retained, as they were, at his home. He even kept the covering note, signed by X and Y, which had accompanied the wedding present of the shirt and tie and which was also produced by the defence.

On the day he received the shirt and tie, Adamson showed them to his wife, opening the parcel in front of her at home. Realising that these were expensive gifts, he tried to return them to X and Y, but the girls refused to take them back. 'I did not think I should run about the school trying to force unwanted presents on two young girls. I just put the present in a cupboard.'

He also received a pen and gifts of after-shave, but did not know from whom they came. Some time in December, he said, the two girls had approached him and invited him to go to a party which was to be held on 20 December. He refused—but to his surprise the two girls came to see him again on the following day. On this occasion he refused even more forcibly.

When he received the Christmas card he had discussed the matter with his wife, and they both decided it was not worth bothering about.

Adamson went on to say that he was off school for a period in February 1978, and on his return he met Mr Dornan, Head of the Lower School, who asked him if he had heard of a girl, Miss X, and if so, was she in any of his classes? Adamson told him that she was not, but that he had been aware for some time that she had a 'crush' on him.

Mr Dornan said to him 'You should hear what she has been saying about you, John.' He did not over-emphasise this, and was not precise as to the nature of the allegations, and Adamson assumed that he had been talking about more of the girl's 'crushes'.

Adamson said he was advised by Mr Dornan to pick on the girl indiscriminately and unfairly in order to give her a distaste for him. 'I felt that this conduct would be unfair to her, but I decided to speak to her about the general matter, when she simply walked away from me.'

In September 1977, he said, he had been working at his house and then left to go to a nearby public house for a drink. When he returned home he noticed that he had left the door unlocked. There was an inference here that possibly X and Y could have entered the house in his absence—but I decided not to push this point in case it was thought that the defence was clutching at straws.

Adamson next spoke to his alibi in respect of the first two alleged incidents—saying that he had been at his parents' home on both occasions. As to the final incident, on 9 March, he had been alone at his home and therefore did not plead alibi in respect of this alleged offence.

When I asked him if he could account for the detailed description of the house supplied by X and Y in the witness box (and, apparently, to the police) he gave the court a detailed account of his meeting the older brother of one of Miss X's particular friends. 'The boy had paid a lot of attention to the house,' Adamson said, after describing how he and his wife had put him up for the night. But he could not say whether or not this boy had later informed his sister—or, indeed, X and Y—of the layout of his house. He thought that it was possible, in view of the fact that the 'crushes' X and Y had on him were common knowledge at Holy Cross.

In addition, two friends of Adamson's helped to decorate his house in August and September of 1977. One of these friends had a sister in the same class as Miss Y. Miss Y would know this fact and through the friend's sister might have gleaned the necessary information.

Adamson also pointed out that photographs of the interior of the house had been shown to the girls months before the start of the trial.

The cross-examination of Adamson for the Crown by Mr David Wilson was good and well-prepared. He did not mince words, taking a very hostile line with my client.

He asked Adamson if he had not enjoyed the girls' flattery to some extent. Adamson replied 'I did not have any feelings about it whatsoever. I thought it was funny.'

Adamson also denied prosecution suggestions that he was sexually frustrated in September and December 1977, at first because his wife was away from home, and later because she was pregnant. Adamson denied this suggestion vehemently, saying 'I love my wife too much to do anything like that!' And he repeated over and over again to Mr Wilson that the allegations were lies.

Adamson remained unmoved and unruffled throughout the cross-examination, hardly raising his voice at any time, and with no signs of indignation or anger. The cross-examination—totally unfavourable to the Crown, so far as I could see—finished at about 3.15 p.m.

When I stood up to re-examine, I intended to spend more time than normal in doing so. My eyes were on the clock. I did not want to have to call my next witness that same day. For my next witness was to be Mrs Adamson.

If I had to call her that afternoon her evidence would clearly be interrupted when the court rose for the day, and would not have the same cogency.

I filibustered with my client until 3.45 p.m. As he left the witness box, I looked at the Sheriff, trying to convey a suggestion that there was little point calling the next witness so late in the day. The Sheriff seemed to know what was in my mind and adjourned the court until the next morning.

I immediately took the opportunity of announcing in a firm, clear voice that Mrs Adamson would be called for the defence first thing in the morning, and watched carefully the jury's reaction to this piece of information. I knew that they would want to hear her evidence about the matter, as there was no-one closer to the accused than she was. If anyone knew the truth, it would surely be her. Now they knew that she was to be called as a witness, and, from that, that she was standing by her husband—something she would not to be likely to do if there was the slightest doubt in her mind about his involvement.

The stage was set for the following morning—and, tactically, I had won a point.

As was normal, Adamson's bail was discontinued as he left the witness box and for the remainder of the trial he was detained in custody. He told me later that on the first night in prison he had overheard some other prisoners discussing what they proposed to do to him if they had a chance. They had obviously been following the progress of his case in the Press—and were jumping to the conclusion that he was guilty.

When Adamson was examined by a doctor on his first night in prison, as is customary, he was told 'Don't turn your back on anyone in here!' One can understand that for the next four days of the trial the strain was considerably increased for him by having to return to Barlinnie Prison each night and to look out for his own safety.

Mrs Adamson did not let me down.

172

She spoke first about her husband's alibi for 16 December and emphasised that he had been at her mother-in-law's house at about 4.25 p.m. when she arrived there after Christmas shopping. She would not and could not be budged.

I asked her if her marriage had been affected by the vile allegations which had been made, and she answered 'No, not at all.' She added that she was certain that the allegations were wholly untrue.

She spoke of being shown the letters by her husband and of opening the wedding present and reading the gift card signed 'X and Y'. She smiled when she recalled her husband bringing home the large Christmas card, on which was inscribed 'Love to you Darling'.

She went on to say that on being shown an obvious love letter from the girls—a defence production—she had advised her husband to show it to someone at the school.

During pregnancy, Mrs Adamson said, she and her husband had had normal sexual relations until it was no longer possible. She added 'We both coped admirably.' And yes, her husband had told her about pupils following him about the school, and requesting locks of his hair—indeed, it became obvious that Adamson had told her everything that happened at school.

Mrs Adamson said that on 8 March 1978 she had gone to her parents' home in Dundee for a long weekend. Her husband was to travel there on the Saturday morning, 10 March—which he did. On the date of the first incident, 19 September 1977, she had been living in Dundee, undergoing teacher-training.

She was cross-examined by the Fiscal, who immediately recalled that her child was born on 5 January 1978. 'You were married on 9 July 1977,' he said. 'Does that mean that the child was premature—or that you had sexual relations prior to marriage?'

Mrs Adamson agreed with the latter suggestion—but it seemed to me that the Fiscal had started off on the wrong track. He had tried to embarrass the witness and had failed abysmally. His line of enquiry, I thought, prompted only sympathy for both Adamsons.

Matters went from bad to worse for him when he suggested to her that in December 1977 her husband must have been frustrated 'because he was not getting his rations'. And even worse was to come when he suggested that at that time they might have been having anal intercourse.

I could see from the Sheriff's expression at this line of cross-examination that an objection on my part would have been successful, and that Mrs Adamson would have been told by the Bench not to answer these apparently crude and irrelevant questions. But I glanced at the jury—and decided not to intervene. I felt that the jury was just a little bit disgusted at the manner of cross-examination, and that to allow the Fiscal to continue could do our case nothing but good.

Mrs Adamson was rightly indignant—and not nearly as phlegmatic as her husband had been. She dismissed the Fiscal's points with scorn; and when she left the witness box I felt that the case was virtually over, and that—given a reasonable jury speech by the Sheriff—only one verdict could follow.

Adamson's father and sister were called to confirm Adamson's alibi—and then the boy who had spent the night in Adamson's house in October 1977. He said he remembered questioning Adamson about the Dundee map and the nineteenth-century Greek ornamental knife and the wargame figures. He could not recall giving a detailed description of the house to anyone, but could not exclude the possibility that he may have mentioned one or two items.

I then closed my case for the defence. There were only the speeches to the jury to follow. I was feeling confident at that stage—subject to my client receiving an impartial jury charge from the Sheriff. This would not take place until after the prosecution and defence speeches.

Judges are human, and occasionally find it difficult to be completely dispassionate—and tend sometimes to over-emphasise good Crown points to the detriment of the defence. This is not done intentionally, but one would be naïve to believe that 'loaded' charges to the jury have not been given in the past.

I will not mention a specific instance of this—but readers who follow cases with interest (and perhaps even attend trials) will understand what I mean. Juries are normally quick to take any lead given by the man in charge of the trial, the judge. The mere intonation of a judge may be of importance, or a facial expression when dealing with the evidence of a particular witness.

Judges are the masters of the *law* applicable to the case—not of the *facts*, which are exclusively the province of the men and women of the jury. Some judges barely deal with matters of fact and evidence, for fear of transgressing upon the jury's function. Others delve into the facts in great detail, and in this situation one of the dangers is that they may inadvertently omit crucial points for either side—which could be construed by the jury as outright dismissal of that point or points.

The situation is not all one-sided, I hasten to add, and there have been occasions when I have been given a very pro-defence charge, in circumstances where a conviction would clearly have been nothing short of an outrage.

The Fiscal's speech to the jury was short for a trial of such length, and I felt that, even by then, he had given up hope of a conviction. From conversations I had had with him in the course of the trial I knew that, as the trial progressed, the Fiscal was becoming more and more concerned—as I was—about the sharpness of the head-on conflict in the evidence.

He must have been impressed, I think, by the calibre of the defence witnesses and he had felt during the trial that the verdict could go either way. The consequences of a conviction were horrendous—moreover the defence evidence had been, I thought, unshakeable. We both realised that the jury's task was harrowing in the extreme.

The Fiscal began his address to the jury by stating that he was 'hanging his hat on the details of Adamson's house as described by the two girls'. He claimed that they could have known certain details only be being in the house—but he did not refer to the other possible explanations for this knowledge which had emerged in evidence.

He conceded that there were many discrepancies in the evidence of X and Y, some of which were of a most material nature. He accounted for these by stressing that both X and Y were merely girls of thirteen and that such discrepancies could be expected.

Of the evidence of alibi he said that there was 'significant evidence of collusion' among the defence witnesses. They were too precise, he claimed, and too exact. As I listened, I thought that in such circumstances witnesses could hardly be faulted for being as accurate and correct as possible. Such a situation as the one in which they found themselves was not by any means an everyday occurrence.

The Fiscal then went on 'You may have been a little bit surprised—if not a little shocked—at the way Miss X gave her evidence. She quite calmly stood up and told you about these intimate details. Although we are in what is called a permissive society, it does not necessarily mean that the people involved in it are any more mature than you or I were at that age. Because they are bombarded with sex almost daily, from magazines and television, they think sex is a great thing. We have a duty to protect these immature minds in these mature bodies, and that is why the Sexual Offences Act of Parliament of 1976 was brought into being.'

He continued 'These girls know of the physical aspect of sex, but as Miss X clearly and calmly pointed out, she was so concerned about getting to love Mr Adamson. It was so sad. She wanted the man. She was desperate to have him.'

The more I listened to his short speech, the more I made up by mind that he had lost a lot of the confidence which he had displayed at the commencement of the trial. I felt that he had almost been won over himself!

While the trial lasted I had made use of the 'wee sma' oors' to check and re-check the evidence that had gone before. I had noted, I think, each and every discrepancy in the evidence given by X and Y. I had memorised the valuable pieces of evidence given by doctors, teachers and other pupils. In short, I had taken the time to know my case. I was determined to address the jury without reference to notes, feeling that this more personal approach was by far the best. The task, as it turned out, proved to be fairly easy and the whole matter seemed to flow because of my detailed knowledge of the background.

I started off by saying that I had noted that in his opening remarks the Fiscal had said he was 'hanging his hat' on the details of the accused's house, as described by the two girls. I commented that I would have been happier had the Fiscal been prepared to 'hang his hat' on the way in which these girls had given their evidence in the witness box. Their demeanour and their inability to answer a number of questions put by me concerning the many disparities in their respective accounts of what had happened was, I said, for the members of the jury to assess and evaluate. It was what they said in the witness box that mattered—not what they might or might not have told the police months earlier.

I made frequent references to the diary which, I claimed, truly read like a fairy-tale. I pulled no punches in attacking the credibility of X and Y, and said that Adamson's appearance in the dock on these charges was a result of 'a wicked, diabolical and monstrous plot by them'. They had fantasised about an imaginary love-life and affair with the dark-haired, handsome young teacher. The seed of the fantasy had been sown, based on wishful thinking, when Miss Y wrote the essay about a camping holiday, and being in bed with a Mr Adams and her girl friend. I claimed that both girls had given entirely different versions as to what had happened during the alleged sex associations, and pointed out that they had seen coloured photographs of the interior of Adamson's house long before the case had begun.

'The sad thing' I said 'is that win, lose or draw, my client's future will never be the same again because of the attendant publicity of this case. Try as he might, there will be no hiding place for him.'

I referred to the questions put to Miss X about the Ten Commandments, and her reply, 'It did not seem wrong at the time.' How could this be explained, other than by being a lie on the part of X, who was constantly trying to justify herself—who would not concede a situation where she must have been wrong?

I told the jury that we had not spent seven full days on the case only to ask them for sympathy. In the interests of justice, there should be no sympathy shown by them towards either the young girls or the accused. The case must be dealt with from the point of view of hard facts. They must consider the credibility, the feasibility, of the evidence given by X and Y. Did it hang together? Did it hold water? I also pointed out how difficult this case was for a lawyer, when the principal witnesses were young girls of thirteen years who could not be seen to be bullied in any way—and yet the defence had a serious job to do!

I said that if these crimes had been committed, then it was the very essence of stupidity—for the accused was said to have committed them in the presence of two emotional young girls on two occasions.

I told the jury 'Your duties are serious and exacting. The evidence must be treated like a cube and you must not go outside its walls. Your decision must be based solely on what you have heard in court.'

As I was speaking I was studying each member of the jury—and realised just how seriously they took their responsibility.

After a lengthy résumé of the evidence, I closed my speech by saying 'We are all here to try to ensure that the ends of justice are met. For me, at any rate, this could only mean the acquittal of Adamson—not by a verdict of Not Proven, which I did not seek, but by one of Not Guilty.'

Sheriff Lovat's charge to the jury was the epitome of fairness and understanding. He had been a Procurator Fiscal in Glasgow for eighteen years before being appointed to the Bench. He and I had had many interesting tussles over that period, and he had been a difficult and skilful adversary.

Sheriff Lovat began by repeating what I had said— that sympathy would not enter the jury's thoughts, or affect their judgment when they were in the jury room. The future of the accused and his family, or the families of the two schoolgirls, was not their concern.

He went over the evidence given by the two girls, and conceded that there were many discrepancies— but he told the jury that they must decide whether or not the evidence was true.

About the sex diary, he daid 'The note-book may be, in essence, a work of fiction, a work of creative imagination, detached from reality. Or it may be a chronicle of events which is substantially accurate. It may contain a blend of fact and fantasy. You alone will assess its character and significance.'

The Sheriff then referred to my speech.

'It was said by the defence that the allegations by the girls were diabolical. Certainly, if you hold that the allegations are false and fabricated by these girls, then the word diabolical would be apt—because the tenacity of the girls in lying throughout to police, parents, Procurator Fiscal and to this court would be tenacity of an evil kind.'

He emphasised that the onus of proving such a case rested with the prosecution, and that the standard was proof beyond reasonable doubt.

'Doubt cannot be assessed from the point of view of mathematical certainty, as this would be impossible to attain—but the doubt which each and every one of you might have in the course of a decision in your everyday business affairs. Every accused is presumed to be innocent until this standard of proof is attained by the Crown. The Crown has to prove guilt beyond reasonable doubt. The Crown cannot be expected to prove the guilt of an accused person to some degree of God-given, mathematical or scientific certitude . . . it is the kind of doubt which appeals to the power of reasoning which you all possess, and to which you would have regard if it arose in some matter of importance to you. . . .If, therefore, when you have considered all the evidence, you are left with any reasonable doubt in your minds as to the guilt of the accused, then the accused is, in law, entitled to the benefit of that doubt, and you must acquit him of the charge.'

I guarantee that it would have been impossible for anyone to assess from his model charge what Sheriff Lovat's views were—such was his impartiality.

The jury then retired to their room, and did not return for two hours—during which time I became more and more anxious, as I had not thought they would be out for more than, say, fifteen minutes.

As they filed back into their seats, their faces were impassive. The Clerk of the Court asked the foreman of the jury to announce their verdict, and one of the men stood up and said that they found Adamson Not Guilty. The courtroom erupted and there were cheers from the public gallery.

Adamson was discharged from the dock, and left the courtroom with his head up, cleared for all time of the dreadful allegations made against him.

Shortly after this—and still acting for Adamson— I advised the Headmaster of Holy Cross School that Adamson proposed to return there to resume his profession. But two weeks later Adamson was transferred to another Roman Catholic school in Lanarkshire.

Professional men, as the American dentist had stressed to me, cannot be too careful when in the company of female pupils, clients, or patients. As further evidence of this—if it is required—on 27 September 1979 Dr Vincent A Harvey stood trial in Glasgow Sheriff Court before Sheriff Gerald Gordon Q C on two charges of allegedly indecently assaulting a female patient. These charges related to incidents purporting to occur on 23 and 25 July 1978. For fifteen months my client had had this grotesque matter hanging over him. The General

180

Medical Council, naturally, were extremely interested in the matter, and Dr Harvey's whole professional career (as in the case of Adamson) was in the melting pot. On 27 September, the second day of the trial, Dr Harvey was found Not Guilty on both counts by the Sheriff in what can only be described as a most proper verdict. At the eleventh hour I was fortunate enough to communicate with the complainer's sister. She was asked to give evidence, and told the court that the complainer had over the years fantasised about her relationship with men. She made it patently obvious that in view of her lifetime knowledge of the complainer she was more than sceptical about the evidence her sister had given on the first day of the trial. In this case the defence was fortunate that such a near relation of a vital prosecution witness was fair and decent enough to volunteer her evidence and allow me to call her as a most crucial witness for the defence.

After the trial, Dr Harvey stated to the Press that since he was charged by the police (July 1978) he had ensured that on the occasions when he required to examine female patients a chaperon was available. In the light of his nightmarish experience his insistence on a chaperon was clearly sensible, and one can only hope that other professional men will follow his example. I do not presume to know what causes women and young girls to fantasise about invented and fabricated situations with professional men. I do know, however, from my many years of practice in the courts, that this does happen and regrettably, as a result, respectable professional men such as Adamson and Harvey have been forced to undergo what can only be described as the most terrible of experiences.

I was loath to incorporate these two cases in this book because I felt that both my clients had had more than sufficient exposure in the national Press. For this reason I conferred with both of them prior to drafting this chapter and, to their credit, each of them expressed the view that their unfortunate and dreadful experiences should at all costs be highlighted—in the hope that others would stand less chance of being smeared in the eyes of the public in the course of clearing their good names and unsullied professional reputations. Regrettably, many of the public fall into the erroneous view that there is no smoke without fire. Some may think that my two clients were fortunate in avoiding conviction. Having come almost to live with them during their lengthy period awaiting trial, I feel I am justified in saying that those members of the public who share such views—without having ever met my clients—have more than a sin to answer for. The verdicts in Adamson and Dr Harvey's cases were the proper ones and had they been otherwise, I would have fought indefinitely to clear their names—in the same manner as I did in the case of Patrick Meehan, an account of whose case will follow this present work.

9

By Reason of Insanity

Of all the many murder trials that I have been involved in, there is one which stands out, perhaps, as the most important—in terms of its far-reaching legal significance.

It was the case of Ian Brennan, whose trial took place in 1976. That case now has an established place in Scottish criminal law. It became the leading case in recent years on questions of temporary insanity, diminished responsibility and self-induced intoxication as a defence to a charge of murder.

Until the determination of this celebrated case, I had held the erroneous opinion that to be found Guilty an accused person had to have been fully responsible for his actions—or, put in another way, that he had to have formed a criminal intention to commit the crime with which he was charged. Conversely, it was my view that if such a person were incapable of rational thought, to the extent of being unable to form such an intention, then he was at least temporarily insane in the eyes of the law.

This view was fortified by a fourteen-year-old case in which I was instructed in the Glasgow High Court. In this matter counsel was the well-known advocate Mr J Irvine Smith, who is now a Sheriff.

In September 1962 a blind man was charged with the murder of two of his children, aged nine and seven. He was accused of administering a barbiturate poison to them at his Clydebank home in May of that year. Having done this, he took poison himself and was later found unconscious, with his two dead children, by the police.

Before poisoning his children the father, a man called Urquhart, told them that he was going to Heaven, and they had asked to go with him. Because of this, he said, he had given them tablets and taken some himself. He had also consumed some alcohol.

I instructed Mr J Irvine Smith to represent my client at his trial at Glasgow High Court. I lodged a Special Defence of Insanity at the time of the crime, and subsequent return to sanity by the time of the trial.

Dr Angus McNiven, psychiatrist at Glasgow Royal Mental Hospital, told the court that he had examined Urquhart on 31 May and formed the opinion that he was insane at the time the crime was committed. He had suffered 'morbid depression' at the time of his acts. He went on to narrate what Urquhart had told him in connection with the offence. Dr McNiven then stated that on examination prior to the trial in September he had reached the view that my client had recovered his insanity and was now perfectly normal. So far as I can remember, there had been no previous indications of insanity on the part of my client prior to May of that year.

In the course of his charge to the jury, Lord Wheatley referred to the English verdict of 'Guilty but Insane'. He said 'In Scotland we regard that as an illogical verdict. If the person is insane, he cannot be guilty, because he has not the capacity to formulate a guilty intent. We regard the English verdict as a contradiction in terms.

I should explain to you, because you are entitled to know, that although the verdict in Scotland takes the form of a formal acquittal the rider that he was acquitted because he was insane at the time means that he is not set at liberty, as would happen in the case of a complete acquittal.'

After retiring for fifty minutes, the jury—ten women and five men—returned a majority verdict of Not Guilty by virtue of insanity at the time of the offence.

Lord Wheatley told my client that, for 'special reasons', he would not send him to the State Mental Hospital. He was ordered to be detained in the Glasgow Royal Mental Hospital for an indefinite period.

So much for that earlier case. . . .

In 1976 Ian Brennan was nineteen years of age and lived with his mother in Easterhouse. His parents had, in fact, separated nine years before and his father, Joseph Brennan, was living in Bridgeton. Although separated, his parents remained on good terms with one another and saw each other regularly.

On Saturday 25 September 1976 Ian and his father met a friend of Ian's named Paul Ritchie, at Bridgeton Cross at about 5.30 p.m. They went to the Monaco Bar in London Road, Bridgeton but the two boys left after a time and went to Queen's Cross to complete some business. During the evening Mrs Brennan joined her husband in the Monaco, and at about 9.30 p.m. they took a taxi from the public house to her home.

In the meantime, Ian and Paul Ritchie had gone to the Blenheim public house in Sauchiehall Street, and while there the two friends had four or five pints of beer each. In the course of the evening they split up for a time, and when Ian met up again with Paul he told him he had 'scored'.

Paul at first thought that Ian meant that he had had some success with two girls that they had met earlier, but it turned out that Ian meant that he had bought two microdots of LSD.

After leaving the Blenheim, Paul and Ian went to the Cactus Bar in Bridgeton where, after some more drink, they bought a 'carry-out' of cans of beer and sherry. They made their way back to Easterhouse at about 10.45 p.m. Ian Brennan later stated that during the course of that fateful day he had consumed anything between twenty and twenty-five pints of beer, as well as some sherry.

When Paul and Ian arrived at the house they had more to drink and put on some records—which did not meet with the approval of Joseph Brennan. After some ten minutes or so in the house Paul and Ian went into the kitchen and each took a microdot of LSD. Ian's young brother Alan, aged nine, saw them take 'wee black pills' and was told by Ian 'Don't tell my Mum!'

185

There was evidently a further argument about the playing of records. Joseph Brennan switched the record player off and proceeded to punch Ian. Ian hit his father back, and Joseph Brennan began to choke him and tried to trip him up. Father and son then wrestled on the couch and Mrs Brennan tried to hit Ian in an effort to stop the fighting. She said that she was going to call the police, and at this point Joseph and Ian fell on the floor, Joseph still retaining his grip with his hands round his son's neck.

Eventually, Paul stepped in and broke it up, and they all sat on the couch. Things quietened down temporarily, but then Ian told his mother to shut her mouth and his father hit him on the cheek with the back of his hand. As Paul later recalled in the witness box, Ian jumped up at this point. 'His eyes were pure white, he was slavering as if he were an epileptic. He said "I'm going!" He shoved his mother and she fell. Ian frightened me. He wasn't all there.'

Alan Brennan giving evidence, said 'Ian said he was going to the toilet, but he went into the kitchen and brought out a knife.'

Paul, in his account, described what happened. 'The door was thrown open and Ian came into the living room carrying a knife. He was crying his eyes out. He fell on the couch and stuck the knife into his father.'

Paul—who, of course, had also taken LSD—panicked at this point, ran out of the house and went home. He later realised he was suffering from hallucinations, and said that he felt unwell for the next two days.

After he had stabbed his father, Ian Brennan ran upstairs to the house of a neighbour, Mr Robert Docherty. He was 'alarmed and excited' and told Docherty 'Phone an ambulance. My Dad's dying. He's been stabbed. I did it. It was an accident, but I didn't mean it.'

An ambulance was called, and the police arrived at 1.40 a.m. When they arrived Ian told them 'I just had a scuffle with my father, and he's dead.' Police Constable John Kane said Ian Brennan then appeared to be very relaxed and quite light-hearted, as if he didn't know he was in serious trouble. Another police constable, Alastair Wallbanks, recalled that Brennan said he was 'spaced-out—double-dosed' which implied, he thought, that he had taken drugs. At one point he asked Mr Wallbanks not to move his silver pen, as flashing lights were coming from it.

When he was eventually fit to be charged with murdering his father, Brennan replied 'Not Guilty.'

I represented Brennan next day at Glasgow Sheriff Court when he made his first court appearance on this serious charge. Even then, he was extremely vague as to what had happened. Clearly, he had stabbed his father for no logical reason. Equally clearly, he had been bereft of his senses at the time.

I recalled the well-known case which had been decided the previous year at Stirling High Court. In this matter a student had been acquitted by the jury by virtue of the fact that he had been considerably under the influence of the drug LSD at the time of an act of attempted murder with which he was charged. In that case the judge, Lord Stewart, had advised the jury in his charge to them that 'assault' was an intentional attack upon the person of another.

' "Intentional" ', he went on to say, 'has a simple meaning. It has to be contrasted with "accidental" or "negligent"—it has nothing to do with ulterior motivation of the mind which drives the hand; and when you have, as here, a situation where the accused emerges from his room and then chases another man and thrusts a knife into his back, you should not have much trouble with the word "intentional".

'What I have said is, of course, quite different from the matter of insanity,' Lord Stewart continued. 'You can have an intentional act directed by a sane mind and an intentional act directed by an insane mind. It is for you, the jury, to decide whether or not there had been some element of temporary mental malfunction at the material time which made him incapable of controlling his actions.

Even if the drug was taken voluntarily, for no therapeutic purpose—as was the case here—yet, nevertheless, if the act charged was committed by the accused while he was insane through the effects of the drug, he is entitled to acquittal in the special form which I will explain to you. In this case the accused has lodged a Special Defence of Insanity at the time of the crime, although both Crown and defence agree that he is sane today at his trial. If you agree that, in all the circumstances, he was insane at the time of the offence, you will return a verdict of Not Guilty by reason of insanity at the time.'

In this case the jury had returned such a verdict, and I considered that Brennan's situation was very much on all fours with the Stirling case.

The trial of Ian Brennan was fixed for the December sitting of the High Court of Justiciary in Glasgow. Usually, in such cases, the defence arranges a consultation prior to the trial at which counsel who will be representing the accused have a meeting with him to discuss the case.

In this case Mr Charles McArthur Q C assisted by Mr James A Farrell, Advocate, were briefed as senior and junior counsel respectively. My assistant, Andrew Glencross, attended the consultation with them, and as a result of that meeting a Special Defence of Insanity was lodged. Its terms were based on the then recent decision in the Stirling case—*Her Majesty's Advocate* v *Aitken* 1975—to the effect that at the time the alleged offence was committed the accused was insane and not responsible for his actions.

Ian Brennan's trial began on 10 December 1976. The trial judge was Lord Wylie; the prosecution was conducted by Mr John Wheatley, Advocate Depute and son of the Lord Justice Clerk, Lord Wheatley. He is now Sheriff at Dunfermline.

It was, of course, never disputed that Ian Brennan had killed his father. The question posed by the defence at the trial was whether or not he was responsible for his actions.

At the start of the trial Mr McArthur, on Ian Brennan's behalf, tendered a plea of Guilty to the reduced charge of culpable homicide, on the basis that he was of diminished responsibility at the time of the offence. This was rejected by the Crown.

The trial lasted three days. The evidence of what had happened on that fateful 26 September was taken quite quickly. Then a certain amount of medical evidence was led, principally by Dr Hunter Gillies, on the question of toxic insanity and the effect that the microdot of LSD, coupled with twenty or twenty-five pints of beer, would have had on Brennan.

When he addressed the jury, Mr McArthur put forward two arguments. He maintained first that at the time of the alleged crime Brennan was so intoxicated by the voluntary consumption of drink, or of the drug LSD, as to be insane within the meaning of the law. He further argued that, in any event, the evidence of intoxication resulting from the consumption of drink and/or drugs was such as to entitle the jury to hold that the quality of his crime should be reduced from murder to culpable homicide.

These arguments were, however, rejected by Lord Wylie when he summed up the case for the jury.

He first of all withdrew from the jury's consideration the Special Defence of Insanity. He said 'I have listened to the very full legal arguments on the legal issues raised by that Special Defence, and I have come to the view, as a matter of law, that it is not a defence which is open to the accused in the circumstances of this case.

The most pertinent circumstance of this case influencing my view on the law is that there was a voluntary intake of the drink and drug . . . which led to the condition in which the accused was found. The question has yet to be authoritatively decided by the Court of Appeal, and it may be that this is the case which will provide the opportunity to do so. . . . It has been accepted for a good many years that where, in the whole situation, an accused person through drink is incapable of forming the intention to kill, he should be convicted not of murder but of the lesser crime of culpable homicide.

Alcoholic intoxication in this kind of case can never be a defence to its consequences, unless it goes the distance of constituting what Dr Hunter Gillies described as toxic insanity. The total alienation of the reason in relation to the act committed ... a condition generated by the intake of alcohol, has got to go the length of amounting to what is, in effect, a temporary state of insanity.'

At a later point in his charge, Lord Wylie said 'I have, however, come to the view that where a person knowingly and voluntarily takes this kind of drug and wilfully embarks upon a journey over such uncertain territory, he cannot later be heard to say that he was not responsible for his actions, however serious; however disastrous to others those actions may prove to be.'

For these reasons Lord Wylie told the jury that they could not consider the question of insanity, and that it would not be open to them to reduce the charge to one of culpable homicide on the basis of the intake of drink and drugs.

The jury were out for just an hour, and when they returned they found Brennan Guilty of murder, by a majority. Lord Wylie then imposed the statutory penalty of life imprisonment.

As Lord Wylie had anticipated, there was an appeal, on two grounds. First, it was claimed that the withdrawal of the Special Defence amounted to a misdirection, and that the conviction should be quashed; and second, that the trial judge should have left to the jury the possibility of returning a verdict of Guilty to culpable homicide— because there was evidence on which the jury would have been entitled to conclude that the appellant was intoxicated to such a degree that he was deprived of all capacity to form the 'specific intent' which is the essence of the crime of murder.

The issues which these matters raised were so important and fundamental that the case was heard before a full Bench of the High Court of Justiciary. This is a very rare occurrence, and the reason for it happening in this case was that the precedents being considered included a number of important Scottish—and also English—legal cases that the Court might wish to overturn. The judges who sat on this appeal were the Lord Justice General, Lord Emslie; the Lord Justice Clerk, Lord Wheatley; and Lords Cameron, Kissen, Avonside, Thomson and Ross.

The appeal was heard on 12 and 13 May 1977, and I attended the hearing with my assistant, Mr Murray Macara. Many a meeting the two of us had in our endeavour to anticipate the Crown's approach to the appeal.

Because of the importance of the case, the Crown brought in the Solicitor General, Lord McCluskey, assisted by the trial Depute, John Wheatley, and the Crown Agent, William Chalmers.

The appellant's case was vigorously argued by Mr C R McArthur, Q C, who had to answer a great number of telling questions, from Lords Emslie, Wheatley, Cameron and Avonside in particular. McArthur had a difficult passage but stuck to his task manfully.

I had two consultations with Mr McArthur and his junior, Mr Farrell, between the conviction and the appeal hearing. As a result of these meetings we were well prepared in the law relating to the case. We knew that several Scottish cases—and at least one leading English case supported our general arguments.

The Court delivered its opinion on 13 June—and refused the appeal.

In rejecting the first ground of appeal, the Court stated that 'insanity, according to the law of Scotland, for the purpose of a Special Defence of Insanity at the time of the crime, means a mental disorder which must amount to an absolute alienation of reason. . . . It means a pre-existing disease fo the mind such as deprives the person of the knowledge of the true aspect and position of things about him.

This situation must be distinguished from the sort of temporary madness which is produced by excess of intoxicating liquors or drugs, or both. To support such a Special Defence as was lodged in this case, there must be proof that the accused was actually of unsound mind at the time.

If a man who, when sober, has no signs of insanity about him, gets himself into a state of intoxication, the presumption is that any abnormal acts he may commit when in that state are to be attributable to the effects of the drink he has taken, and not to mental disease of which there has been no previous indication.'

The Court went on to say that in the circumstances of that appeal Brennan's actions were not caused by disease of the brain but by voluntary intake of drink and drugs, which had affected it.

'If a man is neither insane nor of diminished responsibility when sober, he cannot place himself within this category by taking drink or drugs.'

The opinion continued 'To sum matters up, insanity in our law requires proof of total alienation of reason, in relation to the act charged, as a result of mental illness, mental disease or defect, or unsoundness of mind, and does not comprehend the malfunctioning of the mind of transitory effect as a result of deliberate and self-induced intoxication.

In the law of Scotland, a person who voluntarily and deliberately consumes known intoxicants, including drink or drugs, of whatever quantity, for their intoxicating effect, whether these effects are fully foreseen or not, cannot rely on the resulting intoxication for the foundation of a Special Defence of Insanity at the time— nor, indeed, can he plead diminished responsibility.'

In rejecting our second argument,the Court overruled several leading Scottish cases and distinguished an old English House of Lords appeal decision. These cases had all been advanced by us in support of the appeal. They reiterated that impairment of the mental faculties of an accused person caused merely by self-induced intoxication, however gross the impairment may be, was not insanity in our law. Further, proof of the mere facts of such intoxication, whatever their degree, could not support a defence of diminished responsibility—a defence which is available only when the charge is murder and which, if it is established, can result only in the return of a verdict of guilt of the lesser crime of culpable homicide.

The definition of the crime of murder in Scotland is not the same as that in England. In England, the crime involves "malice aforethought", an expression which requires proof of either the specific intention to kill or do serious injury. In the law of Scotland, however, the crime of murder is constituted by any wilful act causing the destruction of life, whether intended to kill or displaying such wicked recklessness as to imply a disposition depraved enough to be regardless of the consequences.

The criminal intent which is essential to the establishment of such a crime may be proved by satisfactory evidence of a deliberate intention to kill, or by evidence of wicked recklessness, as to imply a person being so depraved as to be regardless of the consequences. For this, and other reasons, the English appeal case which dealt with the effects of self-induced intoxication in relation to a charge of murder does not, and never did, represent the law of Scotland.

There is nothing unethical or unfair, or contrary to the general principle of our law, that self-induced intoxication is not by itself a defence to any criminal charge, including in particular, the charge of murder.'

The appeal judges added 'The learned trial judge gave directions to the jury which are entirely in accordance with our law, and which were, in the circumstances properly given. . . .There was no evidence either of total incapacity to form a kind of "specific intention" nor was there evidence of total alienation of reason, to go before a jury.'

Lord Stewart's jury charge in the Stirling High Court case—on which some of our hopes were based—was disapproved of, and it was stated that he had been wrong to allow the 'Special Defence of Insanity at the time' to proceed to the jury for its consideration. In that case the drug had also been self-induced, and so the accused (who was acquitted) should not have been allowed to avail himself of this defence.

As I said, our appeal was rejected unanimously by the full bench. From that day on, new criteria and guidelines were fully laid down by the most supreme and learned Court of this land. The uncertainty which had prevailed over many years before this case, fostered by conflicting views given by learned lawyers and judges alike, was finally resolved for all time by the Ian Brennan case.

A different situation, of course, might well occur were an accused person plied with strong liquor without his fully appreciating the situation. In this context, his ultimate mental state would not have been self-induced.

The case of Ian Brennan will be quoted in our courts long after his release from prison. Had he been successful in his appeal, the floodgates would have been well and truly opened. Men temporarily out of their minds through enormous intakes of alcohol or drugs would have been given a licence to commit crime by being immune to the full legal consequences.

Looking back, I think the Brennan decision was fair and realistic. But it astonsihes me now to think that the uncertainty among lawyers and judges on this point took so many years to be resolved.

The accused was charged with rape. He was giving his evidence in the High Court in Glasgow and explaining what had happened. He had met a 'bit of stuff', he said, and had taken her into a close and had started to 'mess aboot'.

Here the judge intervened, and asked 'What do you mean by "messing aboot"?'

'You know,' said the accused, 'messin' aboot!'

The judge said that he had no idea what this expression meant—and declared that he would hear the rest of the case *in camera* (which meant in the absence of the jury) in order to regularise the apparent ambiguity. He did not understand the expression, he said, nor did the prosecutor, he was sure—nor did the jury.

The jury was duly sent out and the accused continued his evidence in their absence. 'I met this bit of stuff. I took her into a close and started messin' aboot...'

At this stage the judge lost his temper, threw his pen on to the Clerk's table below the Bench and roared 'I have told you already that I do not understand that expression!'

The accused, exasperated, retorted that he was sure that the prosecutor understood him, and the Clerk of the Court understood him, and the jury most certainly understood him.

'And if you had been in that close with your bleeding camera,' he concluded defiantly 'you would have understood me too!'

195

Father O'Flynn

10
The Seal of the Confessional

Can a priest be made to tell the secrets of the Confessional? More particularly, can he be made to reveal the name of a murderer imparted to him while he gave the Last Rites and Final Confession to a murder victim?

This was the dilemma of Father Jeremiah O'Flynn, who found himself in an agonising position in what was to become a trial unique in British legal history.

Henry Daniels was a sixty-one-year-old Glasgow man charged with murdering his wife at their home in Castlemilk—by punching her, kicking her and jumping on top of her fallen body late on a Saturday evening in June 1960.

Neighbours that night heard sounds of a commotion coming from the Daniels home—punching and slapping sounds and thuds as if someone was jumping up and down. The first neighbour who went to investigate found the door lying open and Mrs Daniels alone and lying in the hallway, covered in her own blood. The neighbour realised at once that she was in a bad way and her first reaction, knowing that Mrs Daniels was a Roman Catholic, was to telephone the local priest, Father Jeremiah O'Flynn.

The priest arrived within minutes and confirmed the view that, although conscious and coherent, Mrs Daniels was dying. He promptly administered to her the Last Rites of the Roman Catholic Church and took from her what was to be her last confession. Mrs Daniels was able to hear the priest and to make herself understood to him.

Some minutes later the police arrived, to find her dead and Father O'Flynn kneeling by her side in the hall. Statements were taken from neighbours, and the priest also made a brief statement about the reason for and time of his arrival and what he did afterwards. The house was searched and there was found to be evidence of a struggle in the living room and hallway, with rather a lot of blood in those places, some of it being on the walls. At least one chair was overturned. There was no sign of a forced entry.

A manhunt was launched for Mrs Daniels's husband Henry, who was known to be the other occupant of the house but who had disappeared. Within hours Daniels was arrested and charged with murdering his wife. He denied the charge, but his clothing was taken from him for laboratory tests. His heavy boots were found to have minute traces of blood on them.

He appeared before Glasgow Sheriff Court on the following day and was remitted to Barlinnie prison. I was asked by Daniels's son to represent his Father. I went to the prison to speak with Daniels, and he vehemently denied any involvement in the assault on his wife.

Early on in the preparation of the case I realised that, leaving out the possible evidence of the priest, the Crown case probably fell considerably short of proof beyond reasonable doubt. I knew that Father O'Flynn was a material witness and looked forward anxiously to precognoscing him, but could not do this until the indictment, with the final charge and list of witnesses and productions, was served on both my client and me as his solicitor. This does not normally happen until at least two months after the arrest and one month before the trial date.

After being in custody for six weeks, Daniels was brought before the court—but on a reduced charge of culpable homicide—and was liberated on bail pending his trial.

I had not been in a position to evaluate his prospects prior to seeing the priest but eventually, on receiving the indictment, I went along to Father O'Flynn's Castlemilk Chapel House with my secretary to take the necessary and long-awaited statement from him. In the usual way, I asked him what he had told the police in his statement to them. He told me about his being summoned to the house, seeing the dying woman, and administering the Last Rites, as well as hearing her final confession. I asked him if the woman had been properly conscious at this time, and if she had discussed with him what had happened to her. I could see from his pallor and demeanour that he was an extremely worried and agitated man.

He told me that the prosecution authorities, when they were taking his statement, had pursued this same line with him, but that he had told them that he could not divulge to anyone what she had told him after he had arrived at the house. I was fully aware of the Seal of the Confessional, but he reminded me that such a conversation, occurring as it had in the process of the Last Rites and Final Confession, was, to a Roman Catholic priest, secret and inviolable. It would go with him to the grave.

He went on to say that he had consulted Archbishop Donald A Campbell about the matter—and, later on, no less a personage than Pope John XXIII. His stand, he said, had been vindicated by his clerical superiors, despite the fact that he would be a Crown witness at the forthcoming trial in the High Court, involving a matter of extreme gravity. His lips were sealed.

Understanding his difficulty, I tried to cheer him up a bit—and promised that I would see him again a few days before the trial began.

When I returned then I could see that Father O'Flynn was almost at the point of collapse. He reiterated that he could not and would not divulge what he had been told, despite the possible consequences which could ensue. He had visions of being held in contempt of court and possibly incarcerated in prison because of this. The Crown had made it clear to him how vital his evidence might be in the case, and had advised him that

199

they would try to compel him to answer their questions. For my part, I told him that there would almost certainly be a legal debate on this point and that the defence would formulate objections to his answering the Crown when they sought to make him break his seal of confession.

I felt—and told him so—that after the matter had been properly ventilated before the trial judge he would almost certainly be advised that he need not answer the questions.

You can imagine the drama here . . . it reminded me of an American film called *I Confess*, starring Montgomery Clift and Erich von Stroheim. This film was made many years ago but crops up from time to time on our television screens. I remember seeing if for the third time in late 1978.

Stroheim was a gardener who committed a murder and confessed it to his priest, played by Montgomery Clift. As a result of a Hollywood twist of plot, it was the priest who was charged and convicted of the same murder—because he could not speak about the information given to him by the actual killer in the confessional box. All ended well, as it usually does in films, when Stroheim had a brainstorm and confessed to the murder outside the courtroom where the priest had just been convicted. In the end he was shot dead by the police, and all was resolved. It all seemed rather unlikely—yet here, in Glasgow, was a real life drama with more or less the same ingredients, and it was not a celluloid plot.

Father O'Flynn was grateful for my reassurance, but we both realised that we were embarking on novel legal ground as there was no precedent in Britain for such a situation. That being so, one could not be certain as to the outcome—but it was clear to me that this real-life priest would go to prison rather than break the seal which had bound him and his predecessors from the earliest days of the Church.

I had again engaged Mr J Irvine Smith, Advocate, as

counsel for the defence. He was one of the finest counsel at the Scottish bar at that time—a sharp legal brain and an accomplished orator. Even now when—as a Sheriff—he has less opportunity to exercise his talent for rhetoric in court, he is in great demand as an after-dinner speaker all over the United Kingdom. As a Burns Night speaker, one requires to book him years in advance.

The Crown prosecutor and Advocate Depute was James Law.

In the course of the first day's evidence, Father O'Flynn was called by the Crown and gave the preliminary facts in his evidence. The crowded court hushed as he was asked by the Advocate Depute, for the Crown, if he had been told by the dying woman how she had come by her injuries, and who had caused them.

His answer was 'Yes.'

'And what did she say?'

The priest said that he was not empowered to divulge this information. 'It is in the nature of a confessional secret,' he told the Advocate Depute.' 'I can say nothing about what passed between Mrs Daniels and me during the confession.'

One could have heard a pin drop in the courtroom.

Father O'Flynn went on to outline the irrevocable confidentiality of the Confessional Seal.

'This is a serious charge of culpable homicide,' the Advocate Depute warned him.

At his point, Mr Irvine Smith intervened to take up cudgels on behalf of the priest, and an enthralling legal debate took place—in the absence of the jury, who had been asked to retire while legal points were discussed. There was no legal precedent and so no previous case and ruling to which one could refer for guidance.

The trial Judge, Lord Patrick, listened intently to the arguments put forward by both sides—and then ruled that the court could not compel the priest to answer the Advocate Depute's question. A greatly relieved Father O'Flynn left the witness box, and the Crown case was thus stripped of evidence which might have been of value to either side. And no-one but the priest knew which.

Juries are not allowed to speculate, and so the evidence had to be disregarded. For all the court knew, Mrs Daniels might have indicated that a complete stranger had been responsible and that he had entered the house after knocking on her door. On the following day, the defence led no evidence but argued strongly that the Crown case could not be proved to the necessary standard. After retiring for three hours, the jury returned with a unanimous verdict of Not Proven and Daniels walked free.

Afterwards, he told the Press 'The death of my wife was a deep loss to me. I just don't know how she was injured.'

Looking back, I am pleased that the judge was not a Catholic, although he must have known nevertheless that a priest would risk imprisonment rather than break his vow to the Church. The ramifications might have been better known to a Roman Catholic judge (at that time there were two) but the important legal precedent established in the High Court that day is most unlikely to be overturned.

Incidentally, the position of a solicitor who has been given information by a client is much more straightforward. Conversations between solicitor and client are of an extremely confidential nature and the solicitor can never divulge such information without the consent of the client concerned. I wrestled with this problem myself for a number of years, after confidential information was imparted to me by William 'Tank' McGuinness in connection with the plight of another client, Patrick C Meehan. It was only after the death of McGuinness, in March 1976, that I felt that I was in a position to divulge the considerable confidential matter gleaned from my erstwhile client. Even then, I took the precaution of having Minutes of Waiver signed by McGuinness's next of kin, who were in full agreement that the police should be advised.

I also requested the Law Society of Scotland to agree that such material should be made public, in order to try to bring to an end Meehan's lengthy and wrongful incarceration. Two months after the death of McGuinness, Meehan was pardoned by the Queen.

I have come across an interesting historical trial with circumstances similar to the trial of Henry Daniels.

In March of 1649 John Dick and his wife, Janet Alexander, were charged and tried with 'crewall murthour by poyssoneing' of one William Dick, John's brother, and Margaret, his sister. The allegation was that both victims were poisoned with arsenic during the previous month and that the poison had been put into bannocks, which had been eaten by them.

Both accused, in late February of that year, had confessed their guilt to their Church of Scotland minister, James Edmistoun (of St Ninian's, Stirling) before any suspicion had fallen upon them. The minister was quick to advise the criminal authorities of the confessions, and the Dicks were promptly detained and charged with murder.

The minister gave evidence for the prosecution at the trial, after which they were found Guilty—with 'mitigating circumstances', in that they had confessed to the minister without pressure, and before they had been suspected. As a result of this, instead of being hanged by the neck, they were given the preferential and more merciful treatment of having 'thair heads struckin fra ather o thair bodeis at Castell Hill, Edinburgh.' In addition, all their movable goods were forfeited to the Crown.

One notices that the effect of their admission to a Kirk minister was very different from the situation when a statement was made at the time of confession to a Roman Catholic priest. The circumstances of the seventeenth-century case, of course, were in line with the Kirk's avowed association with the civil power in the investigation of crime.

11
The Go-Between

Glasgow scrap-metal merchant Alexander Gordon got himself into a complicated legal pickle when he set out to play 'middleman' in a deal involving three-and-a-half tons of stolen metal. In the end, I was called in to help Mr Gordon, who was by then facing charges of attempted extortion and 'resetting'—that is, receiving goods knowing these to have been stolen. It turned out to be yet another of these cases without exact legal precedent. I found it fascinating, and I spent many days researching ancient cases, seeking legal interpretations.

Gordon was a licensed metal refiner, with business premises in Glasgow, who had authority to purchase for resale various scrap metals from business sources or members of the public.

Obviously, there exists a danger that such a person may be offered materials which can reasonably be considered to be stolen, or otherwise unlawfully obtained—in which case he must comply with certain conditions under which the licence was granted, and pass all relevant knowledge to the police. Frequently, in the past, my client had assisted the police in this way and had given evidence occasionally for the prosecution.

On a Monday afternoon in March 1976, a man who would only give his name as 'Willie' came to Gordon's premises. He asked Gordon to make him an offer for a quantity of nickel which, he claimed, was in excess of three tons and was worth about £2000. He produced a sample—two small welding electrodes—and said that the rest was all in a similar condition. My client told him that he was suspicious as to the origin of the electrodes, knowing that the value would be considerably more than 'Willie' had said. In addition, 'Willie' would not give his surname and address, which was even more sinister. The whole transaction smacked of a thieves' bargain, and Gordon was not interested.

At this stage, 'Willie' declared that the nickel was contained in a three-and-a-half-ton parcel of welding electrodes stolen from a well-known electrics firm in Glasgow about a month before. He had paid £1500 for the load, which had a retail value of some £15 000, and had hoped to find a market whereby he would make a sizeable profit. He had since discovered that there was more hope than market, and he was somewhat frustrated about the whole matter.

'Willie' had tried various firms but had been unable to dispose of the load, and the strain of keeping the goods in his garage was taking its toll. He was now at the stage of desperation and wished to abandon his 'get rich quick' scheme and try merely to recover his outlay—with a reduced profit of £500—by selling the metal content as scrap.

Gordon told him that as far as any self-respecting dealer was concerned the material was worthless and that he in particular had no intention of jeopardising his licence by handling stolen goods.

'Willie', by this time a very agitated man, said he would dump the whole lot in the canal, where it would be lost for all time. The threat distressed Gordon, who realised what a considerable loss this would be to the owners, or their insurance company.

The only sensible avenue left open to 'Willie', Gordon told him, was to explore the possibility of getting a reward from the firm for the return of their property. Gordon knew that this was often done in the trade, and that normally the figure was ten per cent of the total value.

At first, 'Willie' was reluctant to fall in with this suggestion, mainly because his deep involvement in the matter might be magnified by this action. It would be safer to dump it all in the canal and destroy all the evidence against himself. Knowing this threat to be a real one, Gordon suggested that he should make enquiries himself at the owner's premises first, to confirm that there had been such a theft from their premises and that the quantity, description and value of the property were accurate. He would also explore, he said, the possibility of embarking on an exercise which, hopefully, would result in recovery of the goods and a reward of at least ten per cent of its total value.

An additional motivation for Gordon was the hope that his intervention might assist his relationship with the firm involved and bring about a reasonable business connection with them.

Reluctantly, 'Willie' agreed and said that he would telephone Gordon within the next forty-eight hours to find out what was happening. In the meantime, he said, he would not dump the electrodes.

The following morning Gordon telephoned the Scottish managing director of the firm and arranged an immediate meeting with him. Gordon told him of 'Willie's visit—and the theft was confirmed, as well as the value. The firm's official told Gordon that he had suffered many sleepless nights since the theft, as there had been a manufacturing loss of £10 500 incurred by his firm, the material not being insured. He was more than relieved to hear that the goods had not been disposed of and that there was a real possibility of their return. He asked Gordon if he had any idea of the size of the reward 'Willie' expected and Gordon said that he had quoted a figure of £2000—but that he felt that 'Willie' would be satisfied if he recovered his outlay of £1500.

Gordon was told that authority to offer a reward would require to be sought from Head Office in London, and that the matter was already in the hands of the police. Both Head Office and the police would have to be contacted, said the Managing Director.

Gordon told him that he could contact the police if he wished but that he, Gordon, would not be able to help them very much at that moment as he had to wait until

'Willie' contacted him. He had no idea of the whereabouts of the electrodes at that time.

A second meeting was arranged for later that day with the Chief Security Officer for the firm, who confirmed that it was common practice within his organisation to offer a reward for information leading to the recovery of stolen goods, but repeated that only London Head Office could agree such a figure. The amount, subject to ratification, would be ten per cent of their estimation of their value. The offer could be reduced if any of the material was found to be damaged.

Gordon was also told that the reward would only be paid after the goods had been returned to the firm and he was again advised that the police would have to be notified—to which he agreed.

An arrangement was then made whereby the two parties would obtain from London a Letter of Commitment to make the appropriate payment to Gordon, who stipulated that the reward should be paid by cheque, made out to his own firm. The security officer asked Gordon for the name and address of 'Willie', but was told that he was totally unaware of these details. The meeting ended with Gordon being told that he would be contacted by telephone as soon as the letter of authority arrived from London at the Glasgow office.

Later that day 'Willie' telephoned Gordon and arranged to meet him at a local hotel. 'Willie' was brought up to date with developments and was told that Gordon was confident that the tentative agreement would be ratified in the near future. Gordon also told him that the figure he could expect would not be £2000, but probably £1500.

'Willie' was having second thoughts by this time, and said that the risk of taking the material from his garage to an agreed handing-over place might be too great. Besides, the reward was a small price to pay in return for information which only he had. However, on the principle that half a loaf was better than none, he agreed— but insisted that the deal must be concluded soon. As soon as Gordon had confirmation that the letter of autority was with the firm in Glasgow, he would be told where the material would be left for collection.

There was no word from the firm on the next day, Wednesday. On the Thursday the firm telephoned Gordon and told him that the letter had not been received because the only person who could approve such action was not expected home from abroad until that afternoon. Gordon, they said, would be told the following day. Gordon said that the matter was now extremely urgent and action would need to be taken soon if the goods were not to be destroyed.

Early on Friday 'Willie' telephoned Gordon and asked if the letter had been received. He was told that the authority should be received later that day. A note of desperation was then detected in 'Willie's' voice, so much so that Gordon promised to telephone the firm within the next half-hour.

'Willie' told him that the goods were still loaded in a lorry at 'Willie's' garage, and that he proposed to dump them during the hours of darkness that evening. Gordon told him to hold off, and said he was certain that the authority to pay the reward would be in the hands of the Glasgow office by next morning. He then telephoned the firm and was told that the document had been mailed in London that day and would arrive in Glasgow on the Saturday morning.

Shortly after midnight 'Willie' telephoned Gordon again and was given the good news. He was told that he had nothing to gain by taking drastic action at that stage—and, accepting Gordon's assurances, 'Willie' told him where the load would be deposited early that morning. He gave Gordon directions as to the exact location—Lumloch Pit, off Robroyston Road—where he would find the goods covered by a tarpaulin.

On the Saturday morning, Gordon went to the premises of the electrics firm and met the same two people, who produced the document. Gordon was at once told that the reward figure was to be £1000—that is, ten per cent of the wholesale, as opposed to the retail, value of the goods. Unknown to Gordon, the police were hidden within the premises and listened to the conversations.

Gordon read the letter, which ran 'With reference to your telexes of 9 and 11 March, we are prepared to offer a *pro rata* reward for information leading to the recovery of the stolen property and the apprehension of the persons responsible.'

This document was properly signed on behalf of the firm.

Having read it, Gordon expressed the view that it was a worthless document, in as much as a *pro rata* reward could mean ten pence or a packet of crisps—and even that could be withheld if the thief or thieves were not arrested and convicted. He was asked what alterations would make the agreement acceptable to him, and said that for *pro rata* should be substituted the figure of £1000, and also that the words 'and the apprehension of the persons responsible' should be deleted.

This was agreed on the spot and the alterations were initialled by all parties present. In addition, it was stipulated that the letter should be re-addressed to Mr Gordon at his business premises. Gordon also insisted that, as well as the initials, the signatures of those present should be appended to the document.

Gordon then explained that he had changed his mind about the method of payment, and said that for tax reasons he should be paid in notes as the money was not coming to him but to 'Willie'. There was no reason why he should pay tax on this transaction as he was not a beneficiary. This was also agreed.

Gordon then suggested that he would expect to have a reasonable business relationship with the firm in future because of the risk he was taking in assisting them to recover their property. He then took the principal copy of the agreement, saying that he would deposit this in his safe en route to the site where the material had been left. He asked the two men to follow his car, which they agreed to do.

He was not to know at that stage that the firm's car would also be followed by a police car with the CID officers who had listened in to the conversation.

Gordon drove from the premises in his white Capri for about a mile and a half, and stopped at his own yard. He was away for about two minutes (the time it took to lodge the document in his safe) then returned and drove off. He went right across Glasgow, over the Kingston Bridge and towards the Springburn and Bishopbriggs area. At one point he seemed to get lost, missing a turning and negotiating a U-turn, and then travelled along a narrow country road, finally turning off into what seemed to be a quarry—according to the Chief Security Officer, who was following.

Gordon got out of his car, opened the boot and took out a fluorescent orange parka and put this on.

The goods could be seen stacked nearby, covered with heavy tarpaulin sheets. It was noticed that under the sheets everything was dry, although the ground in the quarry was wet. The two officials from the firm examined the electrodes and confirmed that they were, in fact, the stolen items. The parties were discussing transport for these goods when a grey Mini van appeared on the scene and two CID officers got out and, making themselves known to Gordon, apprehended him.

They took his name and other particulars—as well as the particulars of the two officials, although these details were already known to the policemen. Gordon was then charged with attempted extortion or, alternatively, reset of the goods, to which he replied 'I am helping them to recover their stolen property.'

Gordon was taken to Pollok police station, where he was questioned about the whole matter. He was then charged again and replied 'I deny both charges.'

I was consulted shortly after his arrest and represented him at his first court appearance, when bail was fixed.

The trial did not take place until about two years later, in Glasgow, before Sheriff Gerald Gordon, QC, and a jury. Sheriff Gordon seemed to me an excellent choice for what was to be an unusual case of this type, being a former professor of Criminal Law and author of two editions of a first-class textbook on the same subject, entitled *Gordon on Criminal Law*.

There was little cross-examination of the Crown witnesses, as most of the evidence was agreed by the defence. This was not to be an issue of credibility but an exercise on the application of the law on reset. Both officials of the firm agreed with me that, as far as Gordon was concerned, a proper legal agreement had been concluded. Their ultimate intentions and bringing in the police were not known to the accused; not even suspected by him. They both agreed, too, that Gordon had seemed to lose his way en route to the pit and appeared to be following instructions as opposed to having first-hand knowledge of the site.

Throughout the proceedings, they said, Gordon appeared not to wish to see the electrodes destroyed by being dumped in water. It was clear, too, that the electrodes had not been long at the pit—the covering tarpaulins had not been disturbed by the elements and the items were dry.

The police evidence given by Detective Chief Inspector Long and Sergeant Russell covered the replies made by my client when he was charged at the site and in the police station.

They said that while listening to the conversation between the officials of the firm and Gordon on the Saturday morning they had heard Gordon say 'I am in a cleft stick—I do not want to be held responsible for theft.' On my pressing them, they recalled his saying that he was doing it as a favour to the company and by doing so could get himself into trouble with the police.

They also recalled Gordon saying that he was in a position akin to someone burgling their homes and then attempting to blackmail them for the return of the property. In addition, he had said that payment must be in notes, because he did not wish to pay corporation tax in respect of any cheque issued as he would not benefit from the transaction.

At the end of the Crown case I called my client as a witness and took him through his evidence. He was questioned closely by the Fiscal, but steadfastly denied that he had seen the goods at any time before the company officials did so. To me his evidence seemed to be of a high standard, and when he left the box I closed my case, intimating to the Sheriff that I wished to debate the law applicable to the evidence—and that this should be done outwith the present of the jury. The Sheriff agreed.

I argued that, for certain valid reasons, there was clearly insufficient evidence to warrant the matter proceeding to the jury for their consideration. The issue, I said, was not one of fact but one of law and was, therefore, the responsibility of the Sheriff, not the jury. In other words, I was asking the Sheriff to hold that Gordon was Not Guilty as a matter of law.

When one wishes this course to be taken one must accept the veracity and truthfulness of all the Crown witnesses—ignoring the evidence of the defence—and argue that, having done this, there is clearly no case to answer in law.

By the time of the trial the charge of attempted extortion had been abandoned and the case had proceeded purely on the charge of reset, which was less serious. The definition of reset is 'the retention of goods obtained by theft, with the intention of keeping them from their true owner.'

The Fiscal argued that Gordon had been in constructive possession of the goods, in that he knew where they were and had taken the officials to them. I retorted that, as matters had turned out, he had known where they were because he had followed the instructions given to him by 'Willie', who had never been traced. If 'Willie's' information had been incorrect, Gordon could not have led them to the stolen material. As to the possible possession of the goods at the pit, I argued that at that stage the goods had ceased to be stolen: they had, in fact, been recovered by someone acting for—and in the company of—the owners.

It was also argued that, from the accepted circumstances, Gordon was acting as an agent for the company. Was there not written authority for this proposition?

To sum up: instead of being privy to the retention of goods from the lawful owners—the essence of reset—

was Gordon not, surely, privy to the return of the goods to the proprietors and were not his actions meritorious, as opposed to being criminal? I pointed out that there had been nothing clandestine in Gordon's approach and, indeed, he had been frank and open, having dealt with the Scottish boss of the company.

'The circumstances constituted a most interesting and unusual twist, quite dissociated from the norm, and an unbiased look at all the evidence clearly supports, this,' I said.

Hard as I had tried, I had been unable to find a previous case on all fours with that one—but, after reviewing the principles of our law governing reset, the Sheriff agreed with me. He withdrew the case from the jury, directing them that they must unanimously find the accused Not Guilty on a matter of law. At this point he gave it as his opinion that the prosecution might have been in a slightly better position had they proceeded with the original charge of attempted extortion. But he agreed that, even in this event, it would have been impossible to infer that the accused had a guilty and criminal intention in his mind. This charge, too, would have foundered.

Gordon was discharged from the dock, cleared of the charge.

Some days later I sent for Gordon and asked him if he wished me to pursue the contract in the civil courts and sue the firm for the sum of £1000 which had not been paid over to him. After reflecting on the matter, he decided against doing this. He felt that, at the very least, they had arrived at only a gentleman's agreement—and although somewhat bitter about their reluctance to honour it, he was relieved at the Not Guilty verdict.

He would settle for that, he said.

I remember being on duty at Glasgow Sheriff Court, interviewing a person charged with breach of the peace. It had been a busy day, and the time allotted to each interview had been about two minutes—sometimes less.

In the limited time available, I had formed the impression that this client was an average type.

As he entered the dock, the Clerk of the Court asked me how he wished to plead. I retorted 'Not Guilty.' I then moved for bail.

The Fiscal stated at this stage that, from his psychiatric evidence, it was clear that the accused was of unsound mind and unfit to plead to the charge. He asked that he be detained in Leverndale Hospital for additional psychiatric reports. I immediately stood up, somewhat affronted, and stated that I had interviewed the accused and was astonished at the suggestion made by the Fiscal. I had had much experience in these courts, I said loftily, and had more than a rough idea as to the state of mind of persons I had interviewed.

I had hardly finished when the accused in the dock began to whistle a plaintive melody. I looked around at him. He was staring at the austere courtroom ceiling, quite unconcerned by events. He seemed more interested in the tune he was trying to put across.

I hesitated—and appreciated that, perhaps, my first assessment had been incorrect. I sat down.

My client, discontinuing his whistling, clenched his fist and shouted that he would annihilate the Fiscal in a 'square go'. He then proceeded to refer to the Fiscal in most disreputable and defamatory terms, and was hustled from the dock by two policemen.

Sheepishly I decided not to oppose the Fiscal's motion for detention pending further psychiatric reports.

12
Chain of Evidence

On a bitterly cold October morning in 1974, four people huddled together at Glasgow Airport and waited to climb aboard a helicopter. They were Mr R E G 'Bobby' Younger, Advocate (now a Sheriff in Falkirk); Mr Michael McDonald, my office manager; my legal assistant, Murray Macara; and my brother, Ray Beltrami, a photographer with the Glasgow *Evening Times*. I myself was engaged in Glasgow High Court and was unable to join the expedition.

They were all there to use a helicopter for the first time ever in preparing a case for the defence in Scotland—the case of Kenneth Burnett, who was charged with murder of a twenty-four-year-old woman. Special permission had been granted by the Law Society of Scotland (Legal Aid section) to hire a helicopter on Legal Aid, and off they went to fly over the scene of the crime—farmland on the banks of the River Gryffe just outside Glasgow.

My brother was there to take aerial photographs of the area as part of our determined attempt to rebut formidable forensic evidence which would be brought against my client. In this case the value of forensic evidence was shown to be considerable. Indeed at times forensic evidence can be stronger than even eye-witness or direct evidence. It is difficult to 'cross-examine', and each piece of forensic evidence forms a link in the chain of circumstantial evidence which can finally enmesh the accused.

During the mid-afternoon of Sunday 18 August 1974, a fifteen-year-old schoolboy went for a walk on the north bank of the River Gryffe in Renfrewshire. As he walked along the river bank near Barnhill Farm, Inchinnan, he saw a jacket floating in the river—and then he was able to make out first the leg of a girl and then her head. She was lying face down in a bed of reeds at the river's side.

The police were notified. They discovered that the dead girl was Catherine Galloway, a twenty-four-year-old machinist. Her body had been protected from the current of the river by the reeds in which it had been lying. There were signs that she had been sexually assaulted, and her trousers and pants were round her ankles. Buttons on her waistcoat were missing, the buttonholes were ruptured and her bra was torn. It was estimated that she had died between twenty-four and forty-eight hours prior to the discovery of her body.

When the police began their enquiries into the murder they found out that on the Friday evening, 16 August, Catherine Galloway had gone to The Doctor's public house in Paisley Road West, Glasgow. The pub was run by Catherine's aunt, and Catherine was at the bar in the company of a number of her relatives. It so happened that another relation of the landlady's was in the bar that Friday—Kenneth Burnett, who was actually a distant cousin of Catherine Galloway, although they were introduced for the first time that night.

Because it was a family gathering, the group stayed on in the public house after closing time, remaining on the premises until about eleven o'clock. The gathering then broke up, and most of the people departed in taxis.

At that point Catherine Galloway decided not to go home with the others, but to remain in the company of Kenneth Burnett. When her relatives last saw Catherine, she was standing on the pavement outside the pub, talking to her new-found cousin.

It was, of course, one thing to establish that Burnett had been seen with Catherine Galloway outside The Doctor's late on the Friday night—but what the police needed was evidence that would connect Burnett with

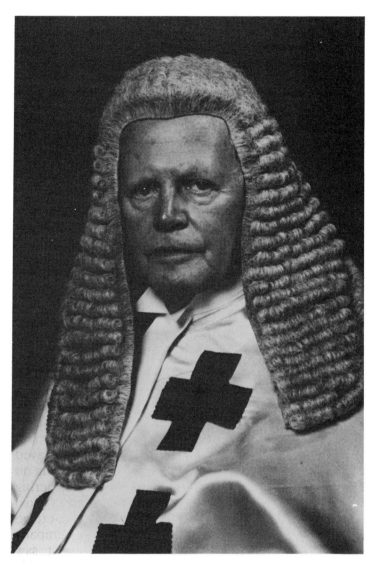

The Rt Hon Lord Wylie

the scene of the crime. There were to be no eye-witnesses to say that Burnett had been seen at Barnhill Farm when Miss Galloway met her death. But the evidence that *was* produced—which led to Burnett being charged with her murder—was of an interesting and unusual nature, and it led to a far-ranging investigation by the defence also.

The police knew that Burnett lived with his parents in Erskine. There had been a suggestion at The Doctor's that he was going to take Catherine to his house for the night.

At 2 a.m. on Monday 19 August Detective Chief Inspector Paul Newell and another police officer called at Burnett's house. Burnett was told that enquiries were being made into the death of a young woman and was asked to accompany the officers to Paisley police office. There Burnett was handed over to Detective Chief Superintendent Arthur Bell.

Mr Bell told Burnett that he was making enquiries into the death of Catherine Galloway, and Burnett apparently replied 'I don't know what you are talking about. I don't know her.' On being informed that relatives of the girl had seen him in her company outside a pub, Burnett said 'You mean the wee blonde bit? You're not on. I left her at the bus garage at Inchinnan.' He added 'I'm in the clear. Check at the bus garage, and you will find I tried to get her a taxi. She was coming home with me and the bus from Glasgow only went as far as Inchinnan. I tried to get a taxi, but they wouldn't let me use the phone. She changed her mind and wouldn't go any further, and I left her to walk. She walked away in the opposite direction at about one o'clock.'

At this stage Mr Bell left Burnett with Detective Superintendent Meldrum while he went to check on the details Burnett had given him. Burnett then asked Mr Meldrum where the body had been found and what condition it was in. After a few minutes they began to talk about football. In the course of this discussion, apparently, Burnett—having already mentioned that he had cartilage trouble—suddenly said 'Look, man, how could I climb these fences with my knee?'

This remark struck Mr Meldrum as being extremely significant, since the place where the body was found could only be reached by climbing over a number of fences—and there had been no mention of fences up to this point in the conversation. Accordingly, he sent for Mr Bell, and Burnett was charged with the rape and murder of Catherine Galloway, to which he replied 'What a load of——. There is only one witness and she is dead.'

It should be noted that later, at his trial, Burnett was to deny strenuously having made these comments to Meldrum. What the police were trying to show, of course, was that Burnett had been with Catherine Galloway after leaving the bus depot and that he had been at Barnhill Farm. These remarks in the police office indicated that this was indeed the case.

The three places of significance—the Western S M T bus depot at Inchinnan, Burnett's house at Erskine and Barnhill Farm—formed the points of a triangle about five square miles in area.

A number of roads lead off from the bus depot at Inchinnan. The A8 Glasgow-Greenock road runs westwards, towards the Red Smithy roundabout. It is possible to walk to Barnhill Farm from the garage along this road—a distance of two miles. Then there is the Old Greenock Road, leading north-westwards from the garage—the direct route to Burnett's house, just over three and a half miles away. From Barnhill Farm to Burnett's house was a distance of almost four miles, by way of the Red Smithy roundabout and the A726 Paisley–Erskine Road.

The Crown case was prepared by Mr John Skeen, then Procurator Fiscal at Paisley, later at Glasgow.

The prosecution managed to trace a witness, Mr James Mitchell, who said he had been driving home at 1 a.m. when he saw a couple walking on the Old Greenock Road towards Bishopton. The man turned round and thumbed a lift, but Mr Mitchell did not stop. Mr Mitchell subsequently identified the man as Burnett. He said that the man had had his arm round a girl's shoulder at the time.

Police officers also interviewed a number of witnesses at the garage, who said that Burnett had enquired about buses for Erskine and was told that the last bus had gone. They said he had a young girl with blonde hair with him, and that the couple left the garage saying they would walk to Erskine.

As agents for the defence, we questioned the geographical link between the garage at Inchinnan, the murder spot and Burnett's house at Erskine. We decided to look at the scene from the air and to take aerial pictures—and that was the reason for the helicopter expedition. A series of photographs was taken, which proved to be of considerable value at the trial and which Lord Wylie, the trial judge, described as 'these rather excellent aerial photographs on which the Crown relied as much as the defence.'

The evidence led by the prosecution at the trial, in an attempt to connect Burnett with the body and with Barnhill Farm, was of such a diverse nature that the preparation of the defence involved investigation across a very wide range—although none of the enquiries was as spectacular as the helicopter flight.

There was another unusual aspect to the case: we approached the Crown to have the trial adjourned from the High Court sitting of November to that of December to allow more time for preparation. Extensions of the hundred-and-ten-day rule—which limits the time an accused can remain in custody pending trial—are rare in Scotland, and indeed unique when the defence requests one! But this we did and it was agreed. We made full use of the extra month.

When the police first examined the body they noted a mark on her chest, above the right breast, which they suspected was a bite mark. The mark was one of the usual size and shape seen in human bite marks, and some of the more damaged areas towards one side of the mark could have been caused by human incisor teeth. However, after examinations carried out by Mr Donald

MacDonald of the Dental Hospital in Glasgow—in which he compared the marks of the supposed bite with impressions taken of Burnett's teeth—Mr MacDonald concluded that he could find no characteristics present. There was, in fact, some doubt expressed by pathologists that the mark had been caused by a bite at all!

I had, however, taken the precaution of having Burnett make a declaration at his first court appearance at Paisley. 'I am entirely innocent of this charge,' he said. 'I wish to have impressions taken of my teeth for comparison purposes.'

The post mortem on the deceased concluded that death in this case was due to asphyxia caused by manual compression of the victim's neck. In evidence, Dr Walter Weir said that Miss Galloway was very close to death before she had been immersed in the water. He added 'At that moment there is evidence that she was still alive, because there was a small amount of water in her lungs to indicate that she had breathed once or twice. I think she was more or less dead anyway when she went into the water.' He added that even if she had not been put into the water, she would still have died.

A vaginal swab had revealed that sexual intercourse had ocurred—probably within four hours of her death.

In presenting the case against Burnett, the Crown relied heavily—indeed, overwhelmingly—on the remarks alleged to have been made by Burnett to Mr Meldrum, and also on the evidence of Mr Mitchell having seen Burnett on the road to Erskine with a blonde girl. The Crown, however, sought to go further than this, and produced a considerable quantity of forensic evidence that attempted to connect Burnett with the deceased and the locus.

They claimed that they had found three dock fruits, a number of chickweed seeds and some grass fragments in the turn-ups of the trousers Burnett had been wearing on the night he had gone to The Doctor's. The police said that they had noted grass fragments on his jacket and two cat hairs on the trousers. But, as Lord Wylie pointed out in his charge to the jury, although the deceased had a cat no-one was disputing that Burnett had been in her company that night. There was also a cow hair on Burnett's trousers—but it would not be surprising to find cow hairs on the clothing of someone who lived in the country.

We covered all the ground (sometimes literally!) that the police did, and more. We consulted Mr Basil Ribbons of the Department of Botany at Glasgow University, and on the day before the trial he went with Mr Macara on a tour of the lanes and fields of West Renfrewshire. Fortunately for the defence, this demonstrated that dock fruits, chickweed seeds and grass fragments of the type examined by the Crown were not confined to Barnhill Farm, but existed all over the area—even in Burnett's own garden! Another strand in the Crown case had been eliminated.

The Crown was also attempting to establish some link between the accused and the deceased by blood grouping. In an attempt to link Burnett with the sperm sample, the Procurator Fiscal at Paisley, John Skeen, presented a petition to the Sheriff at Paisley, asking to obtain a sample of blood from Burnett.

The aim was to determine not just his blood group, but also whether he was a 'secreter'—that is, whether he belonged to that part of the population whose blood grouping can be discovered not just in their blood but in all their secretions, whether urine, saliva, sweat or even semen.

When Dr William Tilstone of Strathclyde University attended Barlinnie to obtain the blood sample, Burnett—who was, presumably, suspicious about the need for the sample and did not wish to provide evidence against himself—resolutely refused to co-operate. I immediately went to the prison to persuade him to do so, as his refusal in the face of the petition could have been referred to at his trial and would not have helped his case.

In any event, the sample taken from the deceased's vagina indicated the presence of sperm and corresponding to the blood group 'O'. Both accused and deceased had blood group 'O'. As this characteristic is shared with about forty-six per cent of the British population, any particular significance attached to the evidence was expunged.

We went to no end of effort in this case. We wondered if the body might have been carried up the river to Barnhill Farm by the tide. Murray Macara went to the swing bridge at Inchinnan and also to the Yacht Club there to consult tide-tables and speak to people with local knowledge of river conditions—only to learn that the effect of the tide at Barnhill Farm was minimal and that the amount of water coming downstream at the time the body was found was insignificant. He also went to the bus depot at Inchinnan and checked the logs for Western S M T buses on 16 August.

At the end of the day, however, much of this effort was in vain. The crucial evidence on which the Crown relied—namely Burnett's comments to Mr Meldrum, and his being seen in the company of the girl at Inchinnan—evidently satisfied a majority of the jury beyond reasonable doubt. Burnett's defence was one of alibi— that he had left the girl at the bus station at about one or one-thirty a.m. and walked home alone. This, of course, was inconsistent with the prosecution evidence which, at the end of the day, the jury accepted.

Lord Wylie, taking Burnett's previous record into account, added a recommendation to the mandatory sentence of life imprisonment: that Burnett should serve not less than twelve years before being considered for release.

Even after sentence, Burnett maintained—as he still does, from Peterhead Prison—that the verbal evidence attributed to him by the police, in particular his alleged remarks to Mr Meldrum, was false and fabricated. The majority of the members of the jury, however, accepted the veracity of the police statements—which had, undoubtedly, been the basis of the Crown case.

13
The Leap Year Case

1972 was a leap year—which was lucky for two of my clients, at least.

Early in 1972 there was an armed robbery at the Stepps Hotel on the Edinburgh Road, Glasgow. Sawn-off shot-guns were used and about £2000 was stolen. A few days after the robbery, one of the men, James H Steele, was arrested by armed police officers. Within hours another youth was taken into custody, and I appeared for them both when they came before the court on the following day. In all, I made three applications on their behalf for bail, but these were unsuccessful—as luck would have it.

The case against each client looked strong on paper and, in particular, various confessions were attributed to them by the police—although the accused at all times denied making any such incriminating statements. However, a substantial amount of money was recovered from both men and I awaited the trial with no great degree of optimism. In addition, there had been an identification parade and several positive identifications of my clients had been made.

Eventually, after a lapse of some three months, my clients were indicted for trial at the Glasgow High Court—but on that occasion the case was not called for trial but merely deserted meantime. I was never aware of the reason for this. A fresh indictment was served on them for the next sitting of the High Court, and about a week before the start of the trial I realised that the Crown had cut matters very fine indeed. . . .

Under a nineteenth-century Act of Parliament—the Criminal Procedure (Scotland) Act, 1887—which applies to Scotland but not England, when bail has been refused to an accused he must be brought to trial within a hundred and ten days of the date of his full committal. Indeed, the trial must be concluded within that hundred-and-ten-day period. Now under a 1975 Act the trial must be merely commenced within this period.

In England, the famous precept of *Habeas Corpus* covers the situation, but very often accused on serious charges are remanded in custody for periods of up to eight months before facing trial. And on the Continent persons charged can languish for inordinate, indefinite periods before being given an opportunity to clear themselves before a trial court. (I have first-hand knowledge of this, having taken part in Spanish, French and Italian cases over the years.)

This robbery trial of ours was scheduled to start on the first day of the High Court sitting—a Monday. And, after much checking and re-checking their period of detention, I could see that the hundred-and-tenth day for my clients would be the Tuesday. That being so, the Crown had two days to complete a complicated trial involving more than fifty witnesses, numerous productions and various Special Defences of Alibi lodged by each accused.

Meanwhile, a third accused had been arrested six weeks after the arrest of the first two. Although he had surrendered himself in my presence to the police at Northern Headquarters, his bail was also refused, presumably because of the serious nature of the charge. With three accused, it seemed most unlikely that the Crown could finish the whole trial in two days.

Again and again I re-checked my calculations—and was satisfied that my arithmetic was right. I had consultations with the three counsel who were instructed for the defence and advised them of the time consideration. The third accused, of course, was well within the hundred-and-ten-day period and was not concerned in this aspect of the matter.

On the Monday, the first day of the trial, the court adjourned at 4.30 p.m. with the Crown case still far from complete. It was now an utter impossibility, I thought, for the case to be concluded the next day. Apart from the number of Crown witnesses to be called, there were also the accused and various other defence witnesses. Both my assistant, Bob McCormack, and I played the matter very close to our chests.

The next day I attended the court and made a point of trying to find out whether or not the Crown appreciated the situation. I formed the impression that they did not. Indeed, the Crown seemed confident and there was no evidence of panic in their ranks.

That day the court adjourned at 4.15 p.m. The hundred-and-tenth day would be up at midnight.

Throughout Tuesday, I must confess, I had expected the Advocate Depute to make a motion to Lord Leechman, the trial judge, to increase the hundred-and-ten-day period by at least forty-eight hours. But no such motion was made. Mind you, there would have been no guarantee as to its success, as the Crown must show cause in respect of their reasons for requiring such an extension. Extensions are in any event rare.

After the Tuesday adjournment I realised that there would be a considerable sensation in the court next day. As I was leaving, I heard two Crown officials saying that the trial would certainly be concluded on the next day, even if the court required to sit late. They had calculated the hundred-and-tenth day to finish on the Wednesday! The Crown had obviously made some kind of miscalculation. . . .

I spent the Tuesday evening at home, each moment expecting the phone to ring and a Crown representative to tell me that they had made a monumental error in their calculations. After all, a court could have been hurriedly convened at the judge's hotel for the purpose of making an extension of the statutory period. There was no such call and, as midnight chimed, I knew that the first two accused must be set free next morning.

At no time had we told the two accused of the hundred-and-ten-day rule, in case they would talk about it carelessly. I remembered a case I had had five years before, when a similar situation had occured. On the day before the trial, our counsel (Mr Nicholas Fairbairn) and I had told the accused of what would happen on the following day. When we arrived in court next morning we discovered that the Crown had come armed with old cases to argue a motion for an extension. They had been alerted to the situation—because the accused had shouted about it to prisoners in adjoining cells and police officers, hearing his shouts, had alerted the Crown authorities!

However, despite the Crown knowing our moves beforehand, the judge had upheld our motion in that 1967 case and the accused had been discharged from the dock.

That case had been interesting in that the hundred-and-ten-day period was not an uninterrupted one.

The accused, a man called Greenshields, had been arrested and charged with attempted murder of a police constable. The allegation was that he had used a hammer and had caused severe head injuries. When he appeared initially, his bail was refused, and he remained in custody for six weeks, until the Appeal Court allowed him bail. In due course an indictment was served and I appeared for him at the High Court Pleading Diet. Greenshields did not appear and a warrant was issued for his arrest and his bail forfeited.

Months later Greenshields was arrested in London and transferred to Glasgow, by virtue of the warrant issued earlier at the Pleading Diet. He was remanded in custody to Barlinnie Prison and no fresh application for bail was made. Eventually, a second indictment was served on him and he was arraigned for trial late in 1967. He had served forty-two days as an untried prisoner before being liberated on bail and had been detained a further seventy-five days between his re-arrest and the date of his trial. Mr Fairbairn and I calculated that, at the time of his trial diet, he had served a hundred and seventeen days in custody—seven days more than the legal limit!

When we appeared in court, this point was put to the trial judge, Lord Milligan. The Crown argued that the hundred-and-ten-day period must start after our client's re-arrest and that only seventy-five days had expired since that date. But it was decided by the trial judge that both periods of custody must count towards the final hundred-and-ten days and that the legal limit for holding him had expired. Accordingly, despite his careless talk in the cells, Greenshields was liberated, after the judge had directed the jury to find him Not Guilty.

In the 1972 case, therefore, we kept our intentions secret, even from our clients.

On the Wednesday—which we calculated was the hundred-and-eleventh day—counsel for the first two accused made submissions to Lord Leechman at 10 a.m. One counsel made the specific motion: 'The first and second accused have now been detained in custody for a greater period than the maximum period permitted by law. They are now entitled to be liberated and declared free for all time for the crime with which they are charged.'

The nineteenth-century Act was quoted and the Advocate Depute, Mr R I Sutherland, was very frank about the situation—and conceded that a miscalculation had been made because that particular year had been a leap year. The Crown were one day out!

Mr Sutherland then told the judge that the Crown could not oppose the defence motion, although he conceded that he could have applied earlier for an extension to the time limit. He had not, of course, done so and it was now too late.

The jury had been excluded from the courtroom during these legal arguments. When they were recalled and returned to their seats, Lord Leechman told them 'A situation had developed which you will have difficulty in understanding. Owing to some mistake, the first two accused have been held in custody for a period too long to enable you to consider their case. Accordingly, without explaining further, I have to ask you simply to return formal verdicts of Not Guilty in respect of them.'

The accused were then liberated.

These arguments did not apply, of course, to the third accused—who had surrendered himself to the police six weeks after the arrest of the first two. The trial against him proceeded that day and finished at 5 p.m. with a verdict of Not Proven.

The next day the Crown Office ordered a full-scale enquiry into the 'Leap Year' technicality. I have never heard the outcome of this probe.

There were various editorials in the national Press about this dramatic turn of events, and some writers stated that it was the duty of the defence to advise the prosecution of such a matter, since it was merely a technicality. They went on to argue that the defence should not take advantage of such a situation. My answer to this proposition is that the two accused were acquitted because of the law prevailing in our country at the time. To have advised the prosecution on the Tuesday and so caused them to make application to the Court for an extension would have been betraying the interests of both clients.

Had such an extension been granted, and had the accused been convicted and sentenced to a substantial period of imprisonment, I feel that they might have had a genuine ground of complaint against their solicitor for acting in opposition to their best interest. Defence solicitors have duties both to the Court and to their clients. The law is there for both the Crown and the defence, and Crown lawyers are presumed to know the terms of relevant Acts of Parliament. The defence is also presumed to have done its homework and, in the foregoing case, it had. It was a simple matter of arithmetic.

Needless to say, on the Wednesday morning, when they found themelves being discharged from the dock, both accused were speechless. They were utterly bewildered, as they had no knowlege of their legal position on the question of custody. It had been news to them—but good news when it came.

There have been no similar Crown 'slip-ups' since then. I believe that, in living memory, these are the only two to have occurred.

14
Gentle Johnny

The late Johnny Ramensky, the Glasgow safeblower—
known as 'Gentle Johnny' because he eschewed violence
of any kind—was a skilled and evergreen cracksman.
This skill, however, was tempered by the fact that most
of the safes he blasted open were empty or yielded paltry
sums—and that he was usually caught in the act or
shortly afterwards. . . .
They say Johnny was freed from a Scottish prison
during World War II and parachuted behind enemy lines
to blow open German safes to get valuable classified
information for the British Government. Certainly, on
the many occasions he appeared in court, this 'legend' of
Johnny Ramensky was often trotted out in pleas of
mitigation before he was sentenced.
But this colourful and likable rogue's best claim to
fame lay in his record of prison escapes. Johnny was the
doyen of Scottish prison escapers. I doubt if his escape
record has ever been equalled, far less surpassed. Why
he escaped from the famous prison at Peterhead so often
is a mystery, as he was invariably recaptured within
hours of his flight. Perhaps the secret lay in the
challenge.
Very much on Johnny's credit side was that he detested violence—and he never broke into people's
homes. His targets were banks, big shops, large offices—
whose losses, he considered, would be well and truly
covered by established insurance companies. Nor did
Johnny waste the time of the Court with spurious defence pleas, and frequently over the years he resolutely
proferred pleas of Guilty to the many charges he faced.

And Johnny was climbing roofs and blowing safes, facing charges and being sent to prison right up to the age of sixty-six!

My first contact with this celebrated criminal—even the police were known to have a good word for Johnny—came in the mid-sixties, after he had been arrested and charged with breaking into a bank in Main Street, Rutherglen—after it was closed, of course!

When he forced entry—on his own, as usual—he had with him a sizeable supply of Polar Ammon gelignite, along with the standard safeblower's equipment of fusewire, tamping sticks, detonators, gloves and so on. The amount of gelignite he used to crack the bank safe—which, as his luck would have it, turned out to be empty—was far in excess of what was needed, and the resultant explosion must have been heard at Bridgeton Cross! The blast cracked many windows in Main Street, and all Johnny's stealth until then was defeated by the noise.

Moreover, when the safe door flew open Ramensky saw to his chagrin that he had drawn yet another blank. He forced a nearby drawer for good measure—but this too offered up no loot. Such was his luck that if he had tried the next drawer he would have found many thousands of pounds in it, all in neat, crisp bundles of tens and twenties!

Although he had deftly neutralised the bank's intricate alarm system, Johnny realised that the din of the explosion would bring people to the scene and decided to flee, leaving all his equipment behind him. He raced through the back yard behind the bank and was promptly pulled to the ground from behind.

His captor turned out to be a young police cadet who immediately realised, on turning Ramensky round, that his prize was Scotland's best known cracksman. Over the years Ramensky's face had seldom been out of the newspapers, and it also featured regularly in the *Police Gazette*. Indeed, Johnny had a distinctive appearance. His was an elderly Polish face—he would be in his mid-fifties at this time—with high and prominent cheek

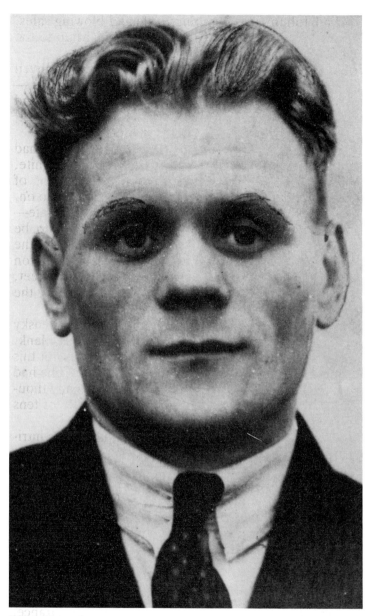

Johnny Ramensky

bones and a head of snowy-white, well-groomed hair. One can imagine the cadet's reaction—and this was his first arrest! But, of course, he was not to know that the old man never used violence.

Ramensky told me afterwards that the excited cadet struck him several times in the face while he was already lying subdued on the ground. And so, said Ramensky, feeling that the cadet had panicked on recognising him, he punched the cadet back—in order, he said, to defend himself.

When reinforcements arrived it was noticed that the young cadet had a minor facial injury. Ramensky was taken to Rutherglen police station, where he was duly charged with breaking into the bank and using gelignite to blow the safe, all with intent to steal therefrom. A second—and minor—charge of simple assault by punching the cadet was also preferred against him.

With his record of dishonesty—which included a sentence of ten years' preventive detention for breaking into a garage at Castlemilk, forcing open a safe and stealing a small sum of money—the first charge at Rutherglen was very serious. The second charge, of course, bore no resemblance to the first so far as gravamen was concerned.

Shortly after his arrest and incarceration in Barlinnie, Ramensky wrote to me and asked me to call upon him there. From our first meeting, he was frank about the serious charge—but maintained vehemently that he was innocent in respect of the minor assault upon the cadet.

'There is a question of principle here, to told me gravely. 'I have never assaulted anyone in my life.' He went on to say that he admitted punching the younster, but explained that he was simply defending himself at the time. If this were true, Ramensky's action would not constitute an assault in law, because every person is entitled to take reasonable steps in his own defence to an attack upon his person.

I subsequently got in touch with the Crown authorities and advised them that my client would plead

Guilty to the serious charge without further ado, on condition that they accepted his plea of Not Guilty to the minor matter. After all, this peccadillo—being a simple case of assault—would not have added one day more to his sentence in any event. But my proposition was refused and an indictment was served on Ramensky which arrainged him on both charges.

He was represented by Mr Nicholas Fairbairn, Q C, and we pled Guilty in the High Court to the attempted bank robbery charge but lodged a Special Defence of Self-Defence to the assault. To Ramensky's obvious and immense delight, the jury seemed to accept his evidence, because he was duly acquitted on the second charge. He received a sentence of four years' imprisonment, however, in respect of the abortive bank robbery.

When Fairbairn and I saw him in the cells below the High Court building in Glasgow, Ramensky was utterly delighted and insisted on shaking our hands.

'I have won my point,' he said. 'I would never assault anyone, and I have been vindicated by the jury.' And he started that sentence quite happily.

Years later he was again arrested, and charged with using explosives to blow open a safe within shop premises in the High Street in Lanark. The charge went on to specify that he had stolen the handsome sum of £46. And once again he wrote to me—from the usual place, Barlinnie Prison. On this occasion, surprisingly enough, he denied the charge and said that he had been nowhere near Lanark at the material time. I looked him in the eye, questioned him further, and decided that his protestations of innocence might well be correct.

He asked me to go to Lanark and try to have bail allowed for him. He could not remember the last time he had been granted bail—he must have been a boy at the time anyway! Realising that he had apparently steered clear of crime for a number of years, I went to the court at Lanark and argued bail before Sheriff M Gillies. My application was opposed by the Procurator Fiscal, and the matter took forty-five minutes to resolve. (Sheriff Gillies had been, in 1958, the Advocate Depute who had successfully prosecuted Peter Manuel at the Glasgow High Court when charged with eight murders, Manuel had been convicted of seven of them and was later hanged.)

Sheriff Gillies was somewhat sympathetic to my plea and allowed bail of £50. This was found within a few days and Ramensky was released pending trial. But before service of his High Court indictment, further disaster was to befall him—he was arrested on the roof of a large store in Ayr. He had been seen by two people from a house overlooking it. When the police arrived they found him hiding behind a chimney. He was in possession of a screw-driver and a pair of white gloves—but no attempt had been made at that stage to violate the security of the premises.

Not being in a position to charge him with an attempted break-in, the police charged him under a nineteenth-century Act—the Prevention of Crime (Scotland) Act—which applies to persons with record of dishonesty who are caught in suspicious circumstances. Very often such persons are arrested while preparing to commit a theftuous crime, although before the physical attempt of entry. The maximum sentence under this Act is one of twelve months' imprisonment because, after all, no damage is normally done to the premises concerned.

Had the police been less anxious and allowed our hero further time, they would almost certainly have caught him within the premises and would then have been able to charge him with a more serious crime.

In any case, Ramensky made his familiar trek to Barlinnie, from where the usual letter was sent and I went to see him. He told me frankly that he had been caught on the roof as he was about to attempt to gain entry to the premises. He said he must plead Guilty to the charge—and this information was duly passed to the Procurator Fiscal at Ayr. Ten days later he appeared in court before Sheriff George S Reid, and I tendered a plea of Guilty on his behalf.

There was not a great deal which could be said in mitigation—apart from emphasising the fact of his advancing years. (He was then sixty-six years old and in failing health.) It was clear to the court what my client's intentions had been and the Sheriff pointed out that only the vigilance of the police had prevented him from gaining access to the building.

I decided to take a slightly jocular approach with the Bench, and mentioned that my client 'had been seen on more roofs than the now famous Fiddler'. The Sheriff seemed to ignore this approach—which was perhaps, somewhat flippant—and sentenced Ramensky to the expected period of twelve months. I remember that, in my address to the Sheriff, I said that if Ramensky were given the maximum sentence he might not leave prison alive. These words were to prove prophetic.

Three weeks after his twelve months' sentence, Ramensky was indicted in Glasgow High Court in connection with the safe-blowing at the shop in Lanark High Street. I again instructed Mr Fairbairn to lead his defence.

I recall that Fairbairn and I had a consultation with Ramensky two weeks before his trial, and Fairbairn was impressed with his total lack of knowledge of the crime with which he was charged. He had always been frank in the past, and this factor led me to the conclusion that this time he was entirely innocent.

The evidence against him was of a wholly circumstantial nature and was basically forensic in type. Ramensky had not been seen anywhere near Lanark on the day of the crime, but the investigating officers must have formed the view that the 'job' had all the hallmarks of his work. Within hours of the discovery of the crime they had arrested him in Glasgow. They found traces of paint on a jemmy which were similar to samples of paint taken from the shop's safe. Apart from paint flakes, the Crown had evidence of certain fibres found on our client's clothing which they thought tied him to the crime, too.

Fairbairn and I spent some time on our homework in this case, as both of us had a liking for 'Gentle Johnny'. We consulted paint and fibre experts—and their reports proved very useful during the trial. Fairbairn cross-examined the police forensic experts inexorably, and completely demolished the Crown case—to such an extent that, after a day-and-a-half's evidence, the prosecutor threw in his hand.

The Crown case, as often happens, was systematically built up to look good on paper but simply could not stand the test of cross-examination based on days of preparation. Both Fairbairn and I had felt that Ramensky was nearing the end and that it was our duty to pull out all the stops on his behalf. Experts can, naturally, be somewhat biased when looking for corroboratory evidence which might fit in with evidence already available. One cannot blame them for this. But Fairbairn knew that various tests ought to be applied to forensic evidence. He knew all the modern equipment used in the most advanced circles. As the trial progressed, once could not help but feel slightly embarrassed when it became clear that such equipment had not been used, or even considered.

In any event the trial judge, Lord Keith, directed the jury to return a unanimous verdict of Not Guilty in what was to be the last trial of Johnny Ramensky.

Johnny still had about four months of his earlier twelve-month sentence to serve—the original sentence in Ayr having been back-dated to the day of his arrest. We saw him in the cells below the High Court again and he pointed out to us that it was the first time he had ever been acquitted by a jury of a safe-blowing charge!

His moment of triumph , however, was short-lived. He was already aged and ailing, clearly on the downward slope, and it was little surprise to me when the Governor of Barlinnie told me of his death there about a month later.

As irony would have it, whereas his criminal career had been a succession of sentences, one after the other, his final trial had achieved acquittal for the first time—and he was unable to benefit from it.

That day underneath the High Court, he thanked Fairbairn and me profusely, shook our hands and went happily off back to prison. We knew that we would never see him alive again.

Many years ago a black-and-white mongrel dog went missing. The owner telephoned the police and enquiries commenced. A few days later a dog of the same description was seen on the premises of another man. The police were summoned to the scene and questioned the man, who claimed that the dog was his and had been for some considerable time.

Despite his protestations, the dog was taken to the police station, and eventually a court case was instituted in the Central Police Court in Glasgow to ascertain the true ownership of the dog.

Both persons were present in court and positively identified the dog as being their respective property.

The judge, Mr Langmuir, was unable to decide on the evidence as to the proper ownership of the dog. In a flash of genius, he decided that Solomon's judgment might well fit the bill. He adjourned the hearing of the court case, at which the parties had been represented by Glasgow solicitors and dear friends of mine, Harry Bradley and Willie Glen. He had decided that there was no way of resolving the matter—apart from ordering the dog to be present in the court in the afternoon too.

With both parties present, he reasoned, the dog was bound to go to one or other of them. And he would award custody to that particular person.

At 2 p.m. the court reassembled and the dog was duly brought in. It immediately approached Harry Bradley, barked and bit him on the right leg.

The learned magistrate decided *ex proprio motu* that the dog was the property of Mr Glen's client.

And so the solemn proceedings ended. . . .

15
The Art of 'Cross'

Cross-examination is truly an art and, no doubt, years of experience of thinking on one's feet can be of great assistance. Sharpness of mind and an innate ability to appraise a situation accurately and succinctly, as well as gauging one's next move, are of paramount importance.

There are familiar axioms—such as, no question should be asked of a witness unless one is reasonably sure of the resultant answer.

I remember, many years ago—indeed, in my first five years of practice—having a Jury trial in Glasgow Sheriff Court. The charge was theft by housebreaking and the prosecution case consisted of two Detective Constables from the Northern Division who claimed to have seen my client running away from the violated premises. They were some distance away and were unable to apprehend him at the time.

The defence was that the positive identification by the two officers was either mistaken or that their evidence was fabricated and a tissue of lies. Such a defence is by no means unique.

Dutifully, I cross-examined the first officer, who was then Detective Constable Joe Beattie, later to become Detective Chief Superintendent and head of the protracted 'Bible John' murder enquiry.

The usual stock questions were asked by me—"How can you be certain of the identity of my client—after all, it was dark and you were so far away that you could not catch him?'

Beattie, wily as ever hesitated—and I pounced, with a bored glance at the jury for effect: 'Come on, answer the question—you surely understand it.' Gaining in confidence, I added, in my euphoric state, "What sort of eyesight do you have anyway?"

I didn't know he was leading me on to the punch. In his own time he looked at me with what I thought might be pity, perhaps it was disdain, and said: 'Sir, (thus giving me my place and about to put me in it) 'my eyesight is perfect. I was a night pilot in Bomber Command during the last war, demobbed in '46.'

It's difficult to follow that. I think all I said was, 'Oh.' At that point the prospect of success for my client evaporated—nay, disintegrated.

I have never forgotten the way Beattie led me to that question and answer, but I have certainly benefited from my acute embarrassment.

Many cases are won by the defence with little or no 'cross'. Regrettably, many accused do not appreciate a situation when few questions are asked.

I have heard the most appalling line of questioning put by a solicitor for a co-accused—questions merely for the sake of asking them, hair-splitting, abject, pettifogging in the extreme.

The judge, I've noticed, can be quite bored by the ineptitude of the 'cross'—sometimes losing his temper and arguing with the agent, not without justification.

At the end of the trial, with the co-accused's inevitable conviction, I have heard his client say, 'You fought like the Devil—you tried hard and you sorted out that nasty judge.'

To the unskilled, shouting and bawling about irrelevancies can often engender praise from a client, despite the fact that conviction might have been avoided had a measure of common sense been applied, together with a degree of reticence.

I suppose that half the battle is to know at the outset where you are going—up which avenue you will proceed, and to reach the end of your journey *post haste* and without aimless meanderings.

Put another way, as the maxim states. ...'Distinguish the wood from the trees.' I try, before the commencement of a trial, to set my target and aim for it as speedily as reasonably possible.

'Cross' can also be used to lay a foundation for one's summing-up. In a very recent Jury trial before Sheriff George Evans my client was charged with throwing a bottle in the direction of an opposing gang of youths (the Tiny Bison), whereby, most regrettably, it struck a young girl on the face and caused permanent disfigurement.

The girl had been standing with her boyfriend, at a bus shelter, close to the confrontation. There were about thirty youths in the vicinity and it was almost dark.

One of the Tiny Bison shouted my client's name, after which the former chased the latter's gang, the Woodhill Young Team.

Statements obtained before the trial showed that the female victim had stated that my client was seen by her to be the bottle thrower.

In her statement she said: 'I saw 'X' (whom she knew) throw a bottle in my direction. I tried to avoid it, but it came too fast and struck me, breaking on impact.'

Her boyfriend supported her statement.

The girl had been taken to Stobhill Hospital, where she had been treated that same night. While there, with her mother, she had met two police constables. The officers, in their statement, said that she had been interviewed about her facial injuries, but had told them that it was so dark that she did not know the identity of her assailant.

In the girl's evidence-in-chief to the Procurator Fiscal she told the jury exactly what she had said in her statement. She pointed to my client in the dock and identified him as the thrower.

In 'cross', I concentrated in the main on her meeting the police at the hospital.

'Did you meet two policemen at the hospital on the night of the unfortunate incident?'

'Yes,' she said, 'but they spoke to my mother mainly, not me.'

'Didn't you tell them that you could not name your assailant because it was dark?'

'No, not at all,' she said. 'I told them who had done it and so did my mother.'

I gave her four opportunities to retract (always hoping that she would not) but she simply would not have it.

She went on to say that, although dark, the street lighting at the scene had been good and she was in no doubt.

At this stage I began to wonder if the clerk who had taken the police statements could be wrong. How accurate were these statements?

The next witness called by the Crown was a Constable Frew, who told the jury that he had been at Stobhill with his mate and had interviewed the young girl. 'Yes, the mother was there.' He told the Fiscal, 'but most of the conversation was between myself and the girl. She told me that the occurrence had taken place in darkness and that she could not say who her attacker had been.'

In 'cross' he told me that she could not even describe her assailant as she had not seen him.

There were many other witnesses called, both by Crown and defence, but the material gained for my jury speech from the clear disparity in the evidence of the first two Crown witnesses proved the death knell so far as the prosecution was concerned. Even her boyfriend wilted under 'cross'.

I started my jury speech with the girl's evidence as to what had occurred at Stobhill and finished on the same theme.

As I remember saying, 'In this case no-one is more independent than Constable Frew—he has no axe to grind and no reason whatsoever to depart from the truth. If you prefer his evidence to hers, as well you might, then you start with the premise that she is quite unreliable. Yet, is she not the corner-stone and linch-pin of this tottering Crown case?'

244

The main purpose of cross-examination is to test the reliability and credibility of witnesses—prosecution or defence—and judge and jury are given the opportunity of assessing and evaluating the evidence by dint of the answers given, cheek by jowl with the demeanour and deportment of the witnesses concerned.

There are occasions when the witness is so good and so well prepared that lengthy 'cross' merely re-affirms the excellence and value of the account.

It is difficult on such occasions for the cross-examiner not to adopt a pained attitude—instead, he should appear to be quite unconcerned by the testimony and the way it has been given. Sometimes this is easier said than done.

It is always helpful if the cross-examiner fully understands the vernacular and habits of the witness. Only too often do we encounter the situation—in serious High Court cases—when the Q C from the East cannot (or will not) step down from his ivory tower and never begins to be on the same wavelength as the witness from the West. Picture the situation many years ago in Glasgow High Court. The principal Crown witness is a tough, cheeky, couthie and 'gallus' girl in her late teens. She said she met the accused 'at the dancin''. In due course, the Q C instructed by me stood up to cross-examine. I had instructed an establishment figure for my own reasons— English public school, Oxbridge ambience, and member of the Queen's Own Archers.

'Miss X,' he said, in an accent that could be cut with a knife, 'did you say that you met my client at dancing classes? Would that be at Warren's Albert, by any chance?'

Her reply was short—'Whit?'

'I repeat, *brevitatis causa*, where did you attend dancing classes? Was it at Warren's or elsewhere?'

The lass from Glasgow's duskier South-side was clearly at a loss to understand.

'Whit's that you're sayin'?'

The Q C was about to demand an answer to his question when I tugged at his gown and suggested that he ask for a brief adjournment, in the interests of sanity. Thereafter, I put it to him, with the utmost tact, that young, tough girls from the Gorbals simply did not have the money to attend dancing classes at Warren's, or elsewhere, for that matter. Whereupon the Q C told me that matters were so bad that he did not propose to address the jury in later course.

Quickly, I disabused him of that attitude and suggested that if he persisted in this line he need not return next day, and that his junior would take over forthwith. For completeness, may I finish by saying that, like General Douglas MacArthur, he did return.

Another case in point, when the wise men from the East made one of their frequent pilgrimages to the West— just to ensure that matters were in hand—was that of serious assault.

On this occasion it was the Prosecutor or Advocate-depute who collected the necessary brickbats. . . .

He was questioning the victim as to how he had received his injuries. The local worthy replied, 'See him there—there between the two polis—he smashed his way intae ma hoose, ran to the mantlepiece, picked up ma cloak (clock) an' hit me o'er the heid wi' it.'

The Prosecutor was clearly having difficulty in following the drift. He was seen to sigh and try to scratch his head (he had forgotten about his wig), then, clearly perplexed, he muttered, 'Do you normally keep a cloak draped over your fireplace?'

I will finish by giving what I consider to be the most telling piece of 'cross' that I can remember—and how it totally backfired. In 1963, Walter Scott Ellis, earlier acquitted of capital murder, had been convicted by a jury of housebreaking with intent to steal. The premises were a bakery in Bridgeton's Bartholemew Street. The charge was hotly disputed but the jury, by majority, convicted him and he was sentenced to four years' imprisonment.

Ellis was furious and constantly maintained his innocence. I, too, had grave doubts about the conviction.

Not long afterwards, threatening letters were received by the Prosecutor and the Sheriff who presided. There was one obvious suspect—and Ellis was charged in Edinburgh High Court with threatening Fiscal and Sheriff in these letters.

The letters, I may say, were vile and sinister—they threatened extreme violence to the recipients.

While giving evidence near the trial's conclusion, Ellis was shown two letter productions and asked if the handwriting were his. He looked at them in a cursory and perfunctory way, saying, 'No, not my handwriting.'

At this stage of the trial it had emerged that the Crown case had not been well prepared. In particular, the Crown had forgotten the obvious. They had not lodged in the process a known sample of the handwriting of Ellis for comparison purposes.

Goodness knows, they had been in possession of a lot of his writings—numerous letters of protest at the conviction, handwritten grounds of appeal and so on—but not a jot had been lodged in the case. Lord Grant, who presided, looked at Ellis in the witness box and said, 'Surely, Ellis, it would have been an easy matter for you to lodge samples of your handwriting so that we could be sure.'

Ellis, unabashed, looked up at the towering, six foot four inch Judge and said, 'Correct me if I'm wrong, but I thought that the defence didn't have to prove anything.'

The Judge realised the trap he had fallen into, almost dropped his pen, and said, 'You're right, Mr Ellis (note the *Mr* here), you don't have to prove anything at all.'

The skilful answer turned the fortunes of the case and encapsulated the verdict that was to follow—Not Proven.

In a recent District Court case the major Crown Witness was a Constable Boyne. After leading him, the Fiscal, a bit of a wag, shouted over to me—in a stage whisper that everyone had no difficulty in hearing—'I take it you won't be crossing, Beltrami'.

247

I have had time only to touch upon the enthralling topic of cross-examination and its effect on cases. Very often, points do not emerge until some stage of the examination-in-chief by the Crown.

Therefore, it is up to skill of the cross-examiner to capitalise on such emerging matters as best he can—all within the spectrum of the interests of justice.

I well remember 1955 and the annual Staff Officers' Conference at Camberley, Surrey. I shall never forget that conference. . . . Two months earlier, the I R A had broken into the R E M E Training Battalion at Arborfield. They had tied up the Guard and had relieved the armoury of a considerable number of rifles, Sten guns, Brens and many, many rounds of ammunition.

I had been called to Arborfield in my capacity as a Sergeant in the Intelligence Corps, in charge of Field Security in that area of England. I had interviewed members of the Guard who had been tied up by the I R A. Within 24 hours, a lorry containing a substantial number of weapons and ammunition was stopped near Epsom and several persons had been arrested in connection with the robbery. Later, a man called Murphy was sentenced to twenty years imprisonment. Naturally, security at Camberley had to be one hundred per cent, particularly as the most senior officers in the British Forces were to be present. It included General Gale, who was in charge of the British Army on the Rhine, Montgomery, Tedder and many other well-known senior officers. There was also General Gruenther, who was the Supreme Commander of the Allied Forces in Europe. Indeed, no officer below the rank of Colonel attended this conference. I had allocated to me a number of Intelligence Corps corporals, as well as a number of members of the Royal Military Police. We were all armed with revolvers and some had Stens. Security was such that all officers attending required to have a Special Pass, with a certain number thereon, and a photograph of the pass-holder.

At around 9 a.m. the senior officers entered the premises at Camberley. I was on the main door. By about 9.20 a.m. most officers had entered the premises. As I stood at the main door I noticed the famous figure of Lord Louis Mountbatten, resplendent in his naval uniform, with many decorations and an armful of gold braid. He was a handsome man. With him was his Aide—a Royal Navy Captain.

As they approached me I saw, with some concern, that Mountbatten was not displaying his Special Pass on his lapel. He approached me and I wondered what I should do. After all, everyone knew Mountbatten.

For a few anxious moments I was undecided, then, when he was within six feet of me, I said, 'Where is your Pass, Sir?'

His Aide told me that this was Lord Louis Mountbatten.

I repeated, 'Where is his Pass?'

It turned out that the Aide had left his master's Pass at their hotel in Camberley.

I said that he would require to fetch same as soon as possible, and that I could not allow him in without the Pass.

Mountbatten was extremely annoyed, and said to me,

'Sergeant, you must know who I am?'

I merely repeated that I would require to see his Pass.

Mountbatten strutted up and down the area of the front entrance and seemed to be considering the prospect of putting me on a charge. However, when he realised that I had no intention of admitting him to the premises without a pass, he shouted to his Aide to get back to the hotel at once and return with his Pass. The troubled Aide hurriedly left the scene. Mountbatten, however, continued to be less than understanding.

After some ten minutes the unfortunate Aide returned with Mountbatten's Pass. He attached it to his lapel and stormed past me into the conference. On reflection, I feel that had I not insisted on the Pass being shown, the same Mountbatten would probably have had me charged with dereliction of duty. The whole incident caused me a great deal of concern, but I feel that I did the correct thing, in that I was not, in any way, a sycophant. Yes, well do I remember the day I stopped Mountbatten, the most famous Serviceman in Britain at the time.

16
Beyond Reasonable Doubt

I do not know who brutally killed 13-year-old Tracy Main in her home at Norfolk Court in Glasgow's Gorbals. But I know who did not. . . .

It was about mid-day on a Sunday, some time in the early 'eighties, when I received a call from a distant relative of a man called Thomas Docherty—I was to go, post haste, to Craigie Street police station, where he had been taken as a murder suspect.

At Craigie Street, I was taken to a small, drab and austere interview room, where I saw Docherty for the first time. He was seated and seemed to be little troubled. Seldom have I seen a man charged with murder—he was, by that time, no longer merely a suspect—appear so exceptionally calm and unconcerned.

Thomas Docherty cut a somewhat grotesque figure. Small and heavy, he wore purple slacks and a navy-blue top. He was odd-looking—indeed, he was ugly. From his appearance it was clear that he must have a low IQ. This was soon confirmed by the conversation that took place.

At the bar counter, and before seeing Thomas, I had been advised that he had been charged with the murder of young Tracy Main—the fact of whose killing had seldom been out of the newspaper headlines in that past week.

I was told there had been no evidence of sexual attack, although her pants had been pulled down.

From the outset it was clear to me that Docherty did not realise he had been charged with murder. It was equally clear that, without difficulty, one could persuade him to say anything at all.

Yes, he knew and liked Tracy. Indeed, he resided on the same floor of the multi-storey—there were six houses on the landing. He had not been in Tracy's house on the day of the murder, although he and other neighbours were directly outside after the discovery of the body and the arrival of the C I D.

Indeed, he had partly seen into the house by reason of the main door being ajar.

I did not make much progress at my first meeting—it is more than doubtful that he realised I was a lawyer. The only reaction I got was when I mentioned the name of the person who had 'phoned me—a Mrs Hipson. He simply smiled at the mention of the name.

I left him after 15 minutes and spoke to Les Brown on my way out. Les was well-known to me as we had been quite friendly over the years, in fact, at that time his son had a summer job in my office, preparing to go to University. His rank was Detective Chief Inspector. I said, 'Les, you must have the wrong man. Thomas knows nothing about it.'

'No,' said Les, 'we have the evidence.'

I inquired further, to discover from him that details of the killing had not been divulged to the media. Yet Docherty was able to tell them the exact number of stab wounds and where the body was found in the lounge of the house.

'Did he admit the murder then?' I asked.

'No, he did not,'

I was puzzled, understandably enough, at the cryptic nature of the information.

I said to Les, 'You're aware of the horrific nature of this crime—I sincerely hope you have a strong, watertight case against him. I don't think you have. Will you not re-consider the position? If you continue to detain him until court tomorrow you might well be signing his death warrant.' No, the death penalty was not in operation at that time as the ultimate sentence for murder, having been discontinued many years earlier—what I had in mind was that the next day, when Docherty appeared in court on this murder charge, his name would be known to everyone.

In murder so foul, many members of the public jump to the conclusion that the man charged *must* have been responsible. They are not interested in the niceties of the law, the principle of innocence and the maxim 'innocent until proved guilty.'

I appreciated at this very early stage that getting off on an insufficiency of evidence was not enough—it would be necessary to prove his total innocence. If not, he would be branded, indeed hounded, for the rest of his unfortunate life.

Les simply said that he was satisfied and that Docherty would be appearing formally at the Glasgow Sheriff Court the following day. I left the station.

Next day I spent an hour with Docherty before his court appearance. The appearance in these circumstances was much of a formality in those days, lasting all of thirty seconds. Since this case new procedures have been introduced by Act of Parliament, whereby an accused, on the occasion of his first appearance in serious matters, may be questioned by the Procurator Fiscal in the presence of the Sheriff and the solicitor acting for him.

This questioning is merely to ascertain whether or not the accused has an alibi, or a special defence of self-defence or incrimination. In these proceedings he is expected to outline the basic nature of his defence with little detail. He is also questioned about the validity or genuineness of any confessions he is purported to have made. He can, if he wishes, deny making such confessions, or state, perhaps, that he made the statement under duress or force from his questioners.

The accused is also advised in advance that he need not answer any questions, but that the record of this procedure will be lodged as a production at his trial, that it may be referred to, and that his failure to answer at this, the earliest stage, could count against him.

As I have said, Thomas did not face such questioning as this was prior to the more recent Act.

Incidentally, I sincerely doubt if the questioning—had there been such—of Thomas would have resulted in anything other than a state of total confusion.

I questioned Thomas for a full hour on the Monday morning before the formality of his first court appearance. I asked him how many times Tracy had been stabbed.

'Seven times,' he replied.

I tried to discover how he could possibly know that.

'Was it not ten times, or twelve?' I asked.

'No, seven times,' was the repeated answer.

I asked him for details of the position of Tracy's body in the sitting room. He told me that she lay on the carpet near the coffee table—facing the window.

How could he know that? I was puzzled. When I asked him how and if he had killed Tracy, he said, 'No, no—she was a lovely girl.'

The formal appearance took place and that same day the name and address of Thomas Docherty was known throughout Britain.

Thomas was remanded in custody to the prison of Barlinnie, to await trial.

The period of waiting is normally three months and, in this country—as opposed to nearby England—no prisoner can be detained longer than a period of 110 days between his committal for trial and the commencement of same.

(In another part of the book I refer to the cases of Greenshields and Steele, when the trial of such persons then in custody had to be *concluded* within 110 days. Since the passing of the Criminal Procedure Act 1975, the requirement now is that the period ends at *commencement* of trial and not its conclusion.)

I saw Thomas on a number of occasions while on remand, but, to be frank, he said little that would help me.

I interviewed his few friends and some distant relatives. It emerged that, unemployed as he was, he spent

254

most of his day watching television. He sat for hours on end, watching. . . .

I talked to him about TV and eventually he told me that a news reader had announced that Tracy had been stabbed seven times. I got in touch with the BBC and Scottish Television and was given transcripts of all news items dealing with Tracy's death, up to the time of Docherty's arrest.

Then I twigged . . . an S T V news-reader, according to the transcripts, had said that Tracy had been stabbed *several* times. I asked to see the actual recording and hear the voice. S T V were most co-operative, as they usually are.

Yes—taking into account Thomas's IQ, his poor speech and even worse grasp of the English language, it could be, I decided, that he mistook the word *several*— the emphasis being decidedly on the first 'e'—for the word *seven*.

Thomas had made a mistake and the number seven had well and truly registered in his miniscule brain. That accounted for the main evidence of so-called 'special knowledge'—or knowledge known only to the killer.

From the post mortem report it was obvious, from the position (on the chest) and the number of stab wounds, that this had been a frenzied attack—and that such an attacker would hardly have counted the number of wounds.

It then emerged that before Docherty's arrest the police had had a theory that the killer might have been a male schoolmate, known to Tracy, and this would account for the complete absence of screaming. After all, the house door had not been forced—it had been opened. The C I D had interviewed some schoolboys before Thomas Docherty. No motive was ever established, although the panties had been pulled down—possibly a young pseudo-lover had panicked.

There was still the position of the body in the lounge. Thomas had been one of a number of neighbours outside the house when the door was ajar and while the C I D were talking and investigating. This knowledge could easily have been gleaned then.

I remembered my conversation with the Detective Chief Inspector months before, when I had doubted if he had a case. It was now toppling like falling debris.

There was something else which had come out at the initial police enquiry, about which I had not been told by Les Brown... well, we often keep something up our sleeve. Had I myself not done so in the shape of counsel's opinion when I had applied for the Dangerous Wild Animal licence in the Hercules the Bear case?

The CID, having learned from Docherty the number of stab wounds, asked him where the body would have lain. They went on to ask him where the knife might be—because the weapon had not been recovered in the house. Thomas had said that the killer could have gone—note the wording—to the Jamaica Bridge and thrown it into the water.

They took him to the bridge and asked him where the knife could have been thrown from. Thomas pointed to a part of the bridge. Needless to say, the area was scrupulously searched, and frogmen brought in—but, no knife.

When I heard about this line of evidence it reminded me of Walter Mitty's fantasies. The whole scenario simply was not real.

Yet, astonishingly enough, that was the Crown evidence—although the ugly, unprepossessing appearance of the accused might have assured them that they had the right person. Of course, being ugly and untidy is far removed from being a murderer.

Thomas was known as the quiet man of the tower block called Norfolk Court. His neighbours seldom saw him—as I said, he spent most of his time watching TV. When seen, he seemed to move about furtively, and was quickly nicknamed 'The Creeper'.

He was small and shambling and had the intelligence of an eight-year-old. He had moved into the tower block only six weeks before Tracy's murder. He arrived with his common law wife, a 73-year-old grandmother. He was 43 years old.

At the time of the murder, Tracy's parents were out working in men's hostels.

Although he had lived there for only six weeks, he could not tell me if it were six days, weeks, months or years. He simply did not know and his memory must have been considerably flawed. During my visits to him in Barlinnie Prison it was obvious that he did not know where he was, or that he was soon to face trial.

Two Crown psychiatrists had examined him and certified that he was sane and fit to face trial. I wondered about this, but realised that if he were to be certified insane and unfit to plead by a defence psychiatrist, then we would be doing him no favours—he would finish up in Carstairs State Mental Hospital for the rest of his natural life.

Against this now ropy and emaciated Crown case was also the fact that unremitting searches by teams of forensic scientists could not bring one adminicle of evidence against this half-witted man. Not a fingerprint, not a fibre, a hair, not a bloodstain—and there had been plenty of blood spilled.

Had Thomas committed this heinous crime, he would not, in my view, have had the ability to clean his tracks as expertly as he would require to have done in the event of his having been the assailant. Further, he had only one minor conviction, years earlier, and loved people, especially children.

I was convinced that Thomas could not murder anyone—he liked people too much, and did not possess an evil thought. The case worried me, as had the earlier case of Patrick Meehan, who was wrongly convicted and sentenced to life imprisonment for a murder he did not commit.

In both cases, I sensed that I was representing innocent men, charged with the most serious crime in the calendar.

This was a case in which there was no substantive defence to put forward—it was unnecessary so to do, as I felt that the Crown would not get off first base in its endeavours to prove the crime.

We could not plead alibi—not because Thomas was at the scene of the crime, but simply because he could

257

not remember where he had been. Almost certainly in his flat, I would have thought. His 73-year-old paramour was of little help either, so far as his movements were concerned. She too, was of low intellect, with little memory to speak of.

Earlier, I had taken the unusual step of writing to the Crown Office and to the Lord Advocate, expressing my fears for the accused—not *if* but *when* he was acquitted. I reiterated my concern about the apparent paucity of evidence. My letter proved to be prophetic—shades of the letter to the same quarter prior to the Meehan trial.

I instructed the eminent QC, Hugh Morton, to undertake the trial, assisted by a young advocate, Ian Simpson. Hugh and I had gone through University together and had graduated Bachelor of Law on the same day.

Hugh is now Lord Morton of Shuna and is a Senator of the College of Justice.

We met Thomas at the prison, and I had warned counsel in advance that Thomas could do little to help us to help him. He simply could not understand his predicament, nor the hard fact that his trial was imminent. The consultation was, accordingly, of a somewhat perfunctory nature.

Trial was fixed for the Glasgow High Court in Saltmarket, before Lord Cowie,* a Judge of then some four years' standing. He was well-known for his fairness, and I was satisfied with the formation of the court.

On the eve of the trial, neither I nor counsel—even in our wildest dreams—had any inkling as to how the whole matter would finally be resolved.

The trial started tamely rather than sensationally. The court heard how the tragedy had been discovered when Tracy's mother returned from work, found the door opened and feared something was wrong. How right she was. She went to a neighbour and, together, they found Tracy's partly exposed body propped against

---

* Scottish Rugby International—capped as wing forward against England at Twickenham in 1953. The writer cannot recall the match result.

a settee in the lounge, her feet towards the window. There were seven stab wounds, all through the heart.

Some formal evidence followed, and I looked at the accused in the dock. I will swear that he did not know where he was and that he was standing trial for murder. He fidgeted a bit in the dock and seemed to take no interest in the proceedings—so much so that I am sure he did not know that the proceedings were for his benefit.

Days earlier I had heard that there would be a contract out for my client if he were acquitted. With this in mind, I asked Thomas where he would go after he left his present place (I used the word 'place' because he simply did not know where he was). He said, 'I want to go back to my flat'. I knew that if he had his wish he would not last a week. Such was his total innocence and his belief in people, he saw no reason why anyone would want to harm a hair of his head.

Prior to the trial, Hugh Morton, Simpson and I had a second consultation—this time outwith the presence of Docherty. We went over the Crown statements carefully.

We noted that according to Les Brown's statement, after taking Thomas to Craigie Street, he cautioned him in the following terms: 'Anything you say will be taken down in writing and may be used in evidence against you'. He went on to say that he wrote the caution into his notebook at the time.

Now, if this information were correct, then the caution was invalid—because every suspect or accused person should be given a caution with the following extremely important prefix—'You have the right to remain silent. . . .'

We discussed the statement and decided that it must surely be a typographical error. Not even a junior constable would make this mistake, far less an experienced Detective Chief Inspector.

However, as a precautionary measure, I told counsel that I would check the Productions next day—in particular, Brown's notebook, which was a Production.

Next day I checked the book and saw that the precognition taken from Les was correct and accurate. There was no mention of 'the right to remain silent' in the handwritten caution.

To compound matters, Brown had said that as he verbally cautioned Thomas, he wrote it into his notebook. That being so, the verbal caution and notebook entry must correspond—they were both wrong and invalid. It proved that anything said by Thomas after this was inadmissible and would not be allowed in evidence. Far from being an emaciated Crown case, there was no case at all.

I 'phoned Morton with the good news. We knew the case was over before one word of evidence was led. Even then, I had second thoughts. If the case were dismissed because of this monumental blunder, the public would claim that Docherty had been acquitted on a technicality. In other words, 'He did it, but got off the hook thanks to C I D blunderers. . . .'

Would it not be better, I thought, for the whole evidence to come out and so prove to the public that Thomas should never have been charged in the first place? I raised this with the counsel, but we decided that we must take the point at the trial. There were no murmurings from the Crown—they had not appreciated the disastrous error. In our law, when a suspect is questioned about a crime there should be two officers present. Sometimes this might be impossible to achieve, but surely not at a police station, where there are suitable numbers of officers.

In Docherty's case, the corroborating, or second officer was Detective Superintendent Ian Smith, who was present at the caution. He, too, had entered Brown's caution in his own notebook and it was in identical tems—no right of silence.

Now we exercised *our* right to remain silent about our discovery and began to look forward to the trial and the ructions it would cause.

The Crown led formal evidence, which included TV film of the murder inquiry and transcripts of all TV, radio and Press accounts of the search for the killer. This was to demonstrate, presumably, that at no time was there mention of seven fatal stab wounds on the chest.

Then the Crown, through the Advocate Depute Alan Johnston Q C, called Detective Chief Inspector Les Brown to the stand, as they say in Perry Mason's courtroom.

Brown took the oath and gave his personal details. He said that neighbours of the Mains were suspicious of Docherty, who was extremely odd and furtive. Some neighbours suspected Thomas, not as a result of hard evidence, but because of his conduct and quaint, bizarre appearance.

Brown said Docherty was taken to Craigie Street police station for questioning. Brown said he was with Superintendent Smith, who had to leave the room for a minute. While he was alone with Thomas he said he asked the man if he had heard about the murder. Docherty told him that it was a terrible killing and that the girl had been stabbed seven times. At that, Brown shouted for Smith to come back at once. On Smith's return, the fatal caution was administered by Brown and noted in their respective notebooks.

Further questioning was to follow, but, at this stage, Morton was on his feet, like a greyhound out of the trap, objecting to the line of evidence, and pointing out the inadequate terms of the vital caution. It is to be noted that, without a caution, the further questioning would have been inadmissible, on the grounds of fairness to the accused—who, at that stage, did not have the benefit of legal advice.

There followed a two-hour hearing, outwith the presence of the jury. This is our procedure when a point of law is being argued—the jury are masters of fact, but the judge is master of law.

What followed was what has been called a trial within a trial, outwith the hearing of the jury—whereby the Judge is given all relevant evidence which will enable him to decide the point.

Brown continued to be questioned by the Depute and admitted that he had not written down in his notebook—now a production—that Docherty was entitled to stay silent. Later, he said that this part of the caution was sometimes given 'parrot-fashion' and that was probably why he had not written it. On recollection, however, he was sure he had verbally advised the accused of his right to remain silent.

In short, Brown was saying in the witness box that the notebook notes were inaccurate, but that he had remedied matters by giving the complete verbal caution at the time—'right to remain silent', too.

In cross-examination, he was asked how he could possibly remember the exact form of the caution given, particularly if he had erred in what he had written down.

Brown stone-walled by saying that he always gave the proper caution and had been administering it for almost twenty-five years. He saw no reason why he should not give the usual complete caution on this occasion.

The Crown, through Brown, were not giving up without a fight. The Depute argued that it would be for the jury to determine the terms of the caution given and that if they believed Brown they could hold that the verbal one was correct. If that were so, the written one would not matter.

The corroborating witness, Smith, was called next—still outwith the jury's presence. He said he had put down the exact caution administered by Brown to Docherty when he was called into the room, and that the caution made no mention of the right to remain silent.

He was asked to look at his notebook and read from it. In his own fair hand Brown's noted caution was repeated—no basic right to silence.

After Smith left the box—not having supported Brown—Lord Cowie asked the jury to be brought back in and said, 'It's with regret that I have to say that Detective Chief Inspector Brown is wrong in saying he administered the full and normal caution to the accused on this occasion.

I would be slow to criticise senior officers on matters of this sort—particularly when something is done in the course of a difficult, protracted and serious police inquiry. But, fortunately, I had the benefit of the evidence of Superintendent Smith, who was present at the time of the caution, and he confirmed that the caution was administered in the terms written in Mr Brown's notebook.'

He went on to rule, in law, that anything said by Docherty after this would be inadmissible. After a brief adjournment, the Depute withdrew the charge.

Lord Cowie then told the jury, 'Whatever one might think about this, it is absolutely essential that justice must be done and seen to be done. Because of this omission in the caution, that the accused was not required to answer questions, anything he might have said after that was inadmissible.' He then directed the jury to find Docherty not guilty.

The way this was done—and I make no criticism—meant that the public would assume that the conversation—no longer admissible—consisted of a confession to the crime. Nothing could be further from the truth. I had the benefit of knowing the full extent of the statement made to Brown and Smith—no question of any admission. But this knowledge has never become public until now.

I often criticise English criminal procedure, which is not on a par with ours on the all-important matter of fairness to the suspect or accused—but, having said that, Docherty might not have been brought to trial there.

Shortly after the charging process Docherty would have been brought before two or three magistrates. Evidence is led on oath, and signed depositions taken. The Crown must show its hand and, in the circumstances of Docherty, it is likely that the whole matter would have been thrown out by the magistrates on the basis that there was no *prima facie* case.

In many cases in England there is ample Crown evidence and little difficulty in establishing a *prima facie* case. In situations such as this, the Defence can agree that no evidence be led before the magistrate at the committal hearing. However, in a case of *penuria tes-*

tium, or paucity of evidence, such as in Docherty's case, we would have insisted on the Crown leading its evidence and then argued that no jury suitably directed, could possibly convict. It should never be forgotten that the onus of proof rests with the Crown and that this is only discharged in the event of proof beyond reasonable doubt—a high standard—and not proof on a balance of probabilities.

Docherty was duly discharged from the dock and, somewhat bewildered, was taken downstairs to be given his possessions before release.

We went down to see him and he confirmed his wish to return to his flat in the South Side. He was quite oblivous to the obvious dangers in store for him.

There had been further talk of a contract on his life— the cash put up by a bookmaker. I could not allow him to return to Norfolk Court.

I asked the police downstairs at the court to detain my client in the meantime. That was not a difficult task— Thomas simply did what he was told.

The court had been over for about half-an-hour when my attention was drawn to the main entrance in Saltmarket. I also looked at the side entrances in Clyde Street and Jocelyn Square. There were groups of undesirables at all the court exits. They were clearly waiting for Docherty to appear.

I remained for a further half-hour and saw that the crowds had not dispersed. There was no doubt they were waiting for the acquitted man—his not guilty verdict was not relevant to them whatsoever.

I called the police, to get rid of them, but was told that they were only standing there. They were not breaking any law.

I did not know what to do. I had never faced a situation like this before—when I was anxious to have an innocent man detained for his own safety. Particularly a man who had no thoughts of danger to himself.

In desperation, I 'phoned a good friend of mine who was head of the Serious Crime Squad. Superintendent

David Frew had not been a witness in the case, but was fully aware of the circumstances.

I told him about the 'lynch mob' outside the High Court exits and sought his good offices. I asked him to smuggle my client out of the court building and take him to Turnbull Street police headquarters for the night. This would give me time to think.

In passing, may I say that the headline in the *Daily Record* next morning was—'Freed to a life of fear'. Regrettably, there was no fear so far as Thomas Docherty was concerned—it would have been easier had there been.

Shortly after my call for help, the Serious Crime Squad arrived and Thomas was whisked away under cover as the angry crowds waited. (An orange Vauxhall Cavalier containing four detectives—one with a blanket over his head—screeched from the Court's side-entrance. Ten minutes later, Docherty was smuggled out in a red Cortina and taken to nearby Turnbull Street HQ.)

Thomas remained in Turnbull Street station for two days in complete secrecy. I visited him there. He did not know what it was all about and kept asking to go back to Norfolk Court.

While he was in Turnbull Street, I was in touch with the Social Work Department as to his future placing. I had several meetings with them.

Nothing could be done in the immediate future, so I appeared before Sheriff S E Bell in his Sheriff Court Chambers and had Thomas sent to Carstairs for a limited period of twenty eight days, as a voluntary patient. This gave me breathing space and, in the meantime, Docherty was in limbo.

Meanwhile, the Chief Constable, Pat Hamill, ordered a full-scale internal inquiry—'to ensure justice for all sides'. Questions were asked of the Lord Advocate and Crown Agent: 'Why had the Defence known of the error and the Crown not noticed it?'

Yes, the error had slipped through unnoticed by the Police, the Fiscal's department and Crown Counsel before the trial. Gorbals MP, the late Frank McElhone, raised the matter in the House.

Solicitor-General N H Fairbairn was irate about the error. He said that under new laws going through Parliament at the time, Docherty's statements would have been admissible in evidence. To date, I have no knowledge of this 'new' legislation. Indeed, I accused my old friend and sparring partner, Fairbairn, of making political capital out of my unfortunate client.

Docherty was now in Carstairs, temporarily, under Part 4 of the Mental Health (Scotland) Act, 1960. The Social Work Department acted quickly and admirably. A place was found for Thomas in England—I cannot say where—and he was taken south to a Social Work hostel, where he was allowed to work and watch his beloved TV during his leisure hours. He is still in England.

There are hard lessons to be learned from this unusual case. The focus of attention was on the error by Les Brown, and some were of the view that had there been no such error, then Thomas Docherty would have been convicted. How wrong they were. The error merely accelerated the inevitable—the acquittal of Docherty.

Error or not, the result would most certainly have been acquittal. It is clear that many pre-judged Thomas—because he was charged with an emotive, dreadful murder in the first place.

In a notorious killing, such as this, many members of the public form preconceived notions of guilt—'The police would not charge someone unless they were certain.'

It is in such horrible cases that the media cry out for the killer to be charged—on some occasions they pressurise the CID into making premature and half-baked decisions to placate the ever-anxious public.

Did this not happen with Patrick Meehan? Oscar Slater? William Watt? And many others?

Finally, in the eyes of the law, every accused person is presumed to be innocent until such time as the case against him is proved beyond doubt—let us never lose sight of this fact. No inferences should be drawn from the fact that a person is charged, nor, if the verdict is Not Proven.

The public should be properly educated in this matter—lynch mobs were for the uncivilised Far West of America, a hundred years ago. We have progressed, surely, from those wayward times and, it is hoped, benefited.

I remember, years ago, a client appearing in Hamilton Sheriff Court on a charge of indecently interfering with his young daughter. When he arrived for a formal hearing, he complained—not having been given bail—that one of the prisoners in the van taking him to court had threatened him when he learned the nature of the charge facing my client.

This was well before the trial—which brought about his acquittal.

Irate, I ascertained the identity of this paragon of virtue, whose aim was to rid the world of persons, he assumed, who were guilty of indecent assaults on children. A very commendable outlook, one would think—until one realised, as I did, that I had represented the same man five years earlier on charges of incest—which were proved in court! Talk about hypocrisy!

I could not finish without thanking Mr Fred Edwards, head of Strathclyde Social Work Department, for his good offices and for using his influence to have Thomas Docherty spirited away to safety—thus making this unique case complete.

It is interesting to note in the very recent case of James Fraser and another—both charged with the murder of David Dunn at a house in Mitchelhill, Fife—that a fairly similar point was taken by Donald R Findlay Q C who was instructed by me for the defence. Here the accused Fraser was confronted by C I D Officers at his place of employment and told that he would be detained pending further enquiries. He was then advised to the effect that he was not obliged to answer *any further questions* (apart from those requesting his name and address) but that anything he did say would be noted and would be used in evidence. Objection was taken to the caution on the basis that Fraser had not been told that he did not require to say anything in answer thereto. In short the right to remain silent was absolute and did not apply merely to the answering of questions put by the Police. The Trial Judge, Lord Mayfield, upheld the objection with the result that a statement allegedly made by the accused was excluded from the Jury—and from the case. I find it astonishing that seven years after the Thomas Docherty case mistakes continue to be made over the apparently simple matter of the terms of the common law caution. Might it be that printed caution-cards should be distributed to each member of the Constabulary? Would this step, obvious as it is, not assist in the administration of justice?

It wasn't yesterday when I represented 'Big Frank' on a charge of murdering 'Big Tam' in the Gorbals.

No lesser weapon than a large sword had been used to smite Tam—a man with many convictions, having been a money-lender, extortionist and an extremely disreputable character all round. Hence, even criminals detested Tam for his bullying activities.

My client Frank was six feet three inches tall and built in proportion. He vehemently denied the charge right from the start—the two witnesses who had picked him out at an identification parade were 'hopelessly mistaken'.

Indeed, the mere thought that Frank would need little short of a claymore to kill Tam in the first place was enough to infuriate my client.

The trial was fought vigorously, but, regrettably, the jury, by a majority, found him guilty of murder and he received the mandatory life sentence.

I spoke to Counsel and said that we would have to see him in the cells. Counsel was none too happy about this daunting prospect—and neither was I.

In trepidation, we went downstairs and I arranged for a number of policemen to be placed at strategic points around the cell area—just in case.

I vividly recall my feeling of great unease as the cell door was opened and my sheer desperation in trying to invent possible excuses for the verdict.

Big Frank emerged and declared—to our immense satisfaction and relief—'Killing that bastard, it was worth it!'

Come to think of it, that was the first time I saw Big Frank smile. . . .

The author with Hercules

17
The Trial of Hercules

There can be no doubt about my biggest client—
Hercules, who happened to be a grizzly bear.

Hercules stood nine feet tall and weighed some sixty
stones. He was born at the Highland Wildlife Park,
Kincraig, some time in the 'seventies, and was 'adopted'
by Andy Robin and his attractive wife, Maggie, when he
was ten months old and a mere thirteen stones in weight.

They built a spacious den for him behind the fine
house and Inn they owned at Sherriffmuir, near
Dunblane.

Dutifully and patiently, Andy trained Hercules.
Andy, of course, was a British Commonwealth Wrestling Champion at heavyweight, as well as being a former World Cumberland Wrestling Champion. Without
such obvious strength and wrestling skills it is doubtful
that he could have achieved what he did with the bear.

His den was surrounded by a huge fence constructed
of iron bars. Inside it were several rubber tyres, and a
few tree trunks. There was also a large improvised bath
—Hercules loved water.

After some time, Andy could control him, within
reason, although even he would concede that he could
never allow the situation to develop where he stood with
his back to the pet.

Maggie, herself a ladies' showjumping champion,
soon got to know him and took her turn at feeding him.

Years earlier, Andy had toured Canada as the Cumberland Wrestling Champion and, on occasion, had
been booked to fight a Black Bear called Terrible Ted.
Pride forced him to see the matter through and he duly
tackled the muzzled beast.

The novelty lasted only minutes, but it was, perhaps, that epic encounter which sowed the seed for his later interest in Hercules.

Not without difficulty, Hercules was trained to wear a collar and lead—and then there was the muzzle.

A large swimming area was built and he began to show off his aquatic skills. As he grew, so did his appetite: he ate like a line-up of horses.

He was allowed to run around the nearby marshland with, by now, an even fitter Andy at the end of the lead.

He would drink from a Coca Cola bottle, kiss the Robins and beg for food like a dog. He would even give a massive paw.

He was taken by the Robins in the early 'eighties to all sorts of charitable occasions and fêtes. The children, in particular, loved him and his antics. He made a number of appearances on national television, appearing on *the Russell Harty Show*. He also starred in *Kleenex Soft Tissue* adverts.

The animal was kept immaculately—well fed, with a beautiful sheen to his extravagant coat. He had a type of covered hayloft where he slept in complete comfort.

We now come to the high watermark of Hercules's public stardom. He was taken to Benbecula in the Hebrides, to star in a video film being made there.

Now Hercules, as we have said, loved water. But he had never swum in sea water. Now he did so—duly tethered by a rope to the bank.

In the relaxed atmosphere, he managed to slip his rope and was next seen by the horrified Robins swimming to a small uninhabited island nearby. He swam at tremendous speed and soon reached the little uninhabited island, thereafter to bound at high speed towards the interior and disappear from sight.

There is a clutch of uninhabited islands in this Hebridean area, separated by narrow straits of water.

Hercules remained free for twenty four long and weary days, despite frantic searches by the Robins and scores of volunteers, using small planes and helicopters.

Even the army and local police assisted in the mammoth search for the 'Big Softy', as he had been referred to in many of the *Kleenex* adverts.

There were, of course, numerous sightings—mainly false. Tales came back of huge footmarks being seen in sandy areas. The search for Hercules captured the headlines of Europe. Prayers were said for the beast, as doubts were expressed as to his condition and ability to survive in the wild. How, for example, could he satisfy his gargantuan appetite?

Eventually, he was spotted on another island by a 'copter crew. The pilot, to be accurate, spotted his ear protruding from behind a large rock.

The terror-stricken beast bolted into the open ground. The co-pilot fired several shots from his tranquiliser gun. At least one struck Hercules, who collapsed in a huge heap—unconscious and bereft of all fight.

He was netted after the 'copter landed, and transported home by way of Lochmaddy. The poor beast was in the sorriest of states—bedraggled, starving and filthy.

He had lost more than twenty stones and it was obvious he had eaten little or nothing during his 'free' period. There was no ravaging of the countryside—even rabbits were safe, although his hunger must have been abject torture.

Hercules had a triumphant hero's homecoming. Lengthy queues again began to form at Sherriffmuir. The huge charity collection drum there was filled time and time again.

The festivities were soon to be marred, however, when Andy received an official document by recorded delivery. It was not a commendation from the Queen— but a summons from the Lochmaddy Sheriff Court in North Uist.

The court summons was worded as follows:

'The charge against you is that on 20 and 21 August and 13 and 14 September 1980 at Petersport, Island of Benbecula, the Island of Wiay and the Island of North Uist, all in the Western Isles, YOU DID keep a dangerous, wild animal as defined in the schedule annexed to the aftermentioned Act, namely a European Bear of the family Ursidae, while not under the authority of a licence granted in accordance with the provisions of the said Act by a local authority, CONTRARY to the Dangerous Wild Animals Act 1976 Section 1(1) and 2(5)'.

It must be explained that Andy had licensed Hercules under the Performing Animals Act of 1925. This registration allowed him to train the animal with a view to entertaining others. Under this act the animal required to be kept in properly designated quarters acceptable to the local Council.

Hercules was medically examined by two vets, his den was inspected and the local police carefully monitored the situation.

There had been no difficulty whatsoever in obtaining the Performer's Licence. Hercules had been entered in the Official Register as a performing animal and Andy thought, reasonably enough, that all was well and that he'd taken all necessary steps to legalise its frequent public appearances.

Resolutely, Andy had refused to apply for a licence under the Dangerous Wild Animals Act (DWA), as— he thought—this would brand his pet as being both dangerous and wild. He saw this as an unwarranted and scathing slur on the unimpeachable character of his favourite bear.

The DWA stated, *inter alia,* that the Local Authority should not grant a licence if it were contrary to the public interest on the grounds of safety or nuisance. (I would not have wished to be the person to tell Andy that Hercules was a nuisance).

The animal, so registered, was required to be kept in premises from which it could not escape. That was entirely reasonable. But Hercules had, of course, escaped on Benbecula, and this strengthened the Crown case.

In the accommodating of Hercules, cleanliness, ventilation, temperature and lighting all had to be reasonable—as indeed they were. The drawback to registration under the Act, so it seemed to Andy, (apart from branding the animal) was that the animal should be locked up, and would not be released from the den except on the authority of the local council.

It was then that I was consulted by the Robins—who arrived at my office, I am pleased to say, without their big pet.

I was struck by the feelings of the Robins in respect of their pet. The thought of losing him in the event of the Procurator Fiscal winning his prosecution could not be contemplated by the couple. They simply could not lose the case—nor could I.

That fact was made very clear to me as I sent my letter to the Lochmaddy Court pleading not guilty to the summons. In the event of conviction, heaven forbid, the Court had power to separate Andy from Hercules and order him to be looked after by the Council.

I was given a trial date several months hence and started my preparation.

I was attracted, in particular, to section 5 of the Act which stated that the provisions, and necessity to register, did not apply to any dangerous wild animal kept in a zoo or 'circus'. Circus, the Act went on to define, includes any place where animals are kept wholly or mainly for the purpose of performing tricks or manoeuvres. That, it seemed to me, would be the excuse and linch pin of the defence. I would lodge the Performing Animals Licence as a production and argue that Hercules's activities came under section 5 and thus he was exempt from the Act.

Purely as a matter of interest, wild animals as delineated in this Act consist of wild dogs, wolves, jackals, foxes, coyotes, alligators, cobras, lions, tigers, leopards, panthers, jaguars, gila monsters (remember the film 'The Treasure of Sierra Madre', starring the much loved and oft-imitated Humphrey Bogart?), Mexican beaded lizards, polar, brown and grizzly bears, to name, as they say, but a few.

I made several trips to Sherriffmuir, meeting my biggest client for the very first time—in the sitting room of their home.

Hercules seemed to be positively frisky on that occasion and I tried to be, and look, relaxed. On reflection, I probably looked terrified.

On those occasions when I was within touching distance of him, Andy was always close at hand. The secret, I was quick to unravel, was to keep him fed with a tankard of his favourite dish, prawns. As long as he was grasping the tankard in his giant paws—provided prawns remained inside same—he was sufficiently pre-occupied not to be bothered by the presence of humans.

On several Sundays I took my three sons to see him in his den. There were always many other spectators. My youngest, Jason, was 'persuaded' to enter the den with Andy and myself. I discovered later that he had secreted a screw-driver in his back pocket—just in case. My two older sons never ventured into the den on the pretext and excuse that 'big softy' was for kids, like their young brother.

Andy decided to purchase a custom-built Volvo bus from Belgium. It was new, huge and extremely well-equipped and air-conditioned. At its rear was a large, strong cage. It had two beds, a fine settee, a modern kitchen and, would you believe, gold taps. Yes, in this, one would travel in luxury.

Andy and Maggie wondered what they should call it. I volunteered 'If batman has a batmobile', then Hercules should have a 'Hercmobile', And so it was officially named and 'launched', with the appropriate number of bottles of champagne.

Frequently, they were invited to fairs all over England and Wales and I remember meeting up with the 'Hercmobile' a few miles outside Bolton. I had been to Preston on business and went to the Bolton Fair. They were being treated like Royalty on these occasions and the queue to get close to Hercules was always formidable.

But, back to business . . . I studied the terms of the '76 Act very carefully as so much depended on the finding of a loophole. This was to be the first prosecution in Britain, so the territory was truly virgin.

276

I re-checked section 5 and decided that Hercules, when he travelled, had to be the star of a one-animal circus. All I had to do was to establish this. There would then be no need to register and so a Not Guilty verdict would follow, as day follows night. We could bring any number of witnesses to prove that they had been entertained by the 'one-man' band.

Clearly, I would also have to familiarise myself with his compete repertoire of tricks.

In the meantime, I discovered that the Procurator Fiscal did not have his troubles to seek. He told me that he had received an inordinate number of 'threatening' letters—but not written as these normally are. Scores of children had written to him—some more upset than others, but all irate.

How dare he prosecute their big pet! How inhuman and savage he was even to contemplate such a heinous move! Most of the kids who had seen fit to pen the Fiscal had seen Hercules at some time during his several Highland tours. Indeed, he had toured the North not long after the Benbecula incident.

It was good to know that the Fiscal was under pressure. I decided to add to the pressure. I wrote and suggested that there be an Identification Parade consisting of the suspect and five other grizzlies of similar height, colour and weight. He, the Fiscal, could ask for a volunteer from the ranks of the local Police Force to officiate at the parade and ensure that there was no foul play.

Seriously, Andy did want a parade arranged. He wished to make it as difficult as possible for the unreasonable prosecution.

Another factor I related to the Fiscal was that the animal would have to be brought to Court under the best evidence rule, in order to demonstrate to the Sheriff that his 'act' could be construed as a one-animal travelling circus and was therefore exempt from registration under DWA.

Moreover, how would the stark Lochmaddy Court room accommodate the Press of the world, not to mention hundreds of spectators? Yes, there were logistical problems. The local hostelry could not cope with the interested parties—so I asked him about caravan sites.

During one of my numerous phone calls to the Fiscal, it became clear that he had obvious difficulties facing him at the trial of the decade. He suggested that were I to register Hercules under the Act before the trial date this would give him the excuse to ditch the prosecution. Technically, this should not cover actions or offences in retrospect but, all the same, he would drop matters— and that was a promise.

I met Andy and Maggie to discuss this reasonable development because, after all, no one can say with certainty what might happen at a Court hearing.

Andy almost had a heart seizure, 'Never', he said, 'never will I register him under the Act. It would be tantamout to an admission that he is a dangerous and wild animal'

I retorted, 'Well, is he not an animal, and is he not dangerous and wild?'

Andy turned on me as if I had betrayed all that he stood for. A heated argument ensued, during which, fortunately, Maggie entered into the arena. She took my part and eventually common sense prevailed. She saw this as being a method of removing the pressure and realised that no prejudice would befall them.

Reluctantly, it seemed, Andy bowed to the inevitable, although I felt that his abhorrence of my suggestion was perhaps not nearly as genuine as his affection for Hercules. Many people ventured the suggestion that Andy deliberately released Hercules at Benbecula for the ensuing publicity, but I dismiss this because of their relationship.

An application under DWA was completed and forwarded with the appropriate fee. I was phoned by one of the Council officials and told that if the licence were to be granted Hercules would require to remain at Sherriffmuir as he would be designated as dangerous and wild, and required to conform to the provisions. 'His travelling days are over', I was told.

I did not show my hand and once again the den was examined, as was Hercules, by two vets. I was later to be told that the local council would not grant the licence without a hearing before the full Chamber.

At this time Hercules was still appearing in London theatres and, on one occasion, I was phoned by the Greater London Council (no doubt having been put up to it by the Stirling authorities) who were trying to stop the act from taking place.

They said there was a criminal prosecution pending in Scotland and that Andy had taken Hercules from the premises specified in the Performing Animals Act (Sherriffmuir) without permission and without registration under the more recent Act.

The crisis was circumvented by my pointing out that there was an escape clause within the DWA—that the animal was a complete travelling circus and that this was our valid defence to the forthcoming trial. The London shows proceeded as planned.

As well as conforming in matters of hygiene and well-being, the DWA also made it obligatory that Hercules be insured against any injury or damage caused by him. However, he had been insured to the extent of three quarters of a million pounds under the earlier Act in any event, although, so far as I am aware, no claim was ever made under the policy.

Before attending at the fine Stirling offices, I sought the opinion of eminent Counsel, Hugh Morton, now Lord Shuna, who agreed with me that it would be in order to register under DWA, but, at the same time, use the Act in its entirety, with reference to section five and claim that, outside Sherriffmuir, the 'Hercmobile' was a 'circus'.

This being so, that part of the licence specifying non-removal was inapplicable as there was exemption from the provisions whilst furth of the area.

For some weeks before the final chapter unfolded the head Fiscal in Stirling , Keith Valentine, had been kept abreast of developments by the police and by myself. I had several meetings with him as we did not wish to face a further contravention of the Act in Stirling. He decided to await the outcome of my application to the local Council.

With my Counsel's opinion safely tucked away in my back pocket, I pleaded Hercules's case before the full Council. I had excellent photogrpahs of the bear, its den and such like. These photographs were clearly most beneficial to my case because the licence was granted by a healthy majority of the Council—it may have been unanimous.

That done, I went directly to the Sherriffmuir to meet the delighted Robins.

I 'phoned the Fiscal at Stornaway (he looks after Lochmaddy, too) and confirmed the grant. The dear old Fiscal was as relieved as we were. He confirmed that the charge would now be abandoned forthwith in terms of our agreement—and the matter ended without the semblance of a blot on the escutcheon of the bold beast.

A well-attended Press conference followed, after which I received a number of congratulatory letters from many members of the public—not by any means restricted to children and teenagers. It had been a long, interesting fight, finishing splendidly.

That same year I holidayed in Florida where there are many zoos and animal and fish-life resorts. These are extremely popular—so much so that, on my return, I suggested to Andy that he could do a lot worse than tour North America with Hercules. In 1982 they travelled to California, where they remained for several years.

Seen on the graffiti-adorned inner cell door at Kilmarnock Sheriff Court... 'F − − K Nelson Mandela—free me!'

Glossary of Scots Law Terms

adminicle any piece of supporting evidence.

advocate the equivalent of the English *barrister*. All advocates are members of the **Faculty of Advocates.** Their main functions are to plead in court and, on request, to advise on points of law. They have sole right of audience in the Court of Session and the High Court of Justiciary, except when an accused elects to represent himself. After some years at the Bar, an advocate may be invited to **take silk,** as in England, and become a **Queen's Counsel (QC).** After this he is known as a **senior counsel,** and until recently appeared in court only when assisted by **junior counsel.**

Advocate Depute a member of the Faculty of Advocates who takes part in the preparation and conduct of criminal prosecutions in the High Court as a deputy to the Lord Advocate (*see below*). The selection of Deputes rests with the Lord Advocate, and was until recent times largely governed by political considerations.

Appeal Court In criminal cases in Scotland, appeals are made to the High Court of Justiciary sitting as a **Court of Criminal Appeal.** This procedure was introduced by the Criminal Appeal (Scotland) Act 1926. Under solemn procedure (*see below*) appeals are heard by three or more High Court judges, one of whom presides and is either the Lord Justice General or the Lord Justice Clerk (*see* **High Court,** *below*). There is no appeal to the House of Lords.

complainer the person against whom a crime is alleged to have been committed.

Crown Agent, Crown Office *see* **Lord Advocate**

culpable homicide homicide arising from an unlawful act or omission where death would not be foreseen as a probable consequence—a killing caused by such an unlawful act but lacking in the deliberate intention to kill which would have made the charge one of murder. In England this crime is called *manslaughter.*

direct evidence *see* **evidence**

evidence The testimony of eye-witnesses is **direct evidence; indirect (circumstantial) evidence** consists of circumstances, admitted or proved, from which the existence of a fact is inferred. Examples are fibres, paint scrapings, fingerprints, traces of blood etc.

High Court of Justiciary the supreme Criminal Court of Scotland, dealing with the graver crimes which are prosecuted directly by the Lord Advocate (*see below*) and his Deputes (*see **Advocate Depute** above*). The judges are the **Lord Justice General**, the **Lord Justice Clerk** and the **Lords Commissioners of Justiciary**. All these are also judges of the **Court of Session**—the supreme Civil Court, of which the Lord Justice General is **Lord President**—and in this capacity are known as **Senators of the College of Justice**. The High Court can also act as an Appeal Court (*see above*).

indictment (pronounced *inditement*) In solemn procedure (*see below*) the **indictment** is the formal written accusation or charge, made out in the name of the Lord Advocate.

indirect evidence *see* **evidence**

junior counsel see **advocate**

Law Society of Scotland the governing body of Scottish solicitors.

Lord Advocate the Minister of the Crown who is responsible to Parliament for matters relating to the administration of law in Scotland, including the investigation and prosecution of all crime. In this he is assisted by a) the **Solicitor General** b) the **Crown Agent** and his staff, who function in the **Crown Office** in Edinburgh, c) the local Procurators Fiscal (*see below*).

on Petition In solemn procedure (*see below*), an arrested person appears in private **on Petition** before a Sheriff on the first day (excluding Sundays) after his arrest. The Procurator Fiscal (*see below*) presents a petition in which the accused is charged with the crime and the Sheriff is asked to commit him to prison pending further enquiries or trial. The Crown, however, may still decide subsequently not to prosecute, or to proceed with a lesser charge. Bail may also be settled at this appearance, and a Judicial Declaration may be made by the accused, as in the cases of Wilson and Burnett. He may also be judicially examined by the Fiscal.

pannel an accused person, in solemn procedure (*see below*).

precognosce, precognition (verb pronounced *precognose*) A **precognition** is a statement taken during the period of preparation of a case, by the prosecution or the defence, from victims and potential witnesses. They are **precognosced** to establish what evidence they would be likely to give in court and, therefore, whether they should be called to testify.

Procurator Fiscal (informally *Fiscal*) is responsible for all prosecutions in the lower courts, under the direction of the Crown Office (*see **Lord Advocate**, above*). The Fiscal reports serious crimes to the Crown Office, who then (after consultation with the Advocates Depute or Lord Advocate if necessary) decide whether or not to prosecute and if so, in which court. Where a prosecution is directed by the Procurator Fiscal, he or one of his Deputes handles the preparation of the case and conducts the prosecution in court.

Q C *see* **advocate**

reset the crime of receiving or dealing in stolen goods, knowing them to be stolen and with the intention of keeping them from their rightful owner. *Receiving* is the equivalent English term.

Senator of the College of Justice *see* **High Court of Justiciary**

senior counsel *see* **advocate**

Sherif Court The **Sheriff Courts**, presided over by **Sheriffs**, deal with most civil and criminal cases in Scotland. Sheriffs are appointed from among advocates and solicitors of at least ten years' standing. They may deal with minor cases on summary procedure or with more serious cases on solemn procedure (*see below*). The Sheriff Court does not, however, deal a) with crimes committed outside the territorial limits of its jurisdiction b) with certain crimes—notably murder, treason, rape and incest—which must be tried in the High Court, or c) with cases in which it is anticipated that a sentence of more than three years' imprisonment (the maximum a Sheriff can impose) will be appropriate in the event of a conviction. The Sheriff may also (in solemn procedure) remit an accused to the High Court for sentence, if he pleads Guilty—or, on occasions, if he is found Guilty at a trial—and the Sheriff feels that a longer sentence is called for than he can impose. In the Sheriff Court, the defence Solicitor usually does the pleading himself, even in a jury trial.

silk, take silk *see* **advocate**

Solicitor General *see* **Lord Advocate**

Special Defence If an accused intends to maintain at his trial that he is Not Guilty of the charge because a) he had an alibi b) he was insane at the time c) he acted in self-defence or d) the crime was committed by somebody else, a **Special Defence of Alibi, Insanity, Self-Defence** or **Impeachment/Incrimination** must be lodged ten days before the commencement of the trial in order to give fair notice to the Crown authorities. If this has not been done, no evidence supporting such a defence may be led at the trial. But the sole purpose of a Special Defence is to give notice to the Crown of the line of defence. It in no way imposes a burden of proof on the defence or relieves the Crown of their overall burden of proving the accused's guilt beyond reasonable doubt. Examples of all four Special Defences are included among the cases in this book. It should be noted that a successful plea of Insanity at the time of an offence (when the accused is sane at the trial) produces the verdict 'that he or she committed the act charged but that he or she was insane at the time and that [the jury] therefore acquit on the ground of insanity'. In England the verdict applicable to the same circumstances is one of 'Guilty but Insane' which seems to me to be a misnomer.

solemn/summary procedure Under **summary procedure** relatively minor crimes are tried in the District Courts—not mentioned in this book—and in the Sheriff Courts (*see above*) before a Sheriff sitting without a jury. The maximum sentence is six months' im-

prisonment. Under solemn procedure more serious crimes are tried either in the Sheriff Court before a Sheriff and jury (maximum sentence three years) or in the High Court (*see above*) before a judge and jury. There are other differences too, such as the fact that in summary procedure the accused is prosecuted on a **complaint**, not an indictment (*see above*).

Index